RECOLLECTIONS

OF AN ISLAND MAN

10/21/06

Blessings !

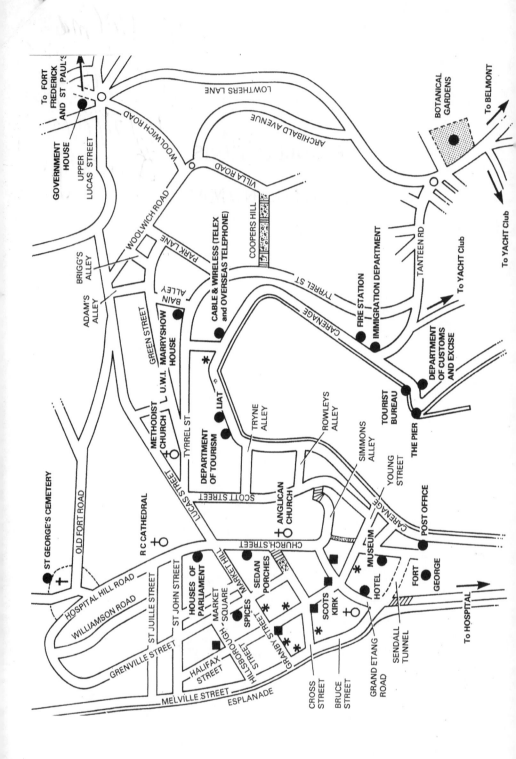

RECOLLECTIONS
OF AN ISLAND MAN

by Anthony W. DeRiggs

Printed in the United States of America
ISBN: 0-9774916-0-9
Library of Congress Control number: 2005910160
2nd Copyright pending.

Cover art from an original phorograph taken by the author.

Editing contributions by
Patricia Boothe
Christopher DeRiggs
Ann Wilder.

Dedicated to the people of Grenada

CONTENTS

FOREWORD

A few years ago, I took a trip to Grenada. Someone gave me a gift to carry for a woman there. I called her when I reached and she asked her son to pick up the gift. He asked me for directions to the house where I was staying and I told him that I was residing close to the spot where Empire Cinema once stood. He told me that he had never heard of Empire Cinema.

Immediately I thought that someone had failed to pass on information, and I recalled the days Grandma spoke to me and told me of places and things that were familiar to her when she was growing up.

She used to speak of the Drill Yard and Ballast Ground and the time when a few motorists had all the streets of Grenada to themselves. Back then, the older people made the time to speak to the young ones and to remind them of their heritage.

I gave the young man a little story about the Empire Cinema and I told him of the times we stood in long lines to purchase tickets for the matinee or midnight show.

This book "Recollections of an Island Man" is made up of stories that I remember. It is not a researched book; it is simply the way I remember certain happenings and people. I did not live in all the areas of Grenada so I can only write about what I know. It is not based on detailed character studies but brief sketches.

When I departed for Brooklyn in 1978, I left with my thoughts of the exciting and not so exciting times I experienced. Lodged in my mind were stories of characters and events that appealed to me. Lurking in my consciousness were stories of Christmas and Carnival and of school days and times I sat and listened to Nansi stories told under the breadfruit tree.

Although I currently live in Brooklyn, I still cannot shake the thoughts of the early morning sea baths and the times I climbed the very tall mango trees. Lingering in my mind is the bush tea that I drank, the spanking I got at school, the coal pot on which we roasted the corn and breadfruit or boiled the ham. I met other Grenadians in Brooklyn who had their own stories to tell. I sat and listened and the inclination to tell stories from Grenada and Brooklyn intensified as the voices of others spoke of similar experiences. Then the outlet for doing so became a reality.

A friend of mine nicknamed Revo told me of a Grenadian Discussion Group Website hosted by Cable and Wireless called Spiceisle Talkshop and moderated by Mr. Brian Steele. I accessed that site and began writing stories and poems, mostly based on my growing up experiences in Grenada.

As I wrote, the wonderful e-mails came from England, Canada, Trinidad, USA, and various other places.

I felt the happiness in the words of those who were hungry for the nostalgic feel of the life they once knew. I laughed with those who found humor in the appealing colloquialisms and expressions.

I read the encouraging words of people on the Talkshop who adopted nicknames as Vanni, 1 Luv, Judy, Queen Maccomeh, Aim, PI, Lavandula, Spiceislander, Tagwa, Spider, Slice, Ackee, Bakes and Fishcakes, Bathway, Kesri, Spanish Eyes, Snow, Corporal Naught, CPD, Skyrone, Gouyaveman, Lord Hungry and Mr. T.

I was moved to action when they advised me to put my work

in book form. My friends, co-workers and family advised me to do the same.

This I have done, but it is not merely a book about Grenada. It is a book of the human experience seen through my eyes. The stories dwell on happenings that mainly occurred during the 1960's and 1970's. It is a book that is intended to grasp the attention of those who believe that the human story is basically the same all over the world.

Somewhere in a distant land, a fisherman will undergo the blazing heat of the sun that Mr. Cliff in the book experienced. Someone will sing a hymn for the dead and indeed there are those who will always curse the politicians.

And all over the world there are those who would find comfort in the bottle just as readily as the rum drinkers of Grenada. People will continue to yearn for the Christmas or holidays they knew as little children and yes, many would find enjoyment in a little exaggeration, nonsense and humor.

I was thrilled when I receive the following e-mail from a woman who was born in Boston:

"Hello Anthony,

I am a woman living California who recently bought a house in Carriacou with my husband. I'm originally from Boston and your pieces take me home.

A Bostonian's childhood is about snowmen and ice skating, but chases, pranks and nabbing sweets are all part of it. A lot of Bostonians go back and forth to Carriacou, and one said to me, "Isn't this like being in the forties" (1940's). That's why we love Carriacou. In the present it reminds us of what we miss from our past.

We live in a beautiful town, Sausalito, right on the water in a houseboat with its special wonders (the soothing hum of boat motors, a resident seal who makes calls underwater every night, our seagull friends who drop mussels on the roof to crack them open). The past, the present, Grenada, Boston, and San Francisco all can be loved the same way that you convey the love of your history. You aren't telling us your past, you are reminding us how to think. Your impact is so great. Thank you-please keep the stories coming."
Stephanie Burns

For those who are concerned with the fading hallmarks of our culture, this is my attempt to help you relive certain aspects of a cherished past.

ME, THIS GRENADIAN

Me, this Grenadian, who stood on the wharf
And watched *sea pum pum* swim in the sea,
Then arrived late for school,
And Palmer got vex like hell,
He pulled out *ah* strap,
And *gee me ah good cut-tail.*
Licks for so!

Me, this Grenadian who was stung
By bee and *maribone,*
Red ants and black ants.
Me who skate down Cooper Hill
'Til ah skate the bottom off
Me new school pants.

Me, this Grenadian who fell in *ah patch*
Of stinging nettles, zootie and *pugatay,*
And *ah* itching still.

Me, this Grenadian who rolled bicycle rim
And rode broom stick pretending it was *ah* horse.
Ah float in the sea with *ah* tire tube,

Where *black sea egg jook* me foot and *bam bam,*
And *ah* pee on me foot to take out the spikes.

Me, this Grenadian who ate
The long thread-like thing from *lambie,*
And made *ah* mistake and ate *sandbox,*
Then *ah* called the *pit latrine* home sweet home.

Me, this Grenadian who made *ah slinging shot,*
Who run down *rainflies,*
And climbed coconut trees,
And dived for Lobster,
And *stoned red crabs* by the bay,
And sucked *tambran* till it cut me tongue.

Me, this Grenadian who jumped in *mas band.*
Me, who played *ah* Viking *mas* and *ah* sailor *mas.*
Me, who was *ah jab jab,* wild Indian and *ah shortknee.*
And *ah* played *ole mas* for all to see.

Me, this Grenadian who played cricket
With breadfruit, lime and *gospo,*
 And hit *ah* man's window with the *gospo,*
And *ah* ran like hell,
But he took the ball (*the gospo*)
He took it to make juice.

Me, this Grenadian who sucked *Chinese plum*
And the big *Jamaican plum,*
But ran from *hog plum.*
Ah stoned mango and grabbed Mammy's fried jacks,
And pulled cane from *dem* big cane trucks.

Me, this Grenadian who walked from Chantimelle
Till *ah* reached Low Town,
And accompanied me lady up Snell Hall,
And shot wild goats in the little islands.

Me, this Grenadian who watched *shango people,*
Ah saw dem drink goat blood,
And watched Leader G *cut they backside* with *ah* whip.
Yes, me, this Grenadian who *mop ah ride*
On *ah banana truck* and *ah Janet truck.*

Me, this Grenadian who spend time in *ah* school
In Six Roads, Carriacou,
Where *ah* big *horse fly* stung me nose.
But *ah* had a wonderful time,
Carriacou people *nice for so*!

Me, this Grenadian who saw horse race
In Seamoon and Queen's Park.
And *ah made ah ting*
Under the big tree in Grand Anse
In the dead of night.

Me, this Grenadian who *drogue cocoa,*
And cleaned pigpen,
And mashed *pig mess,*
And *ah* bawl O....... *GEED!*
Ah walked on *Jumbie umbrella*
And played with *Jumbie bead,*
But hid from *wood slave lizard* and *zandolie.*

Me, this Grenadian who ate *oildown*
Like Jane does make,
And gobbled down pea soup at *Canboulay* time.
And when *ah* bit the dumplings,
They go crix, crix, crix.
Me, who took *ah* ride in Old Man's boat,
And went to shop to buy carbolic soap
But, instead, *ah* asked for *ah* catholic soap.

Me, this Grenadian who hit *ah* six in Tanteen
In *ah* big cricket match
And scored *ah* goal in Windsor Park
In *ah* football match.
Ah fly me kite in the Guide's hut,
And sling me own *compere's* kite
Lord have mercy!

Me, this Grenadian who pushed Angel's Harp's steel pan.

Me, this Grenadian who stood outside
In the burning sun,
But *ah* ran and hide
When the rain came down.

Me, this Grenadian who dug *bush yam,*
And set fish pot
To catch *ah Ca Ca Bari* and *ah Grunt.*

Me, this Grenadian who ate *ah* cake called rock,
And *ah* ginger cake called Fontay.
Ah ate *Leaven bread, Johnny bakes* and *Vienna bread.*

Me, who pound plantain in mortar with *ah* pestle,
And ate cornmeal porridge, asham and pine apple tart.

Me, this Grenadian who *lime ah ting,*
And ran away when she father asked,
"What is your intention?"
Hell, he knew my intention.

Me, this Grenadian who peep
Before ah creep,
Like the *calypsonian* Super P.
This Grenadian who will cuss Susan
Put two *bad words in she tail,*
But we go meet up, *make up* and hug up
Yes *sah!* Me, this Grenadian.

Me, this Grenadian who rolled *ah* dumpling
And pushed it under *ah coal pot,*
While *ah* corn roasted on top.
Ah ate *conkee* wrapped in *bluggoe leaf,*
And *snow cone, soursop block* and Franco's ice cream,
And *ah* put the condense milk to me head,
When Mammy was not looking.

Me, this Grenadian who danced the strongman,
The ska, spooge, rocksteady and Groom's horse dance.
Me, who shake me waist,
In *ah* hula hoop.

Me, this Grenadian who pulled fish net.
Me, Teacher Dunstan and Teacher Kenny.
This Grenadian who cut *watergrass* for goat,

But was afraid to go for the goat when night fell.
Me 'Fraid Jumbie.

Me, this Grenadian who put load on donkey back
And the *dam* donkey refused to move.
The donkey lie down.
Ah pick up nutmeg,
Till me back cry out!
Me who joined *sou sou,*
And *ah* got *the first hand* to buy *ah* fridge.

Me, this Grenadian who *leggo one* in church,
And the priest reacted
As if he got *bazodee.*
After that *ah* forced to keep the rest
'Til *ah* left the Church.

Me, this Grenadian who listened to Pastor Wiggins,
As he preached in *ah* big tent in Tanteen.
He told the women,
"If the men don't want to marry you
Then leave them."
So *ah lot ah fellas* lost *dey* women.

Me, this Grenadian who made Grandma *cuss*
When *ah* opened an umbrella in the house,
Or sang "Ring *ah* round *ah* roses."
"Who you want to kill now?" she shouted,
Grandma said those things brought bad luck.

Me, this Grenadian who sat in moonlight
And told *'Nansi stories*

But was frightened by *ah bluggoe leaf*
Blowing in the breeze.

Me, this Grenadian who teased Zoon,
The red eye *Ligaroo.*
And believed all those stories,
About putting *ah* bowl of sand
To ketch *ah Ligaroo* and keep out *Jumbie.*

Me, this Grenadian who bought *ah* small radio
To listen to cricket game in class,
While Miss Burke taught Biology.
Then all me classmates kept asking for the score,
So she knew and took away me radio.

Me, this Grenadian who was afraid
To say me belly hurting me,
For it was castor oil *in me backside.*
Me, who drank *Coolie Paw Paw, Ven Ven* and *Big Time bush.*

Me, this Grenadian who ate blood puddin',
Potato puddin' and drank Kool-Aid.
And when *tings* was hard,
Ah corn beef and rice
Was really nice.

Me, this Grenadian who made *ah* top,
And with it, ah split me partner's top.
He took away all me marbles,
So, *ah* made *ah bamboo kite,*
Because there were other things to make,
back then.

Me, this Grenadian who studied hard
To pass all *dem* school test,
And was satisfied
When *ah* did me best.

Me, this Grenadians who stood on Pandy beach -
And peeped at political demonstrations.
Big rally on the wharf,
And *ah* saw when fight broke out,
And people ran from the *Mongoose gang,*
Back in Uncle Gairy's time.

Me, this Grenadian now sitting here,
Here in Brooklyn, New York.
Still eating fish cake and drinking *cocoa tea,*
On a snowy day.
Snow flakes dancing on me window,
But *no rainfly, black sea egg,* or *gospo* is visible.

Yes! Me, this Grenadian!

INTRODUCTION BY DUNBAR CAMPBELL

Anthony DeRiggs: The Man at the Window

Several years ago, I was traveling to a city I had never been to before. I bought a map and drove to a number of places I had to visit. But there was one location I could not find on my map. The city was undergoing major growth and signs of construction were everywhere. New buildings, new streets. It was around noon so I stopped at a restaurant for lunch and spread out the map on my table next to a window.

I put my nose to the map and began to study the streets. Just then, the waitress walked up. "May I help you find something?" she asked.

"Sure," I said, and told her the name of the building I was looking for.

She smiled and said. "Don't look at the map. Look out the window. It's over there."

I glanced out the window. The building was just across the street staring directly at the restaurant.

I thanked the waitress and we had a good laugh. But later I

thought of the incident and realized a profound truth. Often we travel through life looking for things with obsolete maps. But if we take the time to look out the window, the things we're looking for might just be staring us in the face.

What does all this have to do with Anthony W. DeRiggs, you ask? Glad you asked. You see, if you read DeRiggs, you realize he's always reminding us to look out the window. His writings encourage us to lift up our noses from many of the obsolete intellectual mapping we've grown up with and to take a closer look at our unique experiences in life, whether you're from Grenada or not. His writings are more accurate representations of our Grenadian reality than many of the foreign interpretations we so readily accept. Wherever you're from, he will inspire you to appreciate the richness of your roots.

I am not saying to ignore the great writers and philosophers of our times. They have provided great maps over the years. But the landscape of life is constantly changing, so when maps become obsolete it's time to look out the window to get a new sense of direction. Whenever I need an accurate fix on where I came from, so I'll know where I'm going, I read Anthony DeRiggs.

When you read DeRiggs, it's an all-encompassing experience, far greater than a flat lifeless map. His writings overcome obstacles of space or time. You can be in North America, and he can take you to Grenada in an instant, on a walk down the stone steps of Cooper Hill, up the steep St. John's street, or across the breezy Carenage. But it's only just begun. You hear the sweet steel band sounds of Angel Harps floating across the harbor, you feel the breeze, you smell and taste the spicy blood pudding, and you laugh with the people. He humanizes people and brings them to life. He transports you to an environment buzzing with amazing characters and incredible stories. It's the view from the window.

So, whenever I feel a little lost, even with my map, I don't panic. I read Anthony W. DeRiggs. I hope you read him too. He's the man at the window.

Dunbar Campbell

INTRODUCTION
BY ANN WILDER

Anthony W. DeRiggs has been telling stories for a long time from his current home in the United States; stories about when he was young in Grenada. Lately he has been writing them down and sharing them, much to the benefit of readers. In this book, his stories and poems are gathered between covers. The publication of DeRiggs' book is not soon enough for his admirers outside and inside Grenada.

My late father, over twelve years ago, told his stories of Grenada, and I helped him get those stories into a book. When I first read A.W. DeRiggs' stories on Talkshop, I was drawn to them out of my love for story-telling.

DeRiggs' stories, like my Dad's, reveal the fondness both men have for Grenada—my Dad from the point-of-view of a retiree to Grenada, and DeRiggs from his childhood memories and ties into adulthood to the Spice Isle.

I am honored to be able to aid A.W. DeRiggs in the publication of his book. I am also blessed to have the opportunity of helping DeRiggs' narrative get into print in the story-telling tradition of Garrison Keillor, Mark Twain, Paul Keens-Douglas, Edwidge Danticat, and the many other unsung keepers of cultures of the past.

The attributes of a good sense of dialogue, a compelling narrative voice and the ability to create a world, resonates with readers.

Ah! But if you were raised in Grenada, the grandest compliment is –

"Your pieces take me back home."

We can visualize, through DeRiggs' tales and anecdotes, what life was like on the Spice Isle and how the people there made a difference to his life – from Ma Rubes to the 'green fig' man.

We are reminded of Grenadian situations through the device of colloquial storytelling—descriptive writing which comes naturally to DeRiggs.

The way DeRiggs writes about how a 'George Otway' bath was taken, or a pleasant rain bath, or a hot water bath straight from the pipe, evokes an atmosphere we can feel. Wouldn't you like to 'breeze out," doing the 'liming' thing?

If storytelling is two-thirds persuasion, DeRiggs convinces us by way of his craft and his skill in relating past events. Humorous storytelling is often subtle because it comes out of honesty. When you read DeRiggs, you carry a soft chuckle along with the reading of his words.

Lying can destroy a good story. If there is slight exaggeration in his stories, though, we don't mind at all. DeRiggs' narratives make sense because he loves his country and cherishes his memories.

The affection DeRiggs has for his country and the people who live there reveals the character of DeRiggs in the tone and attitude of his writings. The stories often make obvious and universal points as if they were wise lessons from our respected elder.

Stories of human activities that endure give us all a common ground for identification; an insight into our human nature. In writing about the characters of his youth, sound of mind or not, and about his joyous experiences, DeRiggs has managed to write about us all.

DeRiggs writes informally. His clear vocabulary and syntax explain matters which we non-Grenadians may not understand. He takes us on a happy narrative journey with his words. Although he writes in the past tense, as readers we feel we are reliving the past. Thus, DeRiggs repeatedly engages us into a moment of the past. Present and past tense are effectively utilized in reading DeRiggs' narratives. We feel like we are there.

The common language or vernacular words of oral Grenadian communication are written down in a manner which carries the storytelling voice. If the words are not explained in the text, DeRiggs provides a glossary. His elaboration of live experiences use colloquial and idiomatic expressions; that is, informal sayings, usually used in the rhythmical, spoken language of Grenada.

DeRiggs captures the cadence of Spice Isle language. Consider this quotation from the book about bus drivers:

"Some people got dey rides and got speeches from the drivers:
'Man, wipe yuh dam foot before yuh come in me car, nah.'
'Whey yuh going wid all dat mud?'"

Discussion could be presented on the origins of the vocabulary and culture, the-specific phrasings used by DeRiggs, but let us leave that for scholars and enjoy.

Enjoy and appreciate this delightful and thoughtful book.

Ann Elizabeth Wilder

RECOLLECTIONS

OF AN ISLAND MAN

WE, THE PEOPLE

As Grenadian as They Come

He was Grenadian. As Grenadian as they come: articulate, witty and a *green fig man* who could take and give a joke. He never walked the halls of any university, but when he spoke, he sounded as if he had just graduated from one. He once told me, "If you can't convince *dem* with facts, then *bamboose dem* with nonsense." He was called home some time ago, but his memory dwells in the hearts of many.

Mr. Rush left Grenada for Trinidad many decades ago at a time when many Grenadians were doing so. He did not remain in Trinidad too long. He gathered his experience of that country, then started working on a boat and soon became the chief cook. His name became synonymous with the pot and cooking. Nothing made him happier than seeing people devour the food he prepared. And if one asked him why he was not eating, he usually joked, "*Yuh tink* ah stupid to eat *dat?* It's me *dat* cook *dat*!"

I first met him on a bus ride to Atlantic City, New Jersey. That was when I found out that he resided in Brooklyn. I was comfortably seated between two ladies in the back of the bus straining my neck to chat with some old friends I had not seen in

3

donkey years. Suddenly, someone handed me a fried *big jack.* It was my good friend Cowie from Florida. My palate wasted no time in making the connection. That was the very same big *fried jack* Mammy Georgie used to prepare for us in Grenada. I immediately sought the source of that fish. It was an old *redskin man* whose hair had long vanished, but who sat there with his merry old self dishing out fried jacks and rice and peas. Then he handed me something in a plate which I immediately gobbled. He looked at me and said: "Down the hatch pal." Next came a piece of *manicou* meat and I begged for more.

It was the first time I had that kind of meat, but it tasted good and it was well-seasoned. Then fish cakes and bakes made the rounds and I mumbled to myself, *"Geeze am bread,* like this man intend to feed the whole bus!" But it was not only the food. It was something warm about the man. He was the essence of Grenadian affection.

He was known for his many good deeds. I have heard many wonderful stories about him and never have I doubted them. I heard of the time he paid for a woman's groceries when she could not come up with all the money to pay for her goods. I heard of the times he offered lodgings to Grenadians who were in desperate need as they walked off the boat or plane. I heard about his charitable contributions to various organizations.

I heard of his mouth too! Yes, that man *cuddah cuss*! He was the first to tell you that he did not have anything in life because he "bought ice and put it in the sun." He said that no one could pull wool over his eyes because he knew of life when many people were still wearing diapers. Once in the midst of a conversation, a woman jumped up and shouted, "Your mouth! Your mouth!" Yes, he had a bad Grenadian mouth. But one that made some people laugh out loud.

He loved to dance. However, if you invited him to *ah* little *drink up;* don't bother to play any of the latest stuff. He was contented if you put on the song about the old time *calypsonian* Terror who was so weak that he had to drink *callaloo soup* to stand up. After that, according to the song, Terror had so much strength he made Elaine and her mother run. He danced to Sparrow's "Saltfish Stew," "Mr. Benwood Dick," and Papitette's "Monica." While others danced, he placed the food on their table and uttered, "Now don't hurt yourself!"

He was Grenadian, as Grenadian as they come!

A Tribute to a Good Ole Friend

He left for England during a different era a different time. It was a period when colonial winds blew strong but his will to succeed raged stronger than the Northeast Trades. Undaunted by critics, Bogart boarded the English boat to a distant land and another clime.

The English boat came and the sadness came too. It was a time of weeping when relatives gathered on the Wharf to see their loved ones depart. Indeed, it was a time of gladness for some. Anyway, the tears flowed so much that people compared the arrival of the boat to the popular Ray Charles song "Crying Time Again." There is often deep sadness when people depart.

Off to England he went, a spirited pioneer with his little *grip,* determined to improve his lot and to secure a better life for himself and his family. For weeks no one would know if he arrived safely because the Trans-Atlantic journey (via ship) was a snail then, compared to the swift BOAC jet that many have used later. He arrived in England and at once knew that there was no large or comfortable cushion to soften his landing.

His struggle began as a house painter and he put his heart and soul into his work. Success eventually came after hard work and with it came some stories to tell. The stories he eventually told me. I will, for just a while, reflect on a few of those stories:

He told me about the white woman who rented a small room for him and his Grenadian friends. She took them straight from the boat and never complained if they were short on rent. She always remained her kind cheerful self. God bless her soul! Grenadians were happy to see each other and gave up space and comfort in order to help those who had newly arrived. It was an admirable thing to do and many went the extra mile to make the lives of those who had just set foot on English soil more bearable.

He delightfully recalled the times he went to see the football and cricket matches. He spoke about seeing the great Sir Gary Sobers in his glory at Lords. He told me about the famous save that Gordon Banks made in the World Cup Football of 1966 when he denied the super-talented Pele a certain goal. His face lighted up as he spoke of his own little Grenadian cricket matches in England.

He told me about the time he urged his friend George to just stay in the wicket and *poke* for they only needed one run and victory was theirs. But George made one big *VOOP* and his stumps went flying in all directions. So they lost the match.

He cited a certain *fella* from Sauteurs nicknamed Chaplet Scrutch who was fond of making speeches in the famed section of England known as Hyde Park.

He climbed up on the box and cursed the Queen. He mounted up and asked his famous question: "Who brought VD to Africa?" Then he would launch into a tirade pointing out all the evils of the white race. When he had enough or had said enough, he walked off hand-in-hand with his white woman.

The stories were many. Too many to repeat in detail here. There were stories of Grenadians who toiled hard in England and saved *every blessed cent* to build big mansions in Grenada. Sadly many of them died before enjoying the comfort of the new structures in the Spice Isle. Some dreams in life never materialize. He spoke of a certain *fella* who on *bouncing up* with some *ole* time friends invited them to his house for a few beers.

He pulled out Sparrow's song "Jean and Dina," and soon music was blasting. A few women heard the music and asked to join the party. Then he told me of that *cheap Grenadian chap* who invited him to his house: "Let's go and drink some *dam* Guinness." The man had only one Guinness in his refrigerator.

He told stories of funerals and of wakes and of Irishmen in

pubs who looked at Grenadians from Grenville hugged them hard and called them "Paddy."

He recalled good times and rough times. He spoke of friendships and betrayal and the abiding spice that Grenadians used to flavor the entire world.

I listened with attentive ears as one would listen to an African storyteller. But alas! His memory dimmed and sickness swept over him. The stories stopped, but not before I had heard enough to tell my child and for you to tell yours if you care to listen.

I Remember Mr. Clouden, a Grenadian Icon

I met him first at Palmer School and I never forgot him. He was a teacher at the St. George's Catholic Boys' School which was previously called Fletcher School before Palmer got the school. There were Grenadians who always gave headmasters the entire school. Fletcher had his school and Hindsey and Morris had theirs. McBarnette had his located in Back Street and Mother Rose had hers on the hill near the Roman Catholic Church. Every headmaster had his school and the names survived long after they expired.

They called him "Fatty Derek" and I never saw him lose his cool over the nickname. He was in charge of the school's choir during an era when the choir was as important as the three Rs. It was as meaningful as attending church on Sundays and behaving oneself in church. One was expected to "keep up the esprit des corps," words handed down from old Fletcher. That meant defeating the other schools in the Junior League football games, excelling in academics and singing in harmony. It also involved telling old people good morning. It was more risky to tell them goodnight as Mr. Palmer, our headmaster, would have tried to find out what we were doing outside during the night.

We stood in line at school to try out for the choir. Mr. Derek Clouden wanted only the best tenors, altos and bass singers. A few students tried to escape by singing in gruff voices, but that only landed them in the bass section. He easily spotted those with the melodious voices. I recall a student called Dolland and another named DeRoache who came from Carriacou and sang better than the three little birds in Bob Marley's song.

Mr. Clouden aimed at perfection. We sang the songs and we had to sing them right. We belted out the tune "The Campbell's are Coming, oh ho, oh ho" and we succeeded in annoying a Campbell classmate from Happy Hill when we stared teasingly at him as we sang it. One can always count on school children for such childhood pranks. There was another song, "O Give Me a Home Where the Buffaloes Roam (and I'll show you a house full of *number two*) Where the Deer and the Antelope Play."

Some *hardheaded* students insisted on saying "dare" instead of "deer" and Mr. Clouden had to struggle with them to get it right. After all those years, his shout still echoes:

"Boy, the word is DEEEEEEER!

Not DAAAAAARE!"

I met Mr. Clouden again. I quietly observed him as he played the organ in the Catholic Church. He cheerfully played during the High Mass and the regular mass. He pounded the notes while the congregation sang, "Come Holy Ghost." He accompanied them as they sang the "Hallelujah Chorus." He was there for the feast of Corpus Christi and was present for the Station of the Cross. He marched in the Church procession.

His was a dedication unmatched and unrivaled since the days of Miss Kate who religiously lit the candles in the Catholic Cathedral in St. George's. Mr. Clouden played and the people lifted their voices towards heaven while his musical fingers touched the inspiring notes.

He was involved in a mass of another kind. He played a significant role in the cultural *mas* with its pretty costumes and sweet, sweet pan. He jumped and he wailed while masqueraders made "mas" on Carnival day. A well-rounded man, Mr. Clouden was. One can take that literally too. He was a talented man, an inspiring soul and a good Grenadian. He taught and he sang and he waved his flag. He, like an Epicurean, sucked life's desirable pleasures and shared his blessings with more than a few. He touched the organ and he played for the Grenadian people. Then at the end of his day, someone played for him

They Call Him Gestapo

He grew up in the village and he knew the village. No one could tell him about the village. He was the eye of the village. He gazed as generations flew by and he took mental note. He was there when Grenadians lit the *masanto* and he recently stood there with his leg and a half under the electric lights in Florida, St John's. He was and still is the cultural notebook.

He was familiar with the estate life in Grenada. He could tell stories of the times pregnant women bent their backs in rigorous toil from morn until eve and often beyond, under the nutmeg and cocoa trees of Grenada. His tales are many. He could recall interesting stories about *Sky Red* and the time the British got angry with Prime Minister Gairy and put him on *ah man ah war* out in the sea.

He could inform you of the time during the nineteen fifties when the boat called the Challenger stuck on a reef off Hope and people came from all over Grenada to witness that. He could give you details of the time in Grenada when every young man wore a *muff* and had a handkerchief in his back pocket. He knew when women wore the pedal pusher and when the tie-dye jersey became popular in Grenada. He could pinpoint the exact time Reds fell from *ah gospo tree* and got a *stone bruise*.

He was around when most Grenadians slept on fiber mattress and the *swizzle stick* was the popular tool to stir the *callaloo*. He knew the name of Miss Mary's *po-po* and the name of the *po-po's* father. He could brief you on the time a certain *fella* returned from Cuba and boasted that he could hide behind *ah cutlass* because he knew *high science*.

He could tell you of the estate worker who decided to take a day off and bravely told a fellow worker:

11

"Tell the overseer *to haul he scrutch*. *Ah ent* feel like cutting no grass today.

Ah taking *ah* break."

The message went out to the overseer who came looking for the one who had uttered such defiant words. And then his tone drastically changed.

"*Sah, ah, ah, coming* right now. A*h* just putting on *me* trousers."

He was there when estate police dragged people to the police station in Gouyave for stealing cocoa and *water grass*. He knew the name of the estate owner who *breed* a young girl and then *breed* another one. He was aware of the time they packed so much load on the donkey's back that the donkey decided to lie down in the middle of the road. The donkey did not want to be *ah* jackass.

He stood and observed as Mandrake ended up in Florida and loved it so much that he never left. Mandrake came from another parish to work on the estate and dropped his anchor there. That was not uncommon then. Gestapo was in his favorite spot to look on as Mandrake made his *simi dimi* in the street after consuming his rum. He peered as Mandrake stood at attention, raised his hands high and announced:

"We, the people of Florida, not *ah* stone shall be *pelted*, not *ah* head shall be *busted!*"

Gestapo forgot no one. When Bogart who had spent *umpteen* years in England decided to visit Grenada, he walked the streets of Florida and quickly realized that no one remembered him. But that was before a loud voice shouted:

"Bogart, you *ole Betche*!

When *yuh* come back?"

The man who saw all recognized all too. Time and distance did nothing to dim his powers of recollection.

There were others who returned to the village. One individual came from America with his head in the clouds. Gestapo looked at him and smiled. His smile turned into a laugh when the man began wearing a polo shirt with a different logo every day. One said, "New York," another had the words, "Yale University." Gestapo wore an ordinary shirt and his foot, his one foot, was always planted on the common ground

He stood in Florida and saw everything. He witnessed the young man *skanking* to the Jamaican reggae beat as St. Paul's jukebox filled the air with the vibrating sounds. He looked on as the boys practiced their martial arts moves in the small church that stood near the Florida crossroad. In those days, many in Grenada wanted to be martial arts heroes. It was a craze that also passed. A young man named Pressy practiced his karate in Gouyave around that time.

He looked on as Kuk Jenga sang his *calypso*. He quietly observed the young man sneaking through the window of his *outside ooman's* house. He stood right there and *scoped the scene.*

He said hello to a young woman who pretended she did not hear. Then she turned around and scolded him.

"*Ole* man, haul *yuh kuk kus*
and keep yuh ole backside quiet!"

A man standing nearby heard and laughed.

Gestapo had a timely response:

"*Doh* worry.

A*h* know where she does pee!"

He lived through Grenada's rough times. He survived demonstrations, Hurricane Janet, fires and guns. And when Prime Minister Bishop was killed, an old man in Florida looked at him and said:

"*Alooooooo there! Alooooooo there!* Grenada is coming like *Odesia.*

Woe pa!"

Gestapo looked at him and shook his head.

The Visagoth

He was no Einstein, not by any stretch of the imagination, but he was no *stupidee* either. Yet the name stuck to him in the same way a *wood slave* lizard attaches itself to a ceiling. People called him *ah pappyut,* another term for a foolish person. Years of experience did precious little to jumpstart an intellect that operated with the pace of a *morocoy.* I am reluctant to join the many and call him a *stupidee.* I will tell you why.

No *stupidee* can be such an expert in pushing the *steel pan.* If you put a *stupidee* to push pan that accommodated *panmen* on a stand around the Carenage, you can bet your *bottom dollar* that the *panmen* will have to be fished out of the sea. He would dump them right into the oil-soaked spot where the wooden vessel called Starlight used to *park up.* The Visagoth pushed, but he pushed Angel Harp's pan right. He pushed while the tireless Mafu pounded the car rim and people danced.

He was a hard person to fool. You tell a *stupidee* to *cutlass ah* big lawn in Westerhall and promise him an invisible gold watch as payment and he will go for it. You could fool *ah stupidee* with that. No one can see an invisible watch, but a *stupidee.* He would believe also, that since no one can see it then no one can steal it. *Dem kind ah ting* could not catch the Visagoth

A *stupidee* can't act a whole Western movie all by himself. That calls for talent, skill and a vivid imagination. The Visagoth was the star, head crook and small crook all wrapped in one. Indeed, he was the "Good, the Bad and the Ugly." He was Pecos, Django, and Fernando Sancho. He was John Wayne!

Hooray for the epic westerns acted out under Teresita's mango tree on Cooper Hill. And when the *fellas* told him they spotted tequila, his reply always was, "*Whey him?*" and he was ready to shoot up tequila. He was a true Gary Cooper and behind every shadow was a gun. Punchy, Tyrone and *dem* used to roar with laughter while his movie was in progress.

His eyes were sharper than that of a ground dove. It was not unusual for him to stand in Marryshow pasture observing the *fellas* play *bat and ball* while keeping his eyes on the Wharf to see when his mother was coming home. Then he spotted her quite over by Jonas Browne. Before one could have uttered *bud pepper,* he was sitting in the base of the big mango tree that stood next to his mother's house. He sat in his famous spot where his *bamsee* transformed the roots into a shiny glow more polished than newly varnished wood. Then his mother arrived and shouted:

"Bwoy! Pass yuh arse in the house!"

The Visagoth was no *stupidee.* No *stupidee* is brilliant enough to put a car's number plate on a wheelbarrow. He placed one on the same wheelbarrow he used to make his *panquaye, droging* goods from shops and occasionally used to tote a gas cylinder. And when someone told him that the police was checking car numberplates and licenses on the street, he was smart enough to hide the wheelbarrow in the *bee bush* in Grand Anse.

Then someone died and he hauled out the wheelbarrow, packed it with flowers collected from the neighborhood and led the funeral procession. His face was as solemn as a monk in prayer.

No *stupidee* will steal a pot of rice and peas and have enough sense to sprinkle some on the ground, and then blame the neighbor's cat. That called for the use of some gray matter.

Now to that unfortunate man who had the nerve to look at him and call him "Cooper Hill *Dum Dum.*"

The Visagoth's mother heard and poked her head out of the window of the pre-cut *Janet House* and addressed him:

"Jackass! *Doh* just sit there!

Tell the *blastid Maco* where to look for the *Dum Dum.*"

The Visagoth sat under the mango tree and smiled.

And I Remember Bobby Too!

I stood and watched as Bobby *hopscotched* his way through the rugged track that led from Morne Jaloux to Springs. Then he continued on to Belmont, his bare feet having grown immune to the burning pangs of the midday sun. He was in a hurry again. There were those who claimed that Bobby was once a brilliant teacher or tailor, but then someone *doo* him. *Dooing* was one way to explain a sudden change in one's behavior. Someone either *doo* you, or put *lite* on you. One thing was certain though; whoever succeeded in *dooing* Bobby, failed to *doo* his ability to spell.

No word was too hard for Bobby to unscramble. He rattled them off with an ease that would have made Mr. Webster smile. School children saw Bobby and instinctively asked him to spell. He never stumbled on the tongue twisters. He even spelled some words in his own fancy way. Mississippi, for instance, became "MI, crooked letter I, crooked letter I, hump back I." He spelled and the people opened their mouths in amazement. If he was asked to spell too many words, though, he became aggravated and mixed them up with some *bad words*. He was good at spelling those too! Then, one was sure to get the message.

Bobby was familiar with words, but he was just as familiar with *praise*. Bobby always learned of someone's death early. And when the people gathered at the home to pray for the dead, Bobby was already there.

It was a common practice for mourners to bring in the Legion of Mary to recite the Holy Rosary while the women and men *knocked down* the Clark's Court or other rum. They drank and sang "O Lord our help in ages past," and helped themselves to more than a few strong drinks.

Bobby would travel all over the place announcing the latest death. He was the telephone link that some people did not have.

He was the death line. Occasionally, he would ask for a piece of bread and if one pretended not to have it, he would raise his voice and demand.

"*Yuh ha* bread *dey*! *Yuh ha* bread *dey*!
Gimme ah piece ah bread."

He then took the bread and journeyed on.

He was very observant too. As he traveled, he took keen interest in what was taking place around him. He acquainted himself with people and things. It was not very wise to ask Bobby to reproduce the sound of the sugarcane factory. It was worse to do so when *big people* were present. His answer was always a graphic, "I F... I F... I F...!" The F stood for a well-known *bad word*. He had the movements to accompany the words. Then children got *licks* for making Bobby *cuss and wine up he waist.*

It was obvious, and indeed natural, that as he hastily trotted the hot pitch, nature would sometimes call. Once when it did, Bobby sought to relieve himself right in front of Back and Neck's front door, Back and Neck was waiting with *ah bull pistle* and Bobby was forced to get up, pull up his pants and move on.

He sought a more suitable place beneath a nearby breadfruit tree. Then he continued on to announce that Miss Mary had passed away.

Andro and Dem

Andro used to take *ah* whole *leaven bread* and push it in his mouth. Then after two bites, the bread quickly disappeared. He then washed it down with *ah Solo, Red Spot* or Fanta *sweet drink*. Next, he took up the *lard pan* filled with *pickin'* and placed it on his head. He then made it down the cobbled steps of Cooper Hill, balancing the *pickin' pan* with considerable ease. He balanced it in the same manner as Miss Charles. She used to carry baskets of food on a tray placed on her head to feed the policemen stationed near Fort George. Miss Charles was a strong woman. She had a pleasant personality too.

The *pickin'* was made up of all kinds of leftover foods. Pigs were never particular about what they ate, so *green fig and dasheen skin* and even rotten mangoes were thrown into the *pickin' pan*. The pigs also ate *bluggoe* leaves and coconut husks.

Cocoawood was unlike the pig. He cared about his diet, but *dat* ungrateful man used to make his wife *ketch she royal tail*. He hated breadfruit soup and every time he drank his grog and *blew all the pesh* in the rumshop, his wife got vexed and retaliated by putting breadfruit soup in his bowl. That was the signal for him to launch into a foul-mouth tirade. He cursed his wife, her mother, her father and everyone he could remember. He even cursed the deceased and the neighborhood dogs when he was angry. When he was drunk and walked up the hill people used to shout, "Look out Castro coming!" The name "Castro" was a reference to Fidel Castro, the Cuban leader.

Mr. Mickey was another character. He vowed never to eat *lambie.* He devoured *callaloo soup, oildown,* cook-up rice and he even *put ah licking* on the *back and neck chicken* his wife bought from the Cold Storage Store. *He used to cut all kind ah style on the lambie.* That was until his wife prepared a wonderful dish of stewed *lambie* with rice and peas

She set a tempting plate before him and he immediately dived into it. In a few seconds the plate was as clean as *ah* baldhead. Mr. Mickey knew what he had eaten, loved it and wanted to ask for more, but he was too ashamed after *cutting so much style* over the years. The lingering taste tortured him. He could take no more:

"Woman!

Yuh ha more *ah dat blastid ting dey?"*

"*Blastid ting?"* she replied.

"*Wha* happen? *Yuh* playing you *cyan* remember the name? It's *lambie*, Mickey, the name is *lambie!"*

Mickey's days of *cutting style* on *lambie* were over.

Moosch's eating habits was similar to that of the pigs that Andro *droged* the *pickin'* to feed. He ate anything. He loved to cook and eat the heads of animals. His friend Shorty from Woburn was always hesitant to eat at his house because he was never certain what kind of beast head Moosch would prepare. Moosch lived in Brooklyn for sometime and he was known to travel all the way to New Jersey to buy goat head and deer head.

When he got drunk, he snatched anything and ate it. He sat in his house one day and bit into a *Vienna bread* packed with corned beef. He did not realize or seemed to care that he was also helping himself to the reds ants that were crawling around in the corn beef. He thought it strange, though, because he knew he did not purchase all that corn beef. That day he got a sober awaking when he felt the sting of the red ants on his lip.

And now I will tell the story of Big George. He loved his food, but the neighbor's cat named Johnny loved his food even more. No matter how much care he took to secure his pot, the cat always found a way to uncover it and sink its teeth into his fried jacks, *corn fish* or stewed beef.

Big George decided to end the cat's *tiefing* ways once and for all. He *set up* one night and waited for the unwelcome intruder. As Johnny jumped on the stove, he grabbed it by the tail. He carried the animal all the way to the Fall Edge near Grand Anse and threw it over the precipice. He walked home a relieved man, sensing that his troubles with that cat were over.

He placed his hands in his pockets and merrily whistled a Sparrow *calypso* tune as he walked up his gap. To his dismay, Johnny was sitting on his step peeping at him and licking its lips. Johnny was peeping like *ah* Grenadian. He had just devoured another big jack.

Big George had only succeeded in depriving Johnny of one of its lives. It had eight more lives to steal his *corned fish*, fishcake, big jack and smoked herrings.

Back then, Grenada had all kinds of interesting characters. George Beard, who pushed his bike from Belmont to True Blue during the time of Expo '69, was a strange individual. He once said that the sun was so hot, he felt sorry for his bike, so he decided not to ride it in such blistering heat.

That was the same George Beard who cut a branch off a tree while standing on the same branch. When he shouted, "Miss Margaret, look out, it's coming down," he was going down also. Daddy-O, that jovial individual, looked on and laughed. And when someone told George Beard his house was burning as he sat in the cinema, his reply was,

"How the hell me house could burn when *ah* have the key in me pocket?"

Walter Dunn was a man with more than a touch of intelligence and he proved how efficient a thinker he was when he was charged with walking around naked. He won his case because he convinced the judge that since he was wearing a tie he was not naked. I can still see him as he made his stately strides on the streets of St. George's.

Dummy James was a fearless individual. He was once charged with an offense and as he stood in court, the judge asked him if he was guilty or not. Dummy James calmly told the judge,

"Ah cyan talk now.

Yuh doh see me mouth full?Ah eating me Rock Cake."

I cannot forget Joe Bain. He claimed that the government stole his land and that was all he spoke about when you met him. I ran into him on Pandy Beach once, wearing his short blue pants and big *waterboots.* I never got to swim because by the time he was through talking about his land, it was time for me to go home.

Many Grenadians will always remember Carriacou Sparrow. I picture him still in his Bermuda shorts and over-sized straw hat as he sang and entertained the crowds in St. George's. His favorite tunes were "Banana Boat for England" and "The Lizard Jump Up." He was a lively and energetic individual who made all kinds of fancy moves as he sang the songs.

Mushay, another eccentric individual, tried to convince people that he was a "damn millionaire." He spoke in a serious tone about all the money he had in the World Bank. He really believed that, but school children only laughed. Another *fella* called "Now Now" used to ring a bell announcing the latest sale bargains in town.

I must not fail to mention Father Paul. He was a priest who hailed from Malta and was noted for visiting women to pray with them just as they were taking their shower. Once while he entered a woman's house, as she was changing her clothes, he placed his hand with the fingers ajar in front of his face and uttered the famous words, "Father Paul can't see!" He said the words as his eyes peered through his fingers.

Politicians

Richard Nixon once made the statement, "I am not a crook." We all know the many troubles that came Nixon's way and how he ended his career. I have high regards for a politician who would tell us up-front that he or she is a crook. We should not have to wait until after we cast our votes to learn that we voted for a *bubul king. Nah!* They should tell us in advance and let us decide if we want to put them in office. There are always people who would vote for crooks once they can gain from the *crookery.*

There are politicians who have more tricks than *dem* monkeys in Grand Etang forest. I remember reading a book in which a certain political contender was crying crocodile tears during a funeral. Suddenly, he peered through the fake tears to ask someone who it was that had died. Big, big tears and the man did not even know who passed away. All done in the name of hauling in some votes and winning an election!

American politicians love to kiss babies while campaigning. Some of them never kiss their own babies at home, but they find time to kiss babies they don't even know. That looks good on the evening news. And don't talk about the handshake! There are politicians who would shake the devil's hand if that can spring a victory. Next time you see a politician, look at the right hand and notice the erosion caused by the constant handshaking. But partner, if *one ah dem* politicians is shaking your hand and sees someone more important than you, it's later for you. Yes, it's *bye-bye Blakey*!

My favorite politician is Justin Crowe McBournie. I have more respect for Crowe and his Good Old Democracy (G O D) party than I had for Nixon. Crowe tells you things in his Manifesto that only people on Mars would believe. I am surprised that Crowe did not offer Grenadians a *tatou* in every pot. Perhaps someone told him that Birchgrove people *dun* eat out all the *tatou* already.

I don't believe there is a politician who would not like to ban George Orwell's book "Animal Farm." That book can open people's eyes and ears too. Most people act like the sheep in "Animal Farm." The sheep like to bleat, and bleat only one thing: "Four legs good, two legs bad." Nice, nice slogan to stall the thinking process. Politicians know they have to give the people a song or a slogan. While the sheep keep shouting the slogan, the unscrupulous politicians drink wine and ask themselves: "How the hell they got that name sheep and not jackass?"

It is even better if a politician can dig up a famous *calypsonian* or musician to make people dance. Give them some wine, rum or *mountain dew* and they *wine* more. Once you get people to *wine* you just have to keep them *wine-ing* non-stop until election is over. Smart people start to think when the liquor wears off. The politician keeps the liquor flowing and the momentum going. Better still if they vote with *wine* in their heads. Just pray they don't put the X in the wrong place while casting votes *under their oil*

Always put the X in the right place. That can decide if you will be able to put bread on the table.

AH HA! DAT'S US!

Nicknames as

Grenadian as Gru Gru

Ask Grenadians in New York, Port of Spain, Toronto or London if they know *so and so* from Grenada. They might stop, think, or reflect a bit and then throw the inevitable question back to you:

"*Wha* is she nickname?"Or simply "*Man doh gee me dat* name, just tell me he *dam* nickname!"

Nicknames can be more important than the names we call Christian names and surnames. People usually forget those names. But for some reason or reasons, nicknames stick to Grenadian people like *sticky cherry* to the hand.

If you don't want a nickname to stick, pretend you like it. When somebody calls you a nickname, just *skin yuh teeth* and pretend you just got christened again. Laugh out loud and that nickname will last as long as the laugh.

I had a problem *pitching marbles.* For some reason the marble used to stick in my knuckles. I don't know if it was nerves or what, but I used to end up falling on *me bamsee* when I released the marble. A friend of mine called Napoleon gave me a nickname that I often hear when I return to Grenada. I should have *grinned me teeth* when he called me that, but when one is but a *young gospo*; the reaction can be one of anger or annoyance. Then the new name stays for good!

There were nicknames we could only use outside the house. Those were the *common* or vulgar nicknames. If Pum Corn hit you in the head while playing cricket, it was not wise to complain to your parents that Pum Corn struck you. You were better off saying Corn hit you; but then they would not know who Corn was. Names like Big Pum, Stink Pum, Bam Bam Head and Big Fart had to be modified for our parents' eardrums.

Things have changed drastically these days. Some of the *bad words* nickname could easily end up in the house. Cable TV helped pave the way for their acceptance. They softened up the reaction to offensive nicknames.

It is possible for one person to be known by one nickname in Gouyave, another name in Belmont and yet another in Grenville. And while Mr. Bush might shake the Prime Minister's hand and call him by his official name, people in the Spice Island look at the picture in the newspaper and say to each other:

"*Allyuh doh* see *Stone* shaking Bush hand?"

And just like Spain had its Ferdinand 1, Ferdinand 2, etc. there were whole families in Grenada that managed to have one nickname stuck to the entire family. The father, son and grandson had the same nickname, only the 1 or 2 was left out after the name.

Some people were happy with their nicknames and eagerly responded when the names were called. Names that were not offensive or made them feel good about themselves were welcomed. They took those names as compliments. They smiled when they were called Strongman, Sweetman Doray, Woodman, Pretty Gal, Sagaboy, or Hero.

It was a different story when names that mocked or demeaned their character were used. No one wanted to be called Elephant Foot, Sambo, Big Chow, Monkey Toe, Bam Bam Head, Crappo Features, or Mud Mask.

There were those who accepted a part of the nickname, but hated the other part. One *fella* responded favorably when he was called Spirit. However, when he was called Jumbie Spirit he flew into a rage. Some people confronted those who called them the unflattering names. They believed that the best way to get people to refrain from calling them those obnoxious names was to voice their disgust. One man, nicknamed Sorefoot Boss, once approached a group of young men. He calmly said in a well-mannered tone:

"Good evening, gentlemen. I will be very grateful if you would refrain from calling me such an unflattering and injudicious name which is inappropriate and demeaning to my character. I thank you all most benevolently. Once again, good evening Gentlemen."

Then he quietly walked away.

People left Grenada with nicknames and traveled abroad where they attained advanced degrees. Some of them forgot their nicknames after a long absence. Then they make a trip back to the Spice Isle and run into someone who remembers the nicknames that they forgot and hail them. Reactions can vary! Many keep on walking pretending not to hear the name, especially if people were looking on. The local reaction could be,

"*Wha' the hell he playing?*

He pretending he *doh* even know *he own* name?"

If you know people like that who intend to make the trip to the Spice Island, advise them to *skin their teeth* or just laugh out loud when old time friends remember their "real" names.

And How Yuh Do. Doo Doo?

Time and distance had cast a wall between us, but then I ran into him on Flatbush Avenue, Brooklyn. I heard the voice first,

"Wendell, you son of *ah* gun! Man, *yuh playing the rass, bwoy! Whey the hell yuh was hiding all dem years? Oh, Goooood, me bwoy!*"

The excitement from that chance meeting was evident in his voice. No, he was not cursing me. It was only another of the many types of our Grenadian greetings. Our forms of greetings are as varied as the spices that abound in our beautiful countryside.

The last time I had seen him, we were students at Palmer School. Then it was normal for us to approach our teachers, place our hands on our foreheads in a smart salute, and say a pleasant good morning.

The salute was mandatory during the days of headmasters like old Mr. Fletcher, who ran the school with strict military type discipline. The salute was no doubt one of the things the English gave Fletcher who, in turn, passed on to us. The salute became customary. I even saluted in front of Brother Schaper, the American, and I saw his bewildered look when I smartly placed my hand on my forehead and begged,

"Sir, please let me out!"

The salute was not only for greeting, but also for seeking permission to answer nature's sometimes unpredictable call. Like many other things, the salute became unimportant with the passage of time.

We are familiar too with the traditional handshake and the knock of the clenched fist. Some even became acquainted with the Black Power salute when the fervor raged during the seventies. Then there are those who just give a pat on the back or shoulder and shout,

"*Wha happening dey?*"

The bear hug, too, expresses warmth and closeness. It is nice to give a brother or sister a comforting bear hug. Just don't squeeze too hard. Some people *doh like dat.* It is much better than having people sneak up behind you, block your eyes with their hands, and say "guess who?" *Ah hate dat*! Sometimes one is able to tell who it is by the smell of the hands.

I like the simple greetings like "How you do?" There is a definite Grenadian feel to those words. My mother's friends, Miss Pope and Miss Paul always used to ask me "How you do?" in that pleasant Grenadian voice.

Some Grenadian men push it a little further when they meet the women,

"*Doo Doo,* darling, *ah* so glad to see you. Come *gimme me ah kiss nah!"*

We use the words "how you do" and we like the words *doo doo.* Sadly, the Americans took our nice little word to mean something I asked my teacher to let me out of the classroom to *leggo* in the toilet.

And then you meet your old time *compere:*

"*Bwoy,* whey the hell *yuh* going with *dat* big belly *bwoy?"*

Don't feel bad! It's just another warm Grenadian greeting. He might follow it up with an embrace and a smile as big as a St. David's breadfruit. That is a kinder greeting than "*Wha* going on mango belly?"

It is not a good idea to lose too much weight either. Another Grenadian might utter,

"*Wha* happen *gal?* Good to see *yuh,* but like *dat* man making *yuh* see trouble or *wha?* Darling, *doh* fraid to tell me *yuh* know!"

Remain calm; it's just another Grenadian greeting. It is much better than the one I received when I first landed at Point Salines and saw my long time friend. He could not hold his happiness:

"*Eh, eh,* dogface. *Ah* see *yuh* come back!"

I laughed and gave him a Grenadian embrace.
Then I saw Ma Rubes, who warmly remarked,
"Lord, bless *me* eyesight, *bwoy*. *When yuh come?* *Ah* have soursop juice and *mauby* in the fridge."

Haul Yuh!

We are a pleasant and loving people; no one can doubt that! But there were times when *niceness* took *ah* back seat. Every time women and men began *cussing,* the Grenadian warmth was temporally halted and placed on the backburner. *Cussing* is as Grenadian as *mace.* There was a time when Grenville Street was called Korea and a part of Gouyave was called Belfast-only no one bothered to draw a 38th parallel as was done in Korea.

One who travels through Gouyave might chance to witness a *bacchanal* in progress. Then the thought is:

"*Bwoy dem* Gouyave people could *cuss oui!*"

But hold it; don't fool yourself! The people using the *sailor words* might not be from Gouyave at all. Perhaps they just ended up there, so don't be too rough on Gouyave people until you are sure who are the ones *letting go* those four-letter words. When one stands in Central, which is located in Gouyave and hears all those words banging against the eardrum, the *bad words* probably are from people who hailed from Grand Roy or Victoria, but just settled in Gouyave. Well, if you got into Sapote's or Shaw's way, you were in for *a good tongue-lashing.* But heck, no area had a monopoly on the use of the *bad words* that aggravated judges like the Honorable I. I. Duncan.

When the women started *cussing* on Cooper Hill, mangoes used to fly off Teresita's mango tree. School children used to hide under their beds.

Much of the quarrel stemmed from *dey say, hear say* and *bad talk.* That was responsible for much of the confusion all over the place. When best friends started to *cuss* all the hidden things were exposed. As Bob Marley instructed:

"Only your friend know your secret,

So, only he could reveal it."

That was the weapon they kept for *your backside* when the friendship was severed.

When the cussing started everybody got to know that you took away someone's man or woman. We learned who couldn't read or write. You got to know who *buss ah shit* down by the bay. They let you know who made *fares* with the sailor from the *man ah war. All ah dat* surfaced when the bacchanal started. Some people shut their doors when the cussing began, but they fooled no one; they hid behind the blind and peeped. Grenadians love to peep. Such *commess* was too juicy to be ignored.

Then one got to hear of the 'bringing up.'

"*Ah go bring yuh up!*"

That was a reference to the courthouse. Pay little attention to that. They were not likely to go before any judge. If a police passed by, a lookout gave a signal for them to cool it until the officer moved on. Then it was back to the exchange of hostile words! In Grenada, police arrested people for using obscene language and they got more infuriated when the obscenities were words the *cuss buds* invented. Policemen hated *cusswords* they could not spell or did not understand.

There was also a traveling part to the *cussing*.

"Ah going in Guyana for *yuh scrutch.*"

Grenada's obeah was not strong enough so some threatened to go overseas. There were those who even threatened to go as far as Haiti which was believed to be the Mecca of Obeah. Others promised to *doo* the offending party. A few spoke of going to Carriacou to *doo* people. I don't know why they sought to include the people of Carriacou in their *taybae.*

This *dooing* thing some took seriously. One *foreday morning,* I met an old man in Springs. He told me that he was on his way to Pandy Beach to *work ah ting* to save his son who was to appear before a judge. He was going to *work ah ting* on that judge. He was carrying two brown eggs and a bottle of rum to *doo* the judge.

Election time was a big time for *cussing.* It was a time when grown men and women argued and cursed each other over politics. Back then, the *cussing* was mostly between the GNP and GULP political parties. The other P's had not yet arrived on the scene. When the election was over and the political candidates were *knocking glass,* the people were still *cussing* and threatening to *buss* each other's head.

Cussing lasted a few minutes to several hours. *Rumshop cuss* lasted for years. Some just cursed until they got tired. It did not take much to ignite a quarrel. A man who was offered a drink and called for expensive whisky, when he was accustomed to drinking Clark's Court rum, stood the chance of getting an *angry tongue lashing* from the one who made the offer.

"Is rum *yuh* does drink; what the arse *yuh* playing. *Yuh* want to kill Santa Claus?"

And then there was the individual who returned from America or England and the butcher neglected his regular customers and sold her all the beef. His customers voiced their anger:

"*You ole macoman*! When she go back, we won't buy *yuh blastid* beef!"

The *cussing* hardly stopped—except at Christmas! Like a basketball game with its timeout, Christmas was the timeout for cussing. Well, except *yuh bounced up* someone whom you had not seen in a long time:

"*Bwoy, yuh* wicked scamp! Where the hell *yuh* hiding since *yuh ha bud in cage? Ah cyan* see you at all!"

But that is ah welcome kind of *cuss* around Christmas time.

Finally, doh get Grenadians vex. After he or she *buss* some bad words *in yuh tail* you might have to unravel this remark:

"*Ketch yuh falling self*".

How the hell you go do *dat?*

Slangs and Expressions

NEN NEN always told me not to eat too much *ASHAM* because *ah go PUFF.* She told me that *ah* was too *LICKRISH.* Well, *ah* put *ah BUNLOAD ah* licks on the *ASHAM,* but thank *PAPA GAWD, ah* never *PUFF.* And the ripe *FIG* that COMPERE TIG told me not to eat in the hot sun was my favorite. *Ah* ate so many of *DEM,* but they never KNOCK ME DOWN as people warned. Teresita peeped through her window once and told me not to suck so many mangoes because ah go get *SHITTINGS.*

Well. *ah* suck mangoes as if they put LITE on me, but *ah* never got *SHITTINGS.* Ah even suck *dem* juicy mangoes that the *CONGOREE* bite.

MACMERE Phillip once told me *ah* that *ah* looked like *AH* WOODEN JUDGE IN *AH* RAM GOAT SESSION. *Ah* still don't know what that meant. And when *ah* woke up in the morning and a little cold sore was on me mouth, they told me that CACAROACH KISSED ME and *ah* resembled *AH JUMBIE BEAD.* They told me to wash me face and take out the *KAKAJAY* from me eyes and the *BRIDLE* from me mouth.

Then *ah* took *ah* quick quick bath under the pipe outside and they told me *ah* took *AH GEORGE OTWAY.* But yuh can't blame me. The pipe was in the middle of the yard and *ah din* want *dem FASS* people to *MACO* me POLICE.

So ah bounced up ah TAYBAE woman.

She said, *"WHA YUH* watching me for?"

Ah replied, *"JOOK* OUT ME EYE *NAH!"*

She said I was *BARRING* and asked me,

"YUH FADDAH IS *AH* GLASS MAKER?"

Ah replied, *"OH GORM, OOMAN. AH TIEF YUH* WHITE FOWL?"

She then said,

"MACO, DEY SEN YUH FOR ME. TELL DEM YUH EN SEE ME."

Ah said, *"LEH ME GO ME WAY EH, IS ME YUH HA STRENGTH ON?"*

Her final words:

"YUH GO MISS ME, *OUI. YUH* LOOK LIKE *AH* DRY OCHRO STICK!"*

Just then ah big political meeting was taking place. All *KINDA WASH YUH FOOT AND COME* were assembled. Two rotten eggs whizzed by. *Ah BAWLED OUT. RUCTION IN DE PLACE!* If that continued it was *BYE BYE BLAKEY* for me. *LAWD, IT WAS FIRE IN THE CONGO!*

But the politician kept using some big *HENGGIBBIT* words like he SWALLOWED *AH* DICTIONARY.

An *OLE RUMBO* from Marshall's rumshop looked at him and shouted, "PREACH IT, *BRUDDAH!* PREACH IT! *DAT* IS NOT MAN TALKING *DEY. DAT* IS MAN *PUPPA!* Someone asked him if he was from *BAHOE* and showed him where the church was.

Sometimes, when we were going through the door, we looked back and remarked, *"AH COMING EH."* We are coming when we are going.

Ah held on to me *GAL* and went inside the house. Me friends got vex and asked me if *AH HA BUD IN CAGE.*

Man, if *yuh* see me, *BREEZE CYAN PASS.*

Who *ah* BOUNCED UP when *ah* came outside, but *FADDAH PRIEST.* He told me that he was shocked that *AH LEGGO AH BIG ONE* in church so close to the pulpit. He told me if that continued, he *GO GEE* me something to *CORK ME.*

Then *ah* made up me mind that no one would catch me with *dem* little tricks they tried on me. Vero caught me once. She made *ah fist wid* she hand and told me to pinch the spot by the pinky

finger. When I did she laughed,
"*AH HA*! YUH PINCHED *FOWL BAM BAM*"
DAT BUGGA!

RUM TALK

I Will Never Condemn a Man!

"I will never condemn a man!" Those were Uncle Lawrence's favorite words and he always uttered them with such deep conviction one would think it was Saint Paul making his famed speech on Mars Hill. My only objection was that he always chose to say them while he was *under his oil.*

Strong rum makes people do strange things. Some people are suddenly hit with a dose of happiness, others make strange antics, some dance and there are those who just find a spot anywhere to *buss ah sleep.* I saw a man slip off to dreamland at a cricket match after he took a sip from a bottle of River Antoine Rum. A friend of mine kicked down my neighbor's cabinet after a shot of Clark's Court rum. The spirit is not for everyone!

We go back to the individual in question. His specialty was to make speeches and he was noted for doing so while we were trying to induce slumber after a hard day at school or work. He cursed Gairy and he cursed Blaize. He cursed Bishop too! Once they told him to go outside and *cuss* Gairy and he immediately answered the challenge. He stood right in the spot where Paddock and Belmont meet and *gave Gairy his clothes.* Then he went back inside, took *ah* strong rum, and said, "I will never condemn a man."

His best drinking days were at *China Town*. I guess his best speeches were made there too. One day, after consuming some Rivers rum, he decided to take a taxi to Blue Danube for more *grog*. But, alas, Blue Danube was already closed so he ordered the taxi driver to turn around and drive him back to *China Town*. The driver raced back, anxious to get away from the rum speeches. Uncle Lawrence even asked the driver to *fire one* with him.

The Grenadian nights can be still except for the occasional croaking of the restless *Crappo*. It is on such occasions that one grasps the opportunity to absorb information in preparation for those tough examinations. As the brain soaks in the details, one becomes confident that the exam will be a breeze. It had to be, after such diligent study! But then, all of a sudden, the tranquility is disturbed:

"I will never condemn a man!"

That was time to put the books away and prepare for rum speeches that would knock the eardrum for the rest of the night.

He passed away. Michael, the Archangel, is hearing those rum speeches now.

The Rumshop—

An Intellectual Center

There is no intellectual center like the Grenadian rumshop. No greater ideas have ever flowed from Cambridge or Harvard than those that arise from the rumshop dialogue.

You want to master philosophy or sociology? Don't waste your money or time attending the University of the West Indies. There is a better university in every village in Grenada. The lecturers are often in good spirits—the spirits that open the mind when they open the bottle. Sit in a comfortable spot on a chair at the University of the Breadfruit Tree in Beaulieu and listen as the rum-filled professors expound on the trials and tribulations of life.

A full bottle of strong is a most inspiring sight for any rum drinker. It energizes the mind and brings it to life. It stimulates the brain and drives away sleep and drowsiness. It instills new energy and fresh ideas and promotes eagerness to converse and, yes, lecture. Rum drinkers stand up and lecture with the conviction of Socrates or Aristotle. Rum is the driving force behind the *ole talk*. You take away the rum and all ideas dry up. The thoughts disappear like the spirits they consume.

No village is complete without a rumshop or two. Some, through the years, have attained more fame than others.

Rum drinkers all have their favorite spots. I can't tell you why a man would leave Marshall's rumshop and journey all the way to Grand Anse or River Road to drink rum. I guess it has to do with the atmosphere—a word that rum drinkers like. When the spirits put them in the stratosphere they do not care much for atmosphere. Then they drink anywhere.

Sophisticated rum drinkers sit near the window at Nutmeg Restaurant and watch the boats make their way in and out of the harbor. Occasionally, they peep like other Grenadians at the spot by Sea Change Bookstore to *maco* women and men talking. Some drank in places where it was easy to stand around and *mop* some rum.

A number of individuals were noted for making all kinds of tricks when they drank rum. Mandrake in Florida used to make the sign of the cross. Ask Cowie; he can tell you! Others *skin up their faces.*

Some drunkards *squinge up* in a corner just like the old-time taxi drivers. Others sway from side to side as if they own the road. Many laugh as if they *catch ah glad.* Some *spin cufform* in the road and dare the motorist to bounce them. Most keep out of the way of people coming in to buy saltfish, pig snout or flour in the shop. A few rum drinkers, however, get in the way of other customers and shopkeepers get annoyed.

The smell of *saltfish* in the shop does not offend their nostrils at all. The more rum consumed the better the *saltfish* smells!

A rumshop never closes. When the front door is shut, there is always the window, side door or back door.

Big shots like to drink in the back. Lawyers and politicians sneak in the back to play dominoes and *throw down ah drink or two.* They like to keep away from the "run of the mill" crowd, except when election is close. All politicians love rum drinkers at election time. That's the time politicians like to call all the boys and girls. One politician in Gouyave once called all the boys who joyfully *drank him out;* then voted him out. They are a wise bunch.

Grenada boasted such individuals who were quite entertaining and whose notable vice was drinking rum. When they drank their *grog,* they all became intellectuals.

Some of them walked the streets and wrote all kind of mathematical symbols on walls and in the road. A big white man called Gater, who never wore a shirt, used to lie on his back with his arms outstretched in the sea and float for long periods.

Ah fella called Tony used to get annoyed and threatened to fight if someone told him that *Red Spot sweetdrink* tasted better than Cocoa Cola. Another individual walked from place to place telling people that "Endless is ah lot, ah lot." He ended up with the nickname "Endless."

Rumshop drinkers could *maco LAWD*! They know who *dey* with who, who pregnant, who leave who, who about to leave who, and who *horning* who. They even know the woman the priest sleeping with.

They are good historians, too. Next time you pass *ah* rumshop, buy a bottle and listen as they tell you about the time your mother had to drag your father from the *outside ooman's* house. That's called rum history.

Those Who Trusted Rum

There were those who trusted rum—that was a different matter! They sometimes ended up paying for rum they did not get the chance to smell. After a few trusted *eights of rum*, shopkeepers laughed and even invited their friends to come in and say hello. They came to say hello and to drink some trusted rum.

Rum debt was hard to pay because one did not always know when, what, or how much he or she ordered. Some of their friends used to help them with the ordering. However, if they wanted rum in the future, it was essential to pay what the shopkeeper had in his notebook. As a man *under his oil* would say, "It was a poooooooint of honor to settle one's debt." That is, whether he owed it or not!

Praise and Rum

Let's continue with *praise*. That was popular in Grenada too. One could not separate *praise* from rum. The more rum, the more *praise,* the more hearty the singing. A little more oil in the lamp kept it burning and a little more rum, kept them singing loudly. People prayed all night with their hearts, but kept their eyes on the bottle.

They sang "Come Holy Ghost" and "Abide with Me" while they *knocked down* the spirit called Clark's Court. One got to know their real intentions when they sang, "keep it burning 'til the break of day." That gave you the warning to have rum 'til daylight arrived. Some sang without knowing the whole song; they sang anyway. When they stumbled on the words, they just grumbled.

I stood between two old men in a *praise* once. They were singing the same song just different words. One was waiting for the chorus to resume his singing, while the other kept on humming when he forgot the words. The words he knew well were sung the loudest and he made up words as he sang along. And when the rum was finished, it was time to find out whom *Basil* had called again. They did not have to wait long because Bobby was always there to spread the funeral news.

ASSUMPTIONS, ATTITUDES & CHANGES

Grandcharge and Grandmove

Most Grenadians are familiar with the word *grand charge.* Some have been good practitioners of the *grand charge* at one time or another.

A *grand charger* is one who likes to bluff. He pretends to do things, but never actually follows up on his pretence. The move is sometimes meant to frighten someone and the word *grandmove* is often used to describe the actions of the *grand charger.*

Even policemen were known to be good at the *grand charge.* They often go through all the motions of making arrests with loud talk and gestures, but usually ended up arresting no one.

Some people have been such masters of *grand charge* or *grand-move* that the nickname stuck to them for their entire lives. There were many *Grand moves* all over Grenada. A certain *Grandmove* fellow in Carriacou had his own slogan.

"Grand is the word,

and move is the action."

Once Grandmove made *ah bunch ah fellas* from the mainland

duck for cover when he grabbed *ah* piece of wood and pretended he was about to fight. The man began flinging his hands in the air and making idle threats. But he was only *pappyshowing.* Those who knew him well laughed because they were aware that all the big *voose* he was making was simply *grand charge.*

A *grand charger* would *buss* your head with an imaginary stone. He would even pretend he has one in his pocket, but the action is only meant to scare you off. You call his bluff and he does nothing. All he wants to do is frighten you with loud sounds and words. He puts his hands in his pockets as if he has something in there, but all the man is doing is playing pocket pool and looking to see if you would run away.

Never worry about the dog with its *grandmove.* Dogs are good at that too. The grandest move is usually made in front its master's gate. It remains a truism that "All dogs are bad in their own backyard"

"Woof, woof, woof" they bark in the streets, but that bark turns into a lion's roar in front their owner's house. Then you make your own *grand move* by grabbing *ah piece ah wood* or big stone, and both you and the dog run away in different directions. It is a case of big *grandchargers* running for cover.

The silent dog is the one to watch. It sneaks up on you without even barking. It never wastes time barking or making any *grand move.* Then you have scamper away to escape its seething anger after it sinks its teeth into your *kajam.* It is a fact that "Barking dogs seldom bites." Barking people too!

I vividly remember the story about the man in Grenville who heard *cutlass pelting* in his land. Someone was obviously stealing his crops. The man wanted to protect his yams and *green fig.* He crept close to a mango tree, knocked his *cutlass* against a stone and shouted,

"Who *dat?*"

The thief, hitting his own cutlass on a stone replied,

"Who *dat, dat* say 'Who *dat dey?*'"
The landowner, angry, but scared, bawled out:
"Who *dat* who ask 'Who say 'Who *dat dey?*'
Come out— *Leh me buss yuh tail."*
The thief in a gruff voice answered:
"Who *dat* who say 'Who *dat;* who ask 'Who say 'Who *dat dey?*'"
Bring *yuh rass* here! *Yuh* go see who *dat!*"
It was pure *grandcharge* on both ends.

"Who *dat?* Who *dat dey?*" was their battle cry. None was brave enough to make *ah* real move. Well, except the *grand move.*

Both were frightened as the woman called Muffin who pretended to be *ah tess,* but then flew into the arms of her friends after a serious confrontation with ah *badjohn* woman in Bluggoe Cottage. She resorted to threatening words -

"*Allyuh* hold me before *ah cripple she backside. Ah* say hold me!"

She said those words as she pressed hard against a man standing nearby. She was *grandcharging,* actually praying for the man to hold her.

And one must not forget the man who drank up his *tania log, sea moss* and *boise bande.* That was his aphrodisiac. He went home to his wife contemplating his intended superb marathon bedroom performance.

In the still of the night the telephone rang. His wife picked it up and listened as her girlfriend inquired,

"How is *yuh* tiger doing?"

Her reply was the perfect description of a *grand charge* man:

"*Yuh* talking about the *grandcharge* man, *dat* big *maco? Lawd,* ah never see *ah* man like *dat.* He told me he drank up some boise *bande, sea moss and tania log* and he was ready for action. Then he kissed me and held me tight. And *BRAPPS!* He fell asleep!"

Trust Me, It's True!

"Come here *bwoy*. Go down to the shop and TRUST *ah* half pound of pig snout, three *leaven bread, ah* quarter pound of keg butter, *ah* carbolic soap, two Red Spot and a pint *ah Lord oil.* Take *dat tin can* and on your way back pass by the *Bowzer* and buy *ah* half *ah* gallon *ah pitch oil.*"

Yes, *Lord oil*! That was the oil of choice. We used *Lord oil* to fry our bakes and to put in our *saltfish souse.* Nowadays people have all kinds of oil: vegetable oil, corn oil, canola oil, olive oil—all kinds of oil. We had *Lord oil,* castor oil, Canadian healing oil, *pitch oil* and coconut oil.

Recently, I bought some nutmeg oil in Grenada. Nutmeg oil can make Grenada famous with its healing capabilities.

Trust *Lord oil?* Yes trust. That was big, real popular. Almost everybody used to trust—even big shots did so. And it says a hell of a lot about the shopkeepers who were a part of the community.

If you lived in St. Paul's, the shopkeepers there got to know you and, more important, your ability to pay when the month ended.

The shopkeepers were a smart bunch. They had a very good idea of their customers' income and disposable income. Even those who had no steady job used to trust and were trusted by shopkeepers. The shopkeeper knew about the *sou sou,* or when the child's father got paid. He knew the man who had the *ooman* on the side and who would pay for the goods she trusted. He also knew the women who loved to *mind men.*

Trust was an important word and it was so significant that many of those who trusted did not bother to mark down what they took or when they took it. It was a nice agreement between business people and their customers. They trusted each other.

The best people to trust were barbers and taxi drivers. They got paid every day. Dock workers got paid regularly too! While others were waiting for the month to end to see a paycheck, those workers had coins jingling in their pockets all the time

There were no computers then. Shopkeepers wrote the names of those who trusted in notebooks, in no particular order. One did not have to worry. The names would always pop up at the end of the month. A number of shopkeepers used the big government ledger books to keep the record; others went to Bryden and Minors store and bought notebooks. There they entered the amount of saltbeef, cooking oil, flour and saltfish the people trusted until payday.

Not all shopkeepers liked to trust . In fact, some even had signs in their shops that read like this:

"Don't ask for Mr. Trust
He is dead and buried."

And there was a picture of the dead Mr. Trust in a coffin.

In one shop, I once saw a sign that said

"Eggs have no right in rock stone land."

One shopkeeper in Mt. Moritz went so far as to call out the names of *bad pay people* while standing in the middle of the street. A few big shots went and paid right away when they heard their names called.

We remain thankful for our shopkeepers just the way we remain indebted to the fishermen of Grenada. Many shopkeepers like Mr. Selwyn Marshall and Mrs. Sandiford were good to poor people and made it possible for them to eat their daily bread and a little butter until they had the money to pay.

Liming and Breezing Out

Yeah bwoy, we Grenadian are a happy lot. When we were going to school, work or church, there were those who just chose *ah spot* and *breezed out*. *Breezing out and liming* were cherished pastimes.

The area in front of Empire Cinema was *ah big liming spot*. People from St. Paul's, Grand Roy, and the Point had their favorite liming sites also. Mato, Conqueror and Cashier had their special *liming area* in St. John's Street. People stood in their selected enclaves and *ole* talked for hours. The *ole talk* and *ah lot ah macoing* always went hand in hand.

Many Grenadians left Grenada years ago and came to Brooklyn where they are still *breezing out*. Take a walk by Cracker's Record shop or Pressureman's auto place and you go *see wha ah mean*. I know a certain woman who took two weeks from her job to *breeze out*.

If you are *breezing* out for a few minutes, you are only *ketching ah five*. *Ketching ah five* was always *ah* regular Grenadian thing. It is always good to *ketch ah five* because all work and no play makes Jack *ah* big jackass. *In truth*! Take my little advice and *doh ketch too many fives* on your job. You might end up *ketching your rass*.

When Last Yuh Laughed Until Yuh Belly Buss?

When last *yuh* laugh until *yuh* belly *buss*? *Ah* mean *ah* real Grenadian laugh. One that made you fall on the floor and bawl,

"Oh God, *ah* go dead!" "*Woye,* hahahahaha! Ho, ho, ho, ho, hehehehehehe, *doh* kill me!"

Now that is what you call a laugh. That's the one the Reader's Digest says is the best medicine.

"Oh God, *ah* go pee!"

Yuh hear dem say *dat*?

To laugh we have to get the jokes. But some jokes can't make us laugh at all. That's the dry kind of jokes. The joke is usually as dry as hard, stale bread.

When they give you a dry joke, the important thing is to know when to laugh. You have to guess the high point, the climax, and then you laugh like them. Just make a chuckle.

Some *ah dem* just *skin their teeth,* but granny always said, "*All skin teeth is no laugh.*" You don't want to make them feel bad, so you have to pretend that you get it. And you can't give anyone that joke because when the joke done, you are still waiting to hear the jokey part. You never get it!

You got the best jokes during school days. Some did not even involve words. A student will make a bench go rat-at-tat and every-one will laugh in unison. The vibration sometimes woke up sleepy headed students.

There was one person in particular that I always ran away from. Every time he saw me, he had a joke to give. They were usually good and made me laugh, but how many jokes could a person take? He wanted to turn me into a laughing-stock while he crammed his schoolwork and got good grades.

That was the same fellow who was not listening to the teacher when she was explaining that Samson took a jawbone of an ass and beat up the Philistines. When the teacher asked him to repeat what she said, he replied: "Samson jammed them in the arse." You see how good it is to pay attention? Even if you are broke, you could still pay attention.

Ah doh noe if *ah* could still laugh at some of those jokes they used to *buss* on me back home. I laughed when they told me of the man who was going to look for a work at Pearl's Airport. On the way, he saw a big Public Works Department truck with the sign PWD. The man thought it meant Pearl's Work Done so he turned around and headed for his home. He wanted to *mop ah ride* on the same PWD truck, but somebody told him that the PWD meant Please Walk Down

The word "thought" is a funny word. A man once thought he wanted to *leggo one,* but he got the numbers mixed up. He ended up letting go *number two.* That guy got everything confused. I can understand why he believed the sign on the building that read "Civil Service Association" (CSA) meant Can't Stand Again!

And there was that lady who was cleaning fish who declared that she was "ofishiating." And when she was cleaning pork, she said she was "oporkiating."

There are people who hate to see others laugh. They get mad like hell when they witness someone having a hearty laugh. They get annoyed when they notice people laughing and they can't hear the joke. The only solution for that is to laugh too.

Laughter can be contagious. There are people who laugh at things that should make them cry. Some people laugh until they shed crocodile tears. You would think their *muddah* kicked the bucket, but the tears are really hilarious tears. That kind of laugh is as Grenadian as *oildown*; the kind of laugh that makes you "roll and tumble down" as the *calypsonian* said.

People laugh even in church. A pastor in Lucas Street once saw a man sleeping in church and asked a young boy sitting next to him to wake him up. The little boy shouted, " You put him to sleep, you wake him up!" Even the pastor laughed.

Changes

Movies showed us that black people all over the world had the same face. Once, a Haitian man came up to me and started rolling out some *patois*. If I had listened carefully to my grandmother, *ah wuddah* answered the man in his tongue! The *patois* was never preserved in Grenada. One reason for that was some of the people who spoke the language did so among themselves when they did not want the children to understand what *big people* were saying.

And the steel pan! Old people *bawl-out* when Brother Brawf played the steel pan in the Catholic Cathedral. Many of the older heads thought it was an outrage. The Trinidadian calypsonian asked, "Who ever thought that the day would reach when steel band music would play while the reverend preach?" The times were changing.

We began to see things differently. Our own day of enlightenment had arrived; just like the Europeans. Women began wearing mini-skirts, hot pants and halter backs. Some started to go to church without hats and enraged their grandmothers.

Men began taking more night dew and started *macoing* and breaking up dance. And almost no one was hiding to buy a condom. We had come of age!

I began to wear sleeveless shirts. An old man looked at me once and asked, "*Wha happen bwoy?* They did not have enough cloth to finish make *dat* shirt?"

And the Catholic priests started saying mass in English, so at long last people knew that it was not bad words they were *cussing* all that time. Poor Joey, he used to *ketch he nen nen* to understand the Latin.

Brothers and sisters, *yuh* see how things change?

Now that we are grown men and women, it is easy to see

what our parents had to go through.

We used to pout when we saw what was prepared for dinner. Some of us refused to eat breadfruit or *green fig*. More than a few hated yams and *coo coo*. Yet, our parents had to provide in difficult times.

A few years ago, I threw a piece of *bluggoe* for a dog in Grenada. The dog looked at me as if to ask, "Who the hell *yuh* giving *dat?*"

Things have really changed; even the dogs are now *cutting style*.

If you intend to go to Grenada for a cricket match, don't forget to wear your pants with the *scrutch* reaching your knees. And when you see Phillip David, remember to say, "Wuzz up, son!" You can call a grown man son these days.

FOND PLACES

Come Sit in Heaven

Come sit in heaven's earthly bliss,
Turbulent chimes you would not miss,
Relax; observe the water flow,
Tranquility nature's kind bestow.

Answer sweet Annadale's call,
A refreshing place that waterfall,
The misty froth ascending see,
As serene a picture as can be.

When life's clamor becomes too loud,
When all around a dreary cloud,
There is a place rare comfort find,
The waterfall that soothes the mind.

Walk along the stony edge,
Or lean from up above the ledge,
The brilliant glow of flowers see,
Pacifies the mind, you feel so free.

Beauty Untold

We should from time to time ponder the immaculate beauty of the isle -Grenada. The place is truly an emblem of geographical wonder.

For those who were born there, I am sure there is that one little spot that you hold dear in your hearts. It might be that quiet area on the beach that you escape to, a waterfall, a lake, or a hillside that arouses fond memories.

Such a place for me is Pandy Beach in Belmont. I have always found solace there, and every time I visit Grenada, I find myself in my little spot. I can freely splash in the calm shallow water and it is also a wonderful place to watch the sun disappear when the day is worn.

Grand Etang! Oh, Grand Etang! What secrets do you hide? Picturesque, mysterious, soothing, Grand Etang shows no signs now of ancient disturbances. Since the first day I saw you on my Boy Scout hike, I remain in awe. Truly, I am impressed!

I must return to Grand Etang,
And rest within its peaceful calm,
I'll dream of past eruptive roar,
A boisterous drum now heard no more.

With waters calm few ripples see,
Mysterious aura now surrounds thee,
While misty charm do cloud your day,
My captive mind no words can say.

Bathway—another wonder! Those bent trees, in harmony with the wind, present a sight to behold. Majestic place. Imperial isle! It has pulled me back twelve times in nine years.

Those are my spots. Which are yours?

That Carenage Picture

I stared at a picture of the Carenage and I was suddenly gripped with nostalgia. As I looked at the awe-inspiring horse-shoe-shaped geographical scene, I was ushered back in time. The Carenage, forever beckoning, ignited thoughts I had long forgotten.

I was taken back to the time when the Carenage, also known as the Wharf, was the venue of Prime Minister Gairy's Easter Water Parade. I thought of the huge crowds that jammed the area to witness or take part in the entertainment.

I pictured Gairy and his political campaign from a wooden vessel in the placid waters close to Empire Cinema. I remembered the sand that was brought from Grand Anse beach to line the water's edge. Yes, the Carenage had its own beach during the Water Parade. The stevedores who assembled at the Seamen's and Waterfront Workers' Union building looked on in amazement and wondered what other strange ideas Gairy had in mind.

The Carnival spectacle on the Carenage came to mind. The wonderfully clad masqueraders used to prance on the Carenage road much to the delight of cheering crowds. The Carnival Tuesday night *last lap jump up* was an especially thrilling affair.

I visualized the famous Angel Harps steel band livening up the area with its scintillating sound. It belted out the catchy tunes while Mafu and Tatoes energetically pushed the stands. Those stands accommodated bass men who pounded relentlessly on their steel drums and sent feet jumping high. There was always a certain urgency on Carnival Tuesday night, as the revelers knew that midnight marked the end of their fun. The *jam session* picked up the pace as that hour approached.

I remembered the restaurants. The Carenage was always the perfect setting for restaurants. There were Nutmeg, Rudolph's,

Portofino and other restaurants.

Rudolph's provided the perfect atmosphere for dining and for absorbing the wonderful scenery the Carenage presented. One could nibble on a *chicken snack* and behold the rushing waves made by massive ships as they propelled out of the Carenage harbor.

Nutmeg Bar and Restaurant was the ideal spot to eat and relax. One could sip on a glass of *sea moss* or a Carib Beer, and be soothed by the beautiful sights around—or just recline on a chair and read a book from the nearby Sea Change bookstore. The atmosphere at the Nutmeg was always enchanting.

When reflecting on the Carenage, the image of boats came to mind. The Rhum Runner was one such boat. Fun-loving people joyfully boarded the Rhum Runner when the sun went down to enjoy a wonderful offshore cruise. The sound of *soca music* from the Rhum Runner always disturbed the quietness as it moved out. Tourists and Grenadians who came home on holiday always spoke of the marvelous time they experienced on the Rhum Runner.

The visitors loved to stand still on the upper deck and breathe in the fresh Carenage air. They sucked in the air and in the process rejuvenated lungs long deprived of purity in the toxic environments of Toronto, New York and London.

I recalled the grayish wooden boats known as *Lighters* that idled on the calm waters of the Carenage. There were also the large wooden vessels that journeyed between Grenada and its sister isle Carriacou. With each trip, the boats tightened the bond between the two islands.

The Carenage had its various forms of entertainment. People flocked to Empire Cinema to see the movies. Even the Saturday matinee drew a large crowd. The CubbyHole was a popular dance spot and a good place to *buss ah lime.*

And then there was that teller of tales called Grubay. He used to pull crowds as he told his farfetched stories on the sidewalks of the Carenage. He spoke of pulling cane from cane trucks, and succeeding in pulling the entire truck. He recalled stories of Hurricane Janet and of parting fights in the sea between barracudas and sharks. Grubay was the comic relief for the citizens of the Carenage.

The Carenage Ghetto I also remembered. I thought of the Rasta men reeling from their grassy high as they smoked their weed in the narrow corridors. I pictured them with their flying dreadlocks dipping themselves into the water of the Carenage to cool off.

There are other memories of the Carenage. The smell still lingers there, engraved somewhere within the brain. Oh, yes, the smell! There was the unmistakable smell of tobacco from the tourists mixed with the scent of fish from the small fishing boats that docked near the bigger boats.

The Carenage was the spot where firemen *breezed out* and waited for the next fire. And when there was a fire, they rode to it in their fire engines and fiercely fought the fire until the building was reduced to ashes. Then they headed back to the firehouse on the Carenage to play dominoes and wait for the next building to erupt in flames.

I looked at the picture and the memories hit me like an avalanche. I pictured the huge political demonstrations that took place on the Carenage. I even saw myself buying a hot *leaven bread* with butter and a quarter pound of salami from Tony in that small shop on the Carenage. The taste is still in my mouth.

PI. Bwoy! We Go Talk About Cooper Hill

I returned to Cooper Hill with its cobbled stones as if set in place by those who constructed the ancient Pyramids.

Cooper Hill, where Grenadians who don't know how to *maco* can get ample practice. Just go to the top of the hill and peep. You might even see a fish or two jumping in the water near the fire station. Don't peep harder, you might spy somebody *horning* your partner. One can observe the firemen hard at work playing dominoes too.

Yes, *me brudda*! At Cooper Hill one does not need a fancy watch because there are church clocks staring right at you from across the pond. For those who could not see the church clock, good souls like Teddy Griffith used to ring the church bell to let us know it was noon. Women then took a break from listening to the soap opera, "None So Blind," to make sure they had food prepared for the *youngsters* on their midday school break. The burning pot sometimes pulled them away from the contagious radio episode.

Cooper Hill, the place where a doctor got so drunk, he made it into a road. He made a short cut through the stony track. People heard that "bong, bang, bong!" coming down and wondered if another Hurricane Janet had struck. It was only the doctor driving down his new road.

Cooper Hill was a place where Prime Minister Gairy used to send the *travo workers* to clean the bush between the stones. All they did was eat and *ole talk* like any true Grenadian. By the time they reached halfway up the hill, the grass was already growing between the stones near R. C. P. Moore's house at the bottom. They were ready to start all over again. And the government was ready to pay again. *Yuh tink* Grenadians stupid?

Cooper Hill had the great Junior, the Visagoth, who sat under the big mango tree until the spot got smooth as a bowlie. I saw him in Grand Anse where he now lives. The people there call him Caca, a very unflattering name.

Cooper Hill and the *cussing!* When women started to *cuss,* every body had to duck. We got to know all the women who stole peas in the market. We got to know the man who was still peeing bed. There is a saying "words is wind," but those four-letter words they used *cuddah* knock down Satan.

God made Cooper Hill so that Grenadians could exercise. You exercise too hard and you end up in another hill—Cemetery Hill. You could not eat biscuit and macaroni and make it up that hill. It called for stamina derived from a proper diet of yams, *dasheen, saltfish* and *sea moss.* You could roast the *saltfish* on a *coal pot* and then throw some *sweet oil* on it. Then you are ready to climb Cooper Hill with ease and in style.

Cooper Hill was the location where a man who came back from Cuba found refuge after confronting the La Diablesse, a female devil. When he saw her cow foot, he ran so fast around a corner it was said that his ears grazed the ground.

O'Gilvie's mango tree stood near Cooper Hill, but Teresita's thin mango was sweeter. I had respect for that mango tree. Sometimes I felt like crying when people called that type of mango *knock-a-bout mango.*

Ah fella, who used to pretend that he did not pick up the mango, got up one morning at four o'clock thinking that Teresita was asleep. As soon as he picked up the first one, her window flew open and she poked her head out. He put down the mango and pretended he was tying his shoelace.

Cooper Hill was noted for the heavy downpour during the rainy season. When the showers fell and water started to rush down the drain on Cooper Hill, one just waited until it subsided a little to sail the small wooden boats. Then the *rainflies* came out in numbers and circled the kerosene lamps. Those kerosene lamps had the famous words, "Home Sweet Home" written on the *lampshade.*

Cooper Hill, where we used to *buss* shortcut to Marryshow pasture to eat *damsel* and suck *governor plums*. They once put a watchman there to prevent us from engaging in our delight. He hailed from Morne Jaloux and we nicknamed him "Brother Watchies." He was an Adventist and a good watchman who did not fall asleep on the job like the other watchmen. He saw me once in the *Skinup* tree. I jumped over his head and ran back to Cooper Hill. I was safe in the confines of Cooper Hill.

Cooper Hill is special. It is special like so many other places in Grenada. Mount Pandy is special too. There was an old man called Mr. Marryshow who used to look at me as I ran on Mount Pandy Beach and shout "God Bless!" He is dead, but his wonderful words still ring a sweet note in my ears.

So I say to you, God Bless!

St. John's Street, a Grenadian Street

There are spots in Grenada that evoke a special fondness. One can think of the Lance and the myriad things that made it a favored place in the minds of Grenadians. The Lance is the Lance and will always be the Lance and there is no other Lance. But there is another place, a sort of "self-contained township" called St. John's Street.

When one eventually peruses the varied chapters in the history of Grenada, somewhere tucked within the informative pages should be the story of St. John's Street. The street, which opens like a river's mouth engulfing the sanctity of the Catholic Church at the top and runs right down to the *rumshops* at the foot, has its own story to tell. St John's Street has a story like all the other places in Grenada.

Grenadians, who obtain great energy sustained from the big jacks, *coo coo*, *sea moss* and yams, climb St. John's Street with relative ease. They walk up the street for different reasons. Some, on reaching the top, go straight to the church and repent after drinking rum at the bottom. Others, who get themselves in trouble, make a right and end up in the nearby courthouse.

School children take easy strides as they head for Presentation Boys' College, Mother Rose and St. Joseph Convent. There are those, who on reaching the top, are afraid to turn left because they will end up among their dearly departed on Cemetery Hill. They prefer to visit those departed souls only on All Saint's night.

St. John's Street is therefore a convenient shortcut to various destinations. It is a designated bus route too. The last time I was in Grenada, I had to scamper to escape the darting buses on St. John's Street.

One cannot speak of St. John's Street and omit its many shops. It is essential to include the part played by shopkeepers of Indian descent who lent their vigor to advance the economic stability of Grenada. I cannot tell you all the reasons why Mr. Peters, Mr. Williams, and Mr. Coomansingh chose St John's Street. It was, however, a good place to purchase pig's snout, saltbeef, sugar and flour.

The Syrians loved the area where Halifax Street kissed St. John's Street. The Syrians walked all over the place selling "teleeleen" cloth and before one could have uttered *brango,* they opened a shop already.

Grenadians grew familiar with names like Nahous and Aboud. Aboud initially sprung up on St. John's Street. I can still remember the Radio advertisement:

Aboud for shoe
Aboud for shoe
Aboud for shoe
Aboud for shoe?
Yes, Aboud for shoe,
Abu, Abu, Abu
for shoe, shoe, shoe.

Syrians started coming to Grenada in greater numbers during the nineteen sixties. They were first spotted toting suitcases and selling "teleeleeeen." They used to roll their tongue as they said the word. Have you ever heard a Syrian say the words "Teleeleeeen, teleeleeeen, five dollaaas?" They sold all kinds of cloth, including *crimpeleen.*

The only cloth the Syrians did not sell to Grenadians was flour bags. Grenadians got that freely from the shops.

There were the other shops. Mrs. Romain's shop quickly comes to mind. I still see the leeches in the bottles. In those days, leeches were important and Grenadians knew how important they were to medicine.

I still visualize Mato, Conqueror, Big Chow, Cashier and a calypsonian called the Mighty Lizard hanging out in front of the shop. Lizard was the *calypsonian* that told Wakax *his mother so and so* when the music kept breaking down in Queen's Park while he was singing.

One must not forget Clouden's shop and the female entrepreneur par excellence called Mama Aird. Mama Aird imported those Volkswagen cars CPD now loves. It's still easy to picture young men *jooking* billiards on the boards Mama Aird provided on St. John's Street.

When they grew tired playing by Mama Aird, they hurried over to McMonroe's place for some more *jooking.* These days Grenadians *jook* pool with style. Many women forgot how to *jook* a *jooking board,* but retained their *jooking* style on Carnival day.

One must not leave out two very important enterprises that sprung up on St. John's Street—Mckie Printery and Photo studio and Clarke's Printery. They were printing pioneers in Grenada.

When one speaks of St. John's Street, it is imperative to talk about the small funeral agencies.

Anyone remembers Papa Hinds and Holas? Stiff competition existed between those two. Their *Huss* were not as fancy as La Qua's, but they served a purpose on St. John's Street.

It was said that undertakers used to go to the hospital and ask people how they were feeling and who were their relatives. Then, they looked to see if they had suitable coffins. A coffin was never too short as they were skilled in the craft of shortening people to make them fit the coffin. Viewing a foot was never important and one hardly got to see the foot anyway.

Have you ever seen a funeral procession go down St. John's Street? Then you have probably seen *old people pull brakes.* Following the *huss* down St. John's Street was never easy. It required, and still calls for, good foot balance and the ability to suddenly halt. If the *huss* suddenly *pulled brakes*, one had to *pull brakes* too to avoid a collision with the coffin.

St. John's Street was the escape route masqueraders took when *blows began to pelt* one Carnival day. The *mas* people ran all the way up St. John's Street and headed for Cemetery Hill. They ran just like people ran when the *Mongoose Gang* got bad in town. They ran the same way people ran from Innocent Belmar, the notorious policeman.

During the big looting in Gairy's time, people carried all kinds of heavy stuff up St. John's Street. Don't ask me how they did it! Perhaps it was the *bluggoe* that gave them the energy. Some ended up, unintentionally, dragging away dog and cat food all the way past the tailor shops that stood on St. John's Street. A woman carried a huge bed up that street.

St. John's Street is indeed an important street. It remains a unique street. It was important when prominent citizens like the Justice of Peace, R. C. P. Moore and the politician Doc Mitchell lived there. St John's Street is as famous as Melville Street, where one can find dead fish in the fish market, dead cows in the meat market and dead people in La Qua's funeral home.

Take Me Back to the Market Square

I vividly recall the St. George's Market Square and the vital part it played in our lives. The small pitched area, bounded by Hillsborough, Granby, Grenville and Halifax streets, is still very important.

It was not only the place where farmers brought their fruits, vegetables, flowers and spices to be sold, but it was also the temporary home of the parked buses, a central stage for political meetings and, at times, the venue for an entertaining film show. It was also the location of the District Board and *Breakfast Shed* and the site of many a religious service.

Somewhere in my mind, the tooting of the vehicle horns still echo and I still see the people squeezing their way through the closely parked Austin, Bedford and Morris wooden buses.

I see the women busily attending their goods in the shed-like structures that were erected there. When the rain fell, people were glad to seek shelter within those buildings. I still recapture scenes of the stalls and the tables that held the *ground provisions,* oranges, soursop, sweet potatoes, mangoes, *bluggoes* and *green fig.*

I picture Dummy James toting a heavy *lard pan,* which he gently set in the back of a wooden bus. Then he receives a small fee as payment for his effort. I still spot the tourist picking up the nutmegs and cloves and sniffing the fragrance. I smell the blood pudding cooking and the corn roasting in the Market. I hear a loud commotion as a customer and a vendor clash over the price of coconut.

The Market Square was especially busy on Saturday. That day was called "Market Day" and the people came out in great numbers to pick the best of the crops that were on display. The fresh fruits and vegetables came from various parts of the country. The early bird got the best worm.

69

My brother George once made a *ballswheel cart,* which he used to carry the goods my mother bought in the Market Square. When we moved to Cooper Hill, an area further away from the Market, she began taking the *One More buses* to transport the stuff. Some of the bus drivers were so kind; they veered off their regular route and dropped my mother as close to her door as possible. When she placed the appealing bananas and golden apples on the table, I smiled.

The wooden buses stood in neat formation, side by side, in designated sections of the Market Square. Policemen were there to enforce that rule. The St. David's buses were in one area and the St. Paul's buses were in their own spot.

The people climbed into the buses and waited until the drivers felt they had enough people to hit the road. The rear part of the buses was often loaded with bags of flour, sugar and rice that people bought in bulk to take to the country.

The wooden bus was an important method of public transportation until its reign on the streets was put to an end in the nineteen-seventies when a number of small Japanese buses made their appearance. They took over the streets and they took over the Market Square. The taxis lined the outskirts of the Market Square.

The Market Square was the place where people gathered to hear politicians speak on their plans for the country and the platform where they castigated each other over the microphone. I remember a certain politician saying,

"Everywhere I go, I see Mr. Blaize following me. When the result of the election is out, he will be following me also."

The people laughed. I also recall another politician asking "Where the hell all the nutmeg money gone?" A *calypsonian* composed a song using those words.

I still hear the loud speakers blaring the famous words: "Tonight, tonight, in the Market Square. Tonight, come hear The

Honorable E.M. Gairy."

On other occasions, the call was for people to hear the Honorable Herbert Blaize. The cars with the microphones mounted on top traveled around the city and someone implored the people to attend the political meetings. When people flocked to the meeting, they stood up and listened and cheered or booed. Sometime a rotten egg became a missile that interrupted the political meeting.

I think of the occasion my mother took my brothers and me to see a film show in the Market Square. The film show was a popular event then. It was in the Market Square that I first saw Charlie Chaplin on the screen. I remember how much I laughed at his funny antics on the little screen they set up near the District Board. We had to stand and look and we were contented to do so. We stood there and laughed our hearts out.

The Market Square was an important place where many of the very important social needs of the people were addressed. The District Board or Town Hall, a sort of Borough Council, was found there. It tended to local matters for the needy.

Below the District Board was the Breakfast Shed, which provided breakfast for school children whose parents were not able to adequately provide for them. The students lined up on mornings and waited until the names of their schools were called.

Curiosity got the better of me once and I went into the Breakfast Shed and I got a cup of cocoa tea. There were students who ate at home, but still headed for the Breakfast Shed.

In those days, the big church meetings or revivals were held in Queen's Park, but the Market Square was also the scene of many Pentecostal and other evangelical services. The people stood on the paved ground and listened as preachers issued the call to repentance.

On Christmas Eve, the Market Square was busier than on any

Saturday. Many of the tables were packed with toys to catch the attention of the children. There were toy guns, balloons, dolls, starlights, cars, and many other toys.

It was customary for parents to give their children a few dollars to go shopping on Christmas Eve and many of them ended up in the Market Square to purchase the starlight or toy gun. They bought their toys and then headed to the area around the Market Square to see what else the people had on their trays to sell. And when night fell, they headed to the cinema to catch the special show.

Whenever I return to Grenada, I visit the Market Square. The old historic houses still embrace the area. The buses are no longer parked there. The coconuts, fruits and ground provisions are still sold, but the Breakfast Shed and District Board are long gone. The noise and bargaining still remind me of my childhood experiences there.

Like the tourist, I pick up the cinnamon and nutmeg and put them to my nose. I purchase them, stuff them in my bags and carry them to my friends in New York City.

The Drill Yard

Have you ever wondered about the spot on Young Street they called the Drill Yard?

Grenadian soldiers fought in the Great War. It is conceivable that they drilled there during that period. It was said that some young Birchgrove men, in order to avoid conscription, used to rub their feet with a particular bush to make them swell. By doing that, they were able to avoid service.

The Drill Yard was once transformed into a calypso tent in the 1960's, featuring singers like the Mighty Lizard, Papitette, the Mighty Dictator and the Lord Melody. It also showcased a singer called The Mighty Pirate who sang a song about pork that had mustache.

SCHOOL DAYS

The Conqueror Revisited

There are many people who can tell you stories of the headmaster known as Fletcher who commanded the respect of students with a belt called The Conqueror. They will tell you stories of the strap soaked in *pee* to give it added weight to make more music on students' *bam bam*. They will recount tales about Hinds, Palmer, Phillip, Redhead, Andrews, and all the no-nonsense headmasters.

A past student, who frequently felt the whip years ago, once confronted one such past principal. He asked his old teacher why he used to flog him so harshly in primary school. The teacher had a simple answer:

"Sonny, I see you are driving an expensive car. It was the belt on your *backside* that turned you into the man who could afford that car."

You will learn about Eli Peters who did not believe in sparing the rod and spoiling the child. The students who attended the Anglican primary school in Gouyave walked circumspectly, for any other walk invited a flogging. Fletcher, who was a strict disciplinarian, stressed obedience and respect, and those who did not fall in line, felt the sting of The Conqueror.

Even the football players knew how important it was to behave on the field of play. That was the same Fletcher who almost fainted when a few boys from the Point threatened to throw him off a window from the school on the hill. They had grown wary of such a strict enforcer of rules.

Students were constantly warned about the consequences of telling lies. They had to memorize the famous words:

"Speak the truth and speak it ever,

Cost it what it will.

He who hides the wrong he did

Does the wrong thing still."

I used to shiver while looking down from the top floor of the St. George's Roman Catholic Boys' School on Canash Hill. It was easy to look down and spot Now Now ringing a bell in front of Franco's ice-cream shop and shouting out the latest and best sale bargains. That school was our skyscraper, a majestic tower on the hill. We could not let a teacher see us peering out of the window as we tried to *scope* the Market Square. We had to look from the corner of our eyes the way the girls looked at boys.

We got *licks* for simple things. Try kicking a box while walking up Canash Hill and vapor would rise from your *bamsee*. If you wore a shoe that cried out for black polish, you were in more trouble. If you threw mango skin in the road you were in hot water.

The most serious looking students were made prefects and the one with the most evil look was called the head prefect. Those were the ones who put you in line for a flogging if you were a minute late for school.

Your fingernails were subject to inspection. One got in big trouble if the teacher ran a comb through his hair and the comb met heavy traffic. And if you laughed out loud while someone *leggo one* in the class, you found yourself in hotter water. You got *licks* for writing *crappo belly*.

At Carnival time, Mr. Palmer never failed to remind the students:

"It's Carnival time and I know from tomorrow it will be *Ting, Bang, Ba, Lay, Lay,* but remember, I will be watching your behavior."

The Conqueror was waiting for those who misbehaved.

I often sit and reflect, and I wonder why the sons of big shots never got *licks*. They passed exams easily without getting any blows. Some of them were not too bright. Intelligent children of poor people got a lot of *licks* to pass the exams. When there was a fair or harvest, the rich children brought expensive stuff so headmasters loved them. Poor children brought an egg or two, a can of condensed milk, or a few pennies. Mr. Palmer always encouraged them to bring "honest pennies".

Once, someone wrote a *bad word* on the wall in one of the school's latrines. The headmaster sent for two detectives from the police station located at the bottom of Fort George to find the culprit. That was not too difficult as the headmaster and teachers knew the usual suspects, and it was one of them that eventually faced The Conqueror.

Don't for a single moment believe that everyone was afraid of the belt. Some *fellas* stood like wooden soldiers and took stroke after stroke. One such student was called Trevor Woods. He conquered The Conqueror. Yes, a few of them managed to conquer The Conqueror.

Students used to pad up like cricketers hoping that putting on two pants would help to ease the pain and absorb the blows. However, the Headmasters had a way of *scrutching* them up like police used to do and pulling their khaki pants to one side to expose and *lace* the next *peg ah Bam Bam.*

A fellow nicknamed "Mackie" got so disoriented once after receiving six strokes across the back that he hid under the stage until school was dismissed. Today many would call that child abuse.

After a tough day at school, one usually ended up *pitching marbles* and an old woman was likely to inform your mother she heard you use a *bad word.* That meant blows on reaching home, and, if Mr. Palmer heard about it, The Conqueror had some more work to do.

The Conqueror, for the most part, kept us on the right track!

Schaper School Remembered

We sat on the rock-hard benches, so hard we sometimes had to put the pressure on one *peg ah bam bam* at a time. We were away from it all, away from the hustle and bustle. We were nicely tucked away in a remote spot at Brother's Estate, which was the past abode of a *cocoa boucan.* There, we nourished the brain and we fed the spirit. Friendships blossomed and like a silk cotton tree grew powerful roots. Then branches spread to New York, London, Toronto and diverse places. We built a lodge-like relationship, but more than that, we became a family—a special Grenadian family. We were a family grounded on good principles.

The school had a rugged start. There are those like Mr. Herman Hall—a teacher from the inception—who can spell out in great detail the trials that existed when the school began. He will point out the conflicts and roadblocks the established churches sought to put in the school's way. The school was a religious secondary school with a difference. Evangelical missionaries from the United States owned it and some of its policies set a new trend in Grenada.

One such policy was allowing over-aged students to attend the school. It was those over-aged students who lifted the school to a level on par with the established secondary schools. One indication of imminent success came when Mr. Hall wrote a play that students performed and even the Governor General took note. One of his students, Mr. George Wilson, later became a principal of the school.

It is refreshing to reflect on the Christmas time at Schaper School when a cantata, musical Christmas hymns and plays that the children performed, echoed in the halls. The many voices rose in perfect harmony engulfing the tranquil air with the inspiring songs. Today, we revert to those songs for further comfort when the times get rough and when our spirits sag. We sang the songs that we articulated with revival fervor. That revival spirit I once felt and I preached some fiery sermons in the auditorium.

The buses streamed from Victoria and Gouyave, Sauteurs and St. George's with students and their parents to attend our "Speech Night" at Schaper School. Speech Night was the time for other speeches. It was the time for the *big lime* by Kong and Miss Maylin's Shop where students used the power of speech to check *out ah ting.* The speech Night for some was the *ole talk* on the outside.

Those of us who took the bus to school had to be punctual. When Labor Reward or Theresa B, revved up their engines and prepared for the journey, and one was still looking for his or her uniform or books, it was *later for you.* Then one had to hop a bus in the Market Square and hope to reach for the third or fourth class period.

Masters and Raymond who drove the big yellow school buses were ready to make the trip and you had to find yourself at the bus stop early.

I recall "Blackboy," Thompson and Dudley controlling the steering wheels of the wooden well-ventilated vehicles they drove with such great skill. When the dismissal bell rang, it was another race for the bus. Some of the drivers had to rush to pick up their other passengers whose daily toil in St. George's was completed by 4:00 p. m. It was a race for the high seat and a bus race up Marigot Hill.

The bus rides were always fun and there were always lots of laughter. The joy was multiplied if we closed our eyes and ignored the many steep hills and sharp corners on the way. I sometimes quiver when I reflect on the near misses, and I can only thank God for the protection he afforded us through the years.

On a few occasions, we had to turn back after passing Happy

Hill and reaching that flattened area in Beausejour. That area was once lined with cane fields on either side. Once, rain fell *bucket ah drop* and it was *water more than flour*, so we had to turn around. An adventurous driver of a car tried to venture forth, but his vehicle became a boat in the middle of the road.

We have a lot to be thankful for. We are thankful for the Grenada Boys' Secondary School, Presentation Boys' College, Anglican High School and the other school connections that gave us brilliant teachers like Dr. Dunstan Campbell, Dr. Keith Mitchell, Dr. Kenny Lewis, Brother Sam from Victoria, Kathleen Peters from Gouyave, the brother and sister Campbell team from Happy Hill, Miss Griffith, Anthony Boatswain, Fitzroy James, Alice Henry, Bernadette George, "Cheese" Lashley, and Peter Thomas.

I must not fail to mention teacher "Mose" Antoine, who in the midst of a Spanish class session would pull out a piece of bread from his pocket and the students would erupt in laughter. He was fond of saying the word "bulto" and raising his hands as he did so. No one knew what he meant by that word. Once while he gesticulated as he said the word, he accidentally struck Miss Marshall, the school's secretary, as she entered the class.

In those days the schools helped each other. When an A' Level English teacher was difficult to find, Brother Schaper made arrangements for "Daddy Bakes" Baptiste of GBSS to teach us English on Saturdays. I am indebted to Daddy Bakes for the English lessons he taught me at his home while I was preparing for the GCE A' Level English examination.

They all did yeoman work that laid the groundwork which helped mold now accomplished minds like the great mathematician "Polar" Henry, the brilliant Sandra Ferguson, the talented Vernon Louison, Shanta Purcell, and many others. We were grateful for the night classes. Schaper in his wisdom put a big floodlight that lit up the whole pasture and its concrete cricket strip. He wanted to be absolutely sure the students would not carry on their own night class in the darkness of the pasture near the concrete strip. Some ended up by the river to indulge in classes of another nature. I remember the concrete strip where a certain teacher tried to bowl *spin* and ended up *bussing* his big toe with the cricket ball.

I recall Robbie and that monstrous motorbike. Robbie, the brilliant historian from the U.S.A. was not too brilliant a biker. He gave me a ride once and when we reached Grand Roy, he started looking back to talk to me. I thought it prudent to refrain from speaking for the remainder of that trip. Robbie was the teacher who taught German and had only a few ambitious souls in his class. Jackie Miller from Belmont, a superb artist, was later speaking German with the tourists on Grand Anse beach.

I think of the mechanic shop and students wondering what further ideas Brother Schaper would introduce. We already had the philosophy class with Bro. Schaper, teaching us about Emmanuel Kant. The students used to laugh when he pronounced the word Kant. It sounded just like a forbidden word Grenadians knew all too well.

Brother Schaper introduced the ten-point West Indian history quiz when we were accustomed to writing essays. Then he made matters worse by reading the names of all those who got zero in the examinations he gave. He stood in front of the class and read out the names of all those who, like cricketers, failed to get off the mark.

The mechanic shop was a good idea and some students gained valuable information about the intricacies about vehicles. Jeffrey Williams told me how much that knowledge helped him. While some students learned about cars, others were taught handicraft by a woman called Dolcie McQuilkin. A space was made in the school's library to accommodate the students who were learning how to type.

I recollect Polar making a speech in the auditorium and saying that as far as God was concerned "there is no conclusion." Polar was branded a heretic and I can't recall him making another speech again. He was such a brilliant individual that it was easy to misconstrue what he was really saying. He went on to earn his Ph.D. in Mathematics and taught for a spell at City College in New York.

I also remember the many sermons of Brother Baber and especially the one about the boy who pounded a nail into a piece of wood. He was asked to take out the nail which he easily did. Then he was asked to take out the hole, which was impossible. The lesson dealt with our actions and the scars that are left even though we take corrective measures.

I recall students laughing at "Trop" when he struggled in English class. He once wrote about the time he "tripped a Dracula" and the class laughed kee *kee kee* for days.

But then GCE time rolled around and Trop told Cambridge about the "full-blooded shots" he learned from the cricket commentators, He put the icing on the cake by telling the Cambridge examiners about the time he got the ball in front of the goal and "that was it!" What a perfect air of finality for such an essay.

Words in place, sah! When the results came and Trop passed English, the laughter was wiped from many faces.

I also think of the time Bro. George told a certain student, "Boy, your English is old-fashioned." I cannot forget the time Lennard "Taloff" told a young lady at the Form Five graduation dinner, "No postponement tonight!" He was thinking of a date with her after the graduation. That dinner we had at a restaurant in Gouyave owned by Mr. Peters. Dunstan, our Geography teacher, counted the few grain of peas we got, after we paid all that money for the dinner.

I think of the time Brother Schaper brought a number of prominent people from Gouyave to teach in the school. They included Mr. Francis of the Bata shoe store, Carlyle Glean, Mr. Raleigh Bhola, the father of Rosie, and that interesting gentleman called Mr. Critchlow.

We also had a Duncan *fella* who called himself "the geogist." He also brought a firebrand from St. Georges called Layne, who almost set off a revolution in the school. He wanted to chase away the white people. That was during the time the Black Power movement was raging in America.

I must not fail to mention those who excelled in sports. Conrad Francis and Jenny Boca were great middle-distance runners who left people gasping in amazement at the intercollegiate sports meeting.

Errol Alexis was always *wicked with the cricket bat*. Prengay was our midfield maestro, also stabilized the powerful Hurricanes football team. Alister Romain excelled both in cricket and football. The school produced a number of notable *netballers* too.

I sit and think of the music classes. The piano was there, but to many students, music class was a big joke. When Sister Wherman asked a student we nicknamed "Prospect" to tell the class the note on the bottom line, he took about five minutes, got up gradually, and then shouted "F," causing great laughter.

However, there were students who took the music seriously and I know they are passing down information about Mozart and Bach and others to their children.

Agricultural science was new. Dr. Dunstan Campbell introduced it in classes as a new discipline. He was a man of numerous talents and he showed us how to plant bananas and cocoa deep in Brothers Estate.

I can still picture Cowie and Reds with their big *water boots*. They planted the corn in Brothers Estate, but the rats ate most of it. They also acted as estate policemen arresting students like Murphy who unlawfully entered their farmed area. Such students were promptly brought to the principal.

Dr. Kenny Lewis built up the chemistry lab all by himself and he showed immense dedication, often remaining after school to aid students who sought his assistance. He, too, was a pillar of the school.

I must include the time a certain fellow had to apologize in front of the students for eating someone's food and hiding the food container in a hole in the wall.

I remember the time pupils from St. George's, like Bugs and Shampoo, were afraid to pass through Gouyave. It was Carnival time and some masqueraders called *vekou* were beaten up in St. George's. That enraged *Gouyavarians* who came to school looking for the St. George's students, to rough them up. The town students were aware of the time Tobias' father came looking for teacher Kenny with a long chain so they took no chances.

Then there were those who always made people laugh—Baku, Augustine, Doubles, Slemmo, and John Duncan readily come to mind. Gordon Briggs, the *fella* who loved his guitar, was always full of life. He was a good table tennis and cricket player too.

I remember the wooden bus in the pasture, which was the site of the *calypso* tent that featured the Mighty Big Balls and Nathaniel, the Mighty Water Cart. Then Sister Burke broke up our *calypso* tent. The religious teachers did not appreciate the *calypsoes*. I think of Tall Joe McBain from Victoria who promised to be the first man to find iron ore in Grenada. His wife, another Schaper product, is a wonderful New York doctor. We always had a strong Victoria contingent that included people like Judy and Jocelyn Dubois, and Chester Cadore.

I can't forget Lapo bringing up the big pot of fish broth that he cooked on the Lance. We sat in the wooden bus, the calypso tent, and gobbled down the dumplings, yams and big jacks during our lunch recess.

I recall Michael "Mashie" bent over some huge books in the library and a *fella* called Webster, who *swallowed a dictionary* by the same name.

I recall the dedication of Michael Hunte. I remember Fraustine, Tinyman, Fedon, Ian and Alwin Salfarlie, and Pepe from Beaulieu.

Then there were those who came after, like Bosco and Jericho from the Point.

I remember the time Hudson McPhail became an economics teacher at Schaper School after he returned from England. He became my good friend and occasionally, he took me to Mt. Granby to pick mangoes from the numerous trees.

My mind reverts to the student who saw me at Point Salines on my return to Grenada and was so happy he shouted:

"Aye, aye, dog face.

Ah *see yuh* come back!"

I laughed because years ago, I had jokingly called him the same name.

My mind goes back to the time a certain *calypsonian,* who worked on a bus, threatened Brother George.

Poor fella, he did not know better. The whole of Victoria came looking for him, but he never showed up.

I remember Mayfair who transported the students from Victoria and had all the young ladies laughing with tales of his real and imagined exploits.

And, yes, that time when we sat in St. Rose Convent to do a GCE "O" Level Health Science examination! The exam was given and everyone was shocked. Nothing that we prepared for was on that test!

Students sat with sad, long faces already resigned to their ultimate failure. Then suddenly, the tension was broken—a fellow (I will not call his name) *leggo ah* thunderous one.

Immediately pens set to work. That jolted everyone to life and ignited our intellect.

Father Evelyn, the test monitor, said, "That boy eats well!" That student was the same individual who ran Miss Burke from the Biology class when he changed the composition of the air with an odor similar to that of sulfur dioxide.

There is so much to reflect on. Past students are urged to help out the school in anyway they can. It is your Alma Mater.

Tribute to Brother Schaper

For many of us, it was the second chance. It was the second, last and most crucial opportunity for us to salvage a secondary education. The prestigious schools like the Grenadian Boys' Secondary School and St. Joseph's Convent had their stipulations, one of which was an age limit for entrance. Many of us had passed that age.

Then Brother Schaper opened a school in the late 1960's, which forever changed the hopes of many Grenadians. He did not just open a school, but a huge opportunity for many poor Grenadians to advance academically.

There were those who had already given up hope for further education. Many had failed the under twelve and under fourteen examinations. One individual was painting the school when Brother Schaper encouraged him to enroll. He did so and excelled both in academics and sports. He went on to sit the General Certificate of Education and later immigrated to the United States where he earned a Master's degree.

Another, who was working at Buy-Rite grocery, was encouraged to seek education at the St. John's Christian Secondary School. He, too, proved that given a second chance, one could make significant strides. He became a teacher at the school and later went on to England where he pursued knowledge even more.

Brother Schaper is a remarkable man. He was acquainted with the class structure that created dents and divisions in the Grenadian society. He did not favor one student over another. As the school excelled, it gained the attention of many of the well-to-do, who enrolled their children there. Brother Schaper ensured that all were treated equally once they were within the confines of the school.

A few years ago, the Grenada government gave Brother

Schaper an award for the part he played in educating the minds of Grenadians. That was well earned! It was a deserved commendation given to one who took the initiative and laid the foundation for many of us. Today, past students of the school, well-acquainted with their initial struggle, are happy that Brother Schaper gave them a second chance.

Ah Tell Yuh!

Children had duties to perform before they took off for school in the morning. Many went to tie the goat or clean the pigpen and clear *pig mess*. Others got up to cut *water grass* for pigs and rabbits.

Talking about rabbits, I am convinced some children used to keep rabbits just to see them eat. You ever saw *ah* rabbit eat? There were children who got up at five in the morning because they really believed in sayings like "early to bed, early to rise, makes a man healthy, wealthy and wise."

So it was off to school to learn about Brer Anansi and about Mr. Joe who built a house for years. They also taught us about Mother Hen and Percy the Chick. Later, *ah* whole lot of Nolas came around: Nola on the Farm, Nola at Work, and Nola at Play are a few examples.

But we still managed to pass HSC and GCE and then, much later, the CXC. If you were bright and loved letters, you would get your GCE and then buy a BSA—that was a Bike. You might prefer a BA, or you could just stick with an ABM—that was an able bodied man.

Let me pause here to "big up" some people, as the young people would say. We must always be grateful to those who struggled with us to make us what we are.

We had a Spanish teacher called Professor. Everybody knew him as Professor. He went from Palmer School to Hinds School to Morris School and Backstreet School, where McBarnette was the headmaster. Professor was a good Spanish teacher and he punctuated his lessons with talk of fried bakes and cocoa tea. The man loved to talk about bakes.

He even taught us to sing in Spanish when he grew tired talking about bakes. Some of the songs I sometimes sing for my amigos from Santo Domingo. One of the songs was entitled "Perfidia" and the words "Mujer si puedes tu con dios hablar" is still fresh in my mind.

Mr. Clarie, the scoutmaster, was one we looked up to for advice and leadership. He had a son called Don. We learned the scouts' motto, "Be Prepared." When the scouts laughed at my shirt that was made different, Mr. Clarie told me it was okay to wear it.

Mr. Clarie took us to Fort George and gave us a test to see if we could pass the tenderfoot. The questions were always simple—the color of the Union Jack, the name of the Queen of England. One can easily get that one right today because England has the same queen. We did not get any questions about *Leapers' Hill* at all. Despite that, we must, however, be proud of people like Mr. Clarie who got us on the right road to life.

We should also be glad we had individuals like Corporal Bartholomew and Ben Roberts around. Parents sent their ill-disciplined children to them to be *straightened out*. They struggled hard to turn children into responsible human beings. Though some of the lessons were hard as Miss Gertie's `*nigger boy sweetie,* we got to learn why it was not good to *bom tourists* disrespect our parents or pelt stink mixtures called *jun jun* in Empire and Reno cinemas.

Mr. Joe Builds a House and Nola on the Farm

Ah wonder when Mr. Joe finished building that house? The strange thing is that we were never told what kind of house Mr. Joe was building. After all those years, we still do not know if Mr. Joe was building a *pre-cut Janet house,* a wall house, a wooden house or a coconut shack. All that the English writer told us was "Mr. Joe builds a house." We had to figure out the rest. We are still trying to `do so.

We are still wondering what became of Percy, the Chick, who *buss ah fall.* All we knew was that Percy, the Chick, had a fall. He had a fall when my father was reading the book and he still did not get up when I read the book. That was some fall, *eh?* That was *ah* harder fall than the one Humpty Dumpty had.

I am trying to find out what became of Mother Hen and Mr. Grums, the goat, Brer Anansi and Brer Rabbit! Anansi, the spider, believed that if a piece of wood could float he could do so also.

Where are Peggy, Laura, Pamela and Joan? Where is compere Ziah and compere Tig? Where did everybody disappear? Is Brer Anansi still taking back those plantains from his wife and children? Is Rainstorm still stuck in the hole in the sky? Is she still weeping and causing rain to fall?

Brer Rabbit and the tar baby was a classic. The hare and the tortoise ran a race and the tortoise won because *ah bunch ah* other tortoises also ran the race and the hare could not tell the difference.

Then those Nola books hit the scene! We read Nola on the Farm, Nola at Work, Nola at Play. They did not even bother to write one entitled Nola Eating Breadfruit!

Don't forget about the Student Companion. One learned all kind of things in that book. When you were finished reading that book you were brighter that a politician.

The Royal Reader must get special mention! We learned about Sir John Moore, but nothing about our own Grenadian R. C. P. Moore. These days Grenadian children are learning about Oprah, Jerry and Dr. Phil on American television.

I will always remember Mr. Joe. The only man I knew in Grenada who did what Mr. Joe did was *ah fella* we called Kong. He lived in Brothers, Saint John's. The man came back from England during the late 1960's and did exactly what Mr. Joe did. He built a house all by himself. He mixed the concrete, he nailed the wood and he put up the roof. He built a house just like Mr. Joe but he finished it.

A Grenadian did what Mr. Joe did! The only difference is that no one is reading what Mr. Kong did.

Palmer School

Palmer school stood like a bastion on Canash Hill. Mr. Palmer used to peep from his secret spot to see who was *liming* by Franco or who was casually strolling to school. Grenadians have been in the peeping business from those days.

Palmer was a strict man and he did not like to do much talking. The leather belt eloquently spoke for him and it usually spoke in a language many students understood. There were students who got blows for simple things like making loud noises in the street.

Those who begged the tourists were punished harshly. It was a serious offense to *bom* the tourist, use obscene language or to *skull school*. Those days, one was lucky to get off with only a spanking. Detention after school became popular and one had to listen to the perennial lecture about keeping up the "espirit des corps" every time the belt came down. Mr. Palmer loved those words he got from the famed Mr. Fletcher. He shouted those words while Mr. Andrews bellowed "Swallow it up!" or "You little rascal!" as the strap came down.

In those days, school children were afraid to *cuss*. One never cursed, or even *strupped* in the presence of grown people. If an elder person caught you using those *sailor words* you were sure to get a licking from your teacher and another flogging when you got home.

School Children Laughed [at Me]

They laughed at me because I wore a shirt bought from the little store Miss Wallace had near the intersection of Melville Street and St. Jules streets. Before that, they laughed at me because my scout uniform was different from those the others wore. They laughed when I came to school in *fliers pants*. They told me to stay away from the Fort George because the strong wind would blow me and that *fat pants* straight into the harbor. They laughed when someone *mooshed* me in Empire cinema.

Miss Wallace's store stood close to the sea on Melville Street, not far from our little bathing spot we fondly called Miami Beach. Sometimes the traffic police directed traffic when the street in front of Miss Wallace's shop became congested.

GETTING AROUND

Wooden Buses

Why would a bus driver leave a whole *busload* of people and chase someone who jumped from his bus to escape paying? Sometimes, he never managed to catch the person and other passengers, meanwhile, seized the opportunity to dart from his bus.

Sounds silly? A tough *fella* called Man Man used to do just that. Other drivers threatened to *break people scrutch* if they did not pay.

People said that Selwyn used to beat up passengers for his money when they tried to run. I guess it was tempting to jump from the wooden bus, which was the best *air-conditioned transportation* that ever graced the streets of Grenada.

Nowadays, it's hard to jump from those fast Japanese-built sardine cans because a conductor sits right there pulling up seats and putting them down. One takes a good five minutes to squeeze in or get out.

The bus drivers of yore not only liked to beat up *bad pay* people—they had superb instincts or a sixth sense. They knew who was likely to pay or not. They did not trust some people.

There was a smart bus driver called Mayfair. He used to stop the bus in an isolated place as Woodford and tell everyone to *"COME UP!"* You had to come up with the money or he *dropped your skin* right there. Then you had to walk the rest of the way!

A funny thing about the wooden bus one should know. It used to change from a bus to a truck and then back to a bus again. That was during the time when they were used to *drogue* cocoa, nutmeg and bananas. I always wondered if they put the *dam* thing back together correctly after they removed the top section.

There were occasions we got stranded in Schaper School because the truck did not change back fast enough to a bus to pick us up and take us home. Then we were lucky if we managed to *mop ah ride* with a van or even a *Janet truck.*

Everybody on the wooden bus wanted the *high seat.* The *high seat* was situated above the rear wheels. Occasionally you sat on the *high seat* and you became a seat. Of course you did not mind if you were the seat for a pretty lady. When you sat there and the bus jerked on the bumpy road, you laugh, *bwoy,* you laugh! But never let her see you laughing.

Me? I always wanted to sit near the driver. When those wooden buses *turned over* in the road, the drivers always crept out alive. Do you remember Elmo (Breakie) and that bus that *turned over* and broke up? Everybody thought that Breakie was dead. The man crawled up from that shattered bus! That was more fantastic than the time a car *bongaway* and blasted away Herbert's house which was situated at the foot of the Park Lane hill in St. George's. Lo and behold! Herbert crawled out!

The wooden buses used to sing. The engines sang going up Marigot Hill and they sang on Lucas Street. The Bedford buses could not sing as well as the Austin and Morris buses that were imported from England. Theresa B, Hey Leroy, Monkey Toe, Reliance, Florida Pride and Sweet Roses were good singers. They sang better that some people.

The conductors are strange too. They always want to put you in a bus. They don't care if you just came from Grand Anse. That is not their business. As soon as they see you they shout "GRAND ANSE!" and they are ready to put you in a bus and carry you back to Grand Anse again.

Yes, my friend, those were the same wooden buses like the one the American medical students from the St. George's School of Medicine bought and rode around in. That should tell you how valuable those buses were! If Boraggy was still around, he would be chasing them on his motorbike.

Traffic Police

The traffic police on motorbikes kept a close eye on the wooden buses and their drivers. The bus drivers did not like the police on motorbikes. The traffic police were *something else*. They chased the bus drivers the same way they chased the little boys with their homemade scooters and wooden carts. They did not even like to see the boys who skated down hill with their ripe-breadfruit greased skateboards. Those were the police who loved *scrutching up* people, but, better still, chasing them down on their Triumph and BSA motorbikes. Boraggy, Black Angel and Church were not easy. Redhead, who came later, gave people a break, but Boraggy was like a Marshall from the old west with his BSA horse.

One thing I can say about the Grenadian traffic police, they were trendsetters! They wore pants with the *scrutch* almost at their knees. The hip-hop crowd in America copied that directly from Boraggy and the Black Angel.

Traffic police in Grenada hated to hear bus sing. They hated that more than seeing an overcrowded bus. They hated that more than viewing a conductor hanging out like a Grand Etang monkey from a wooden bus. At times, the policemen sitting there playing dominoes (as the firemen do these days) sprang to attention when they heard a bus singing as it moved up Lucas Street. It was a signal to jump on the bikes and engage in the chase.

Nowadays, I see policemen in Grenada riding some little things they call motorbikes. Those small scooters hardly make any noise. They have it easy too, no cranking! They put in a key and the bike is ready to go!

They should have seen policemen and other bike men *ketch dey nen nen* to make a bike start years ago. Everybody in Grenada have it easy these days, even the Loupgaroux (*Ligaroo*). They refuse to fly; they are taking vehicles too!

When Boraggy or Black Angel cranked up the bike it was races up Lucas Street or by the little stretch near Queen's Park. Now don't get me wrong; some policemen in Grenada today are as *bad as crab* too.

Once I was in a bus in Lagoon Road when the bus driver suddenly stopped to pick up a passenger in a spot where that was prohibited. The door was already ajar, and then suddenly, the conductor shut the door and the driver raced off leaving the passenger stranded outside. When I looked back, I saw a policeman on a motorbike. That driver must have had eyes in the back of his head to spot the approaching policeman so quickly.

The traffic police were noted for *keeping duty* in style. They employed fanciful movements while calling the cars and trucks. They put on a show on Canash Hill. I can still picture a certain officer with his snow-white gloves making his *saga ting* antics in the little hut overlooking Scott Street. There were times he sent the cars back down the hill because they approached before he had summoned. They had to reverse all the way down the hill and they did not like it.

'Moping a Ride'

When we were ready for school or work, it was time to *bom ah ride*. We never called dat hitch-hiking. We *bom ah ride, pope ah ride*, or *mop ah ride*. Same *ting*!

Ah *fella* was so brave; he once tried to *pope ah ride on ah* bicycle. He ended up mashing up poor Man on the Run's back wheel. Some people *moped* rides on Janet trucks, banana trucks, Land Rovers and motor bikes. Women loved to *mop rides* on motor bikes and *dem fellas* used to be in *donkey heaven* when the women rode behind them and squeezed *dem* tight.

People had some real fancy ways of *moping rides*. Some just stood on the sidewalks; legs crossed and pointed their thumbs in the direction the vehicles were going. Others jumped in the vehicle without even asking and were *bol' face* enough to say, *"drop me down dey."* One lazy *fella bom ah ride* from the Seamen's and Waterfront Workers' building on the Carenage to Renwick and Thompson just a few yards away.

The greatest *moping* feat accomplished in Grenada was done by *ah fella* from River Road nicknamed Mopy. He holds the record. He *moped ah ride* on a plane from St. Vincent to Grenada.

I saw him once *posing off* in Mr. Prime's car on the Wharf. The man was sitting there in style waiting for Prime to return. He offered me *ah ride* in Prime's car

Some people *got dey rides* and got speeches from the drivers:
"Man, *wipe yuh dam foot* before *yuh* come in me car, *nah.*
Whey yuh going wid all dat mud?"
"Yuh only popeing, popeing.
Wha happen?
Is me and you dat buy this car?"
"Yuh want ride?
When ah asked you to pick the breadfruit, wha you tell me?"

Dis is ah new car, doh blam meh door"
"*There is nothing like ah free ride yuh noe, this car runs on gas and oil*"

By the Sweat of His Brow

I glanced back into time and I saw Old Man. I saw his slender frame sitting in his little *oaring boat* named Polar Bear as it constantly rocked in the choppy waters of the Carenage. I saw him waiting patiently on the passengers. There were other boats that idled there, but Old Man's boat caught my eye. I sat on a chair in the Nutmeg Bar and Restaurant and observed the cheerful, but determined, look on Old Man's face.

He sat there and continually steadied his boat with the oars while he waited. He tarried there to make an honest dollar. He was a hard worker who had experienced difficult times in Grenada. He was acquainted with hardship and his boat had pulled him through the rough times.

During the periods when tourists flocked to Grenada, Old Man did well. The tourists loved to be taxied across the Carenage. Then the time came when boat owners affixed Johnson and other engines to their boats and that threatened to put Old Man out of business. But he was a survivor in the heat of stiff competition.

I quietly observed him as he sat in his water-taxi. All those who sought a pleasant ride across the Carenage took the small boats. Those who were too lazy to walk all the way around found a savior in the water-taxis. Indeed it was a desirable relief from the stress one experienced while dodging cars, trucks and buses on the Carenage road.

It was difficult to pull the oars. It was strenuous to do so all day in the punishing heat. It was, however, more rewarding than *liming* on the streets and doing nothing. Old Man sought to make his living the old-fashion way, by doing honest work.

I looked on as a man jumped in and the boat began to dance in the water. Old Man grabbed the oars to stabilize it. Two more passengers got in and Old Man settled himself and prepared to

104

pull. I peered at him as he effortlessly leaned forward and then jerked himself back. The motion was easy for him after so many years of rowing. He settled into his rowing mode. The muscles in his arms showed as he propelled himself into high gear. Beads of sweat formed on his forehead. By the sweat of his brow, he was earning his bread.

As the little boat moved, the beauty of the surroundings captivated the passengers. They saw Fort George on the hill and the brilliantly attired *flamboyant trees* in full scarlet splendor. Those with good vision spotted the ko-*ke-o-ko* hanging from the branches. They viewed the old steeples of the Anglican, Presbyterian and Roman Catholic Churches. They observed the cement and lumber workers hard at work in front of Hubbard's and the other stores that lined the Carenage. They saw the men loading goods onto the vessels that traveled between Grenada and the sister isles. Old Man rowed and the passengers smiled. Above them, the sun was a blazing ball of fire.

As the boat made its way across the Carenage, the passengers looked into the water and saw the mullets, butter fish and other fishes swimming around in the clear water. They glimpsed the starfish and the speedy green eel. They saw the *sea cat* with its many arms cuddled between the rocks at the bottom of the sea. And they looked on in amazement as a *balla-hoo* with its long snout swam close to the boat. They noted the tourist standing on the concrete pavement next to Empire Cinema, snapping pictures of the harbor. While their eyes roamed the surroundings, Old Man's arms were pulling the oars.

And then he reached the other side. The passengers paid him and got off near the Fire Station. Others got in to and he grabbed the oars once more. There was hardly any rest for Old Man. He summoned his strength and prepared for the return trip. Back and forth he went all day. He paused occasionally for a quick bite or to respond to the voice of nature, but he did not get much time to relax.

Then the sun went down and it was time to tie the little boat. He had done his work and had earned his pay. He went to his home for a comfortable night rest.

The following day, he grabbed the oars again.

All Kinda Boats

All kinds of boats were found in the St. George's Harbor. Many were fastened by rope or chain to the Pier while others like Starlight and Rhoda L were braced against the sidewalk near W. E. Julien's Store or Hubbard's on the Wharf. Long before the schooners powered by engines arrived, the Windjammers sailed between Grenada, Carriacou and Trinidad. Some boats, like Sea View, made the trip from Grenville on the other end of the island.

The boats were important for the brisk and important trade. I used to look on, as merchandise and animals were loaded on Emmanuel C for the journey to Carriacou.

Emmanuel C, I remember very well. I traveled on it during the early 1970's when a group of us made a trip to Carriacou. It moved a little faster than a *morocoy.* Emmanuel C was the snail on the sea and Western Hope, the wooden bus, was a slow coach on land. I will always remember that trip. Indeed, it was a trip!

At the time of that journey, there was a drought in Carriacou and many of the trees had wilted under the onslaught of the stinging sun. There were radio and other announcements urging us to "Carry a tree to Carriacou." That became a sort of slogan.

A church group was going there, so I joined them. It was the first time I was leaving the mainland and excitement welled up within me. I was, however, very anxious to reach because sea water and I were never buddies.

The journey was a crawl and when I thought we were already in Carriacou we were only somewhere off the northern coast of Grenada. A few people got sick and they were given lime. Lime was a cure for sea sickness I learned. I took some lime and looked at the dolphins as they jumped up and down in the water.

We finally inched our way to Carriacou. I was more than a little confused when a young lady politely asked me if I was from

Grenada. I always believed Grenada and Carriacou was the same place. However, her question made me feel that finally, I had traveled somewhere. I spent some glorious days in a school located at Six Roads. I often wonder what happened to the tree I had planted there.

Emmanuel C was just one of the many boats that used to *park up* on the wharf. I paused often and stared as the traffickers packed their sugar apples, *ground provisions* and *bluggoes* to be carried to Trinidad.

When the *bluggoe* arrived in Trinidad it was immediately called *moko*. One cannot underestimate the importance of the trade between Grenada and Trinidad and the part initially played by the Windjammers and then by the engine-powered vessels. They took the cargo and made it past the Bocas to Trinidad. Then the boats returned from Trinidad, laden with foodstuff and household items. It was another busy scene in front of Hubbard's store as goods were unloaded and people moved briskly.

There were other boats that came into the harbor. I used to hear Mammy Georgiana speak of the Carib Clipper and the Madinina that frequently journeyed between Grenada and Trinidad. I saw the Federal Maple and the Federal Palm a number of times. While the English boat was carrying Grenadians to England, the Carib Clipper was transporting others to Trinidad.

I often get a reminder of that wave of immigration when I meet people from Trinidad who reside in Brooklyn. They tell me about grandma *so-and-so* who hailed from Mount Rich, Grenville and Belmont, but settled in Trinidad years ago. I tell them of the times I got up early to tune in to the Trinidad radio stations and listened to people like Dave Elcock in the morning. I resurrect thoughts of Auntie Kaye. There is a strong link between the two islands that did not begin yesterday.

The St George's harbor through the years welcomed all kinds

of boats. The tourist liners that were small enough to be tied to the pier came in. Some of them, however, looked so massive that their oversized structures dwarfed the pier. I wondered how they made it in. A Grenadian man named Mr. Otway, who lived at the top of Cooper Hill, was usually called upon to maneuver the boats into the harbor.

There were occasions when a *man ah war* came into the harbor and people were allowed to board the boat and tour its various sections. Some ladies of the night gladly rejoiced when the *man ah war* came with the restless sailors. I still picture the sailors in their white uniforms wandering around the Carenage. I still hear the heart broken drunken sailor cry:

"Have you seen Muffin?

The lady with the twisted jaw

She stole my boots."

Occasionally, one had to choose between a visit to the battle-ship or an evening at Reno or Empire cinemas. When we visited the ships, we were able to view the huge engine rooms. A huge US aircraft carrier once stayed out in the sea off Melville Street. That one was much too big to venture into the harbor so people just spied at it from afar.

People observed the aircraft carrier in the same way they took note of the *Piole boats* that docked in front of the Fire Station on the Wharf. Those were small boats that used to come all the way from Venezuela.

The *piole boats* resembled fishing boats, but their owners were more interested in a cargo of whisky and cigarettes than fish. They were also interested in the ladies of the night. They frequented the Wharf so much that some of the people began talking the *piole twang*. They learned the *bad words* first. Grubay spoke real *piole* and he made up some *piole* where he ran out of words.

There was a certain boat in the harbor that became a home.

It was Rabbit Man's boat. Yes, a few people lived in their boats. They were foreigners who settled in Grenada and chose to do all their settling in their yachts.

Rabbit Man was one such individual. At times he took his home to the quiet spot at Old Harbor in Westerhall or the tranquil little inlet near Woodford. But his favorite haven was on the Wharf. He relaxed there in his small yacht while the little oaring boat called Polar Bear made its way across the harbor.

Then another boat came in near Cable and Wireless on the Wharf. It had succeeded in dodging a fast-moving speed boat propelled by a powerful Johnson engine. It rocked slowly in the disturbed water. Then someone blew a *lambie shell* to signal that a fishing boat had arrived.

While Kick Em' Jenny Slept

I slept close to Kick Em' Jenny. I did not realize that I peacefully snoozed close to an active underwater volcano. Grown man that I am today, I'd give it more than a fleeting thought. It is certainly true that 'Where ignorance is bliss, 'tis folly to be wise." My ignorance was bliss then. It was a time when the chaotic potential of submarine volcanoes was not a debated topic within my consciousness.

I had not too long emerged from childhood innocence, and the thought of spending a splendid weekend on the little island fired my imagination. My girlfriend's family had issued the invitation and although it was the Carnival weekend, I decided to shun the fun and frolic of Carnival and opted for the quiet mystery of the little isle known as La Tante.

We set off from the shore near Low Town early that Saturday morning. Everyone took their seats in the small boat and we pushed out to sea. The captain of the boat was a man nicknamed "Boss." They told me that boss was not only a good seaman; he was also extremely good at shooting wild goats. I looked out to sea and felt assured that I was in for a smooth and pleasant journey. It looked so placid out there. That was before we met the angry waves.

We were tossed into deep holes in the sea and the boat had to ride some very tall mountains of water. My spirit constantly sank as I beheld the frightening columns of water approaching. The Carnival bacchanal flashed through my mind and I wondered if I had made the wrong decision. I thought of the colorful costumes and big parties that I was missing.

But I was so wrapped in the romantic feel of the young woman next to me that the Carnival thoughts did not linger long. I had to keep the faith. There was no better place for me to nurture my love than the secluded haven of a spot on the miniature island; away from the disturbing prance and clamor of jumping Carnival feet.

Boss did not seem too perturbed at all. The raging water did not bother him. While most of us sat there frightened and shivering, Boss kept asking me to *"Pass the bluggoes."* He was enjoying the *saltfish souse* and *bluggoes* that were prepared for the journey.

We survived the furious waves and breathed a collective sigh of relief. We pulled up to shore and unloaded the pots, water jugs and seasonings we had carried. The whiteness and glitter of the sand immediately impressed me. Then I realized that we had company.

A few fishermen were in a couple of boats near the shore. The boats were similar to those used by the fishermen of Gouyave. They remained in their boats and reeled in a net, loaded with jumping Round Robin fish. They gave us a portion of their catch and we thanked them for it. Later we cleaned the fish, salted them and placed them in the sun. We hoped to delight our taste buds with the appetizing corned fish. *Corned fish* goes well with yams, green bananas and a little *sweet oil*.

I stood on the shore and stared at a solitary coconut tree, its branches bent under the load of the thirst quenching *water nuts*. A weather-beaten wooden hut stood nearby. That was to be our place of abode for the next two days.

The gentle seawater rolled onto the shoreline and I was strongly tempted to dive right in. The rocks appeared parched and dried, and I wondered what the wild goats there were feeding on. Wild goats survive even in deserted areas with little food.

Boss got to work. He proved how excellent a shot he was and soon a pot of goat meat was on the wood fire. We cooked our food like the buccaneers of the Seventeenth Century. The smell of goat meat filled the air.

Two delightful days we spent on that enchanting isle. We climbed the rocks and looked out to sea. We filled our lungs with the fresh air. We ate goat meat and drank coconut water. We sipped rum punch and drank *fish brawf.* In the cool of the day, we enjoyed relaxing walks on the sandy beach and refreshing dives in the tranquil water. At night, we stared in amazement at the starry sky as the soothing wind hit our cheerful faces.

We found time for some *ole talk* under the glow of the full moon. Then we slept.

While we slept, Kick Em' Jenny also slept.

FRUITS, TREES, RAIN & ANTS

There is Something in the Banana

During the nineteen sixties, a situation developed with the banana industry in Grenada and the importers. For some reason the bananas were left in the St. George's port. People who used to *cut style* on the *green fig* became its best friend, for when Geest ships would not take the bananas to England, bananas went down their bellies.

Green bananas were everywhere. Bananas were found in the kitchens, living rooms, bathrooms and even the bedrooms. People had to invent places to put the bananas.

They made the trips to the docks and loaded the bananas on their heads and carried them home. Some people filled their vehicles, others their wooden carts and wheelbarrows.

We ate bananas in style. When there was no place to put them, we hung them from the ceiling. It was a banana fiesta!

Someone recently told me that he believed there is nutrition in bananas that scientists have not determined yet. He said that during that period his sons became strong and healthy after feasting on the bananas. He suggested that there is something besides the rich potassium for which bananas are noted. He told me of the time the old men boiled the *green fig* and drank the water it was boiled in. Then they went to the garden and worked like tireless mules for the entire day cultivating their crops. The green banana was their source of strength.

The green banana combined well with various other foods. Green banana and *saltfish souse* or smoked herring would set the salivary glands in high gear. Stewed chicken and green bananas would energize the feeblest limbs.

As long as Grenadians keep planting bananas, they will never starve.

It is true—there is something in the banana!

Time to Pick Cocoa

"My two-pointed ladder sticking through a tree

Toward heaven still,

And there's a barrel I didn't fill—The scent of apples. I am drowsing off.

I cannot rub the strangeness from my sight. "

Those words were penned by Robert Frost, one of the many poets found in the book "Choice of Poets." Frost, in his poem, told us about apple picking, but I will reflect a little about cocoa picking.

We Grenadians love our *cocoa tea.* Many of us will gladly enjoy a cup of *cocoa tea* or chocolate as we sometimes call it. We drink it to wash down the fried bakes and fishcakes. We love the mouth watering fried bakes that our Granny used to make. Those who don't like fried bakes might settle for a *Johnny bake* or coconut bake.

Cocoa tea is nice, but cocoa work is hard. Some like to drink *cocoa tea,* but run from the work. We need the energy derived from the *cocoa tea* to do the tough cocoa work. Grenadian families were acquainted with the cocoa work because cocoa processing was a family affair.

The work begins with the cocoa knife—a curved piece of metal at the end of a bamboo rod. Then we head for the cocoa trees in the land. Our eyes are kept peeled as we look out for the *Crebo,* a large snake. We carry *lard pans* in which to place the cocoa pods. You need cocoa strength to carry a *lard pan* full of cocoa pods.

Then the *jooking* begins! We take our time to *jook* down the cocoa. That is not difficult when plucking them from the short trees, but the taller ones can be problematic. We have to look up constantly and *jook.* We look up and *jook* down cocoa until our necks get stiff and sore.

We are then ready to cut the cocoa with a *cutlass* and throw the seeds in the *lard pan,* then dump them into a large box for *sweating.* The cocoa is covered with *bluggoe* leaves to facilitate the *sweating* process. It is left to sweat for about five or six days and stirred periodically. The seeds attain a light brown color. There is still more to be done.

We put the cocoa in the sun to be dried. We spread large *crocus bags* on the ground and scatter the cocoa on them. It is important to keep an eye on the weather because at times the sun gets stingingly hot and then, without warning, it starts raining. We rush to pick up the cocoa; then the sun reappears and we lay the cocoa out again to complete the drying process. Then the rain comes again. It is a drill—a kind of cat and mouse game, with the sun and rain combining to make us sweat. The running up and down causes us to sweat just like the cocoa.

When the cocoa is properly dried, it is parched and the shell removed. A brick oven is useful for parching the cocoa. Then grinding commences. That is tough work too. To grind the cocoa, we use the same mill we attach to the table to grind our pepper when making hot pepper sauce.

Spices are added to the cocoa paste and it is then rolled into balls, sticks or spread in a shallow pan and cut into cubes.

Acknowledgment is due to all the families who planted the cocoa trees in the backyard. They deserve commendation for their patience and hard work as they diligently toiled to process the cocoa they enjoyed and gave their neighbors to drink. We are happy they sent some to warm our hearts as we labored in the deep freeze of America and Europe.

Frost wrote about the drowsy effect of apple picking, but a warm cup of cocoa would have lifted him from that stupor induced by the smell of so many apples.

Cocoa tea anyone?

Not Only Spice, But Fruits For So!

So *ah hear dat* you go and tell people *dat* we *doh* have apples? Well, march right back and tell them of our custard apple, mammy apple, golden apple, sugar apple, star apple and pineapple. Then they might feel to suck some plum; offer them the yellow *Chinese plum* or the big *Jamaican plum*. Make sure you offer my good *Trini* friend some *pomsetay* before *dem* greedy manicou eat all. Remember to try *ah* piece *ah zaboca* and *ah shebbo* mango from *ah* tree in Morne Jaloux.

You passing by Grand Anse? Please save some of the sea grapes for me. Hope to gobble a few in July. The ones that the sun burned a bit are my favorites. Those are the sweetest ones. And leave *ah* stone around so I can buss an *orman*—or two.

Don't eat all the *damsels*. Save me some *governor plums*. I might need some *gospo* to make some juice or to use as a cricket ball, as in days gone by. *Gospo* opens *yuh* appetite so that you can devour some *fat pork* or French cashews.

If my blood pressure goes up, I hope to have some soursop juice. I will mix it with condensed milk and put it in the fridge to make blocks like Mammy Georgiana used to make.

In case I *can't go off*—mango might do the trick. Hell, if mango doesn't work, I will grab some *sandbox*. Then I will prepare for the battle of Waterloo in the toilet!

Coconut water is good for your daughter, but it's good for you too. *Dem* fellers by Grand Anse Post Office sell them one for a dollar. Where are their coconut trees? I might even feel to try *ah* palmiste, like I did as a little boy. Little boys eat anything! Those palmiste trees *ent* playing they can grow tall, *nah!* Who knows? Palmiste might be good for something too. Perhaps *dem* doctors don't even know *dat*.

We have *ah* lot of citrus. Make some lime juice and *cut your nature* if you are *too hot*. Then suck some grapefruit, orange with the green skin, or *ah* tangerine. You could even make orange peel tea with the orange skin. Then go back to the reliable *gospo*.

The Lady in the Boat with the Yellow Petticoat, *Mama Seaport*! That is our fitting description for the mammy apple.

Thank God for our many fruits.

They Cut Down Dem Trees!

Bwoy! Ah doh noe what we Grenadians have against trees! We like to cut down trees too *dam* much. They already cut down all *dem* tall coconut trees in Grand Anse. Now *dem* Grand Anse people have to go all the way to Westerhall to steal coconut to sell.

They cut down the skyscraper palm tree that was near Mr. Moore's house at the foot of Cooper Hill. The big tree that stood like a Titan on the Esplanade—they cut that down too! *Ah* nearly cried when they cut that tree.

Ah glad I am not a tree. They would have cut me down already. A nice big tree like that in the heart of town, they cut down. That was our Christmas tree and all the kids used to be so happy when they looked up and saw the beautifully decorated boxes wrapped in Christmas paper hanging from the branches. Do you know another country that has a nice big tree like that in the capital?

There was another tree like that in Tanteen. That disappeared too. School children used to admire that tree. Some used to just cool out there. Brown and his friend *pitched marbles* under the thick branches. The GBSS and Anglican High School children used to relax under that tree. When Tanteen hot sun was *bussing* cricketers' tails, they found shade under the well-clad tree. It was the perfect canopy. That tree is history. A nice, nice tree like that!

Mount Granby people cut down many trees to build big mansions. *Doh* worry! When times get tough, *dey go eat dem* houses!

Gouyave people cut down trees in the area known as Central.

They cut down Teresita's mango tree. Depo, my friend, cried for days. The best *tin mango* in the whole of Grenada, and they chopped it down! *Ah* could still taste *dat* mango—it was so sweet!

It's a shame some people called a good mango like that *knock-*

ah-bout mango. That was the best mango to devour when one was finished *knocking about. Ah put so much licks* on *dat* mango, they made up a song about me:

"Who say run the mango down?
Who say run the mango down?
Western cowboy in the town
Running all the mango down."

They made that song because *ah used to clean up all the mangoes* before they got them. When the movie in Empire was over and people walked up Cooper Hill looking for mangoes, they were already gone—gone down my gullet. They then had to cool it with a half-ripe Ceylon mango or two from Ogilvey's.

Another mango tree stood in the middle of Park Lane. They cut that down too. *Wha yuh expect?* Crowe and "Iceman" Smith had a monopoly on that one. Rawle was lucky if he got a few. Smith who became a famed and influential Grenadian radio personality was our cricket commentator. He sat under that mango tree!

Yes, Tyrrel Street is now called Herbert Blaize Street. These days, it's like every man in Grenada is getting a street. *Ah* hope they save Cockroach Alley for me. Please *doh* name *ah* mango tree after me—it will not last long.

Island Rain

I stood in waist deep water at Grand Anse Beach and keenly observed as the rain showers bathed Fort George and the surrounding areas. As the refreshing seawater soaked my limbs, I wondered if the rain would make its way to the beach. On numerous occasions, I had noticed how rain drenched some areas while it left others as dry as a mango seed after Tatoes had sucked it.

An old man who was familiar with the area noted my concern and advised me not to worry. He pointed out that because of the way the rain was falling that day, it would not reach the Grand Anse area. Indeed, he was right, but I wished the heavy drops had descended on me as I playfully ducked in the water.

There is something special about the rain falling while you are in the sea. It is a rejuvenating experience: you can bathe and rinse simultaneously. You can use the raindrops to wash the sun-burnt sea grapes before you stuff them into your mouth. You can dive under water from the rain showers, and then resurface to feel the effects of the pattering rain on your head. And you can run on the sand and feel the freshness of the rain as it washes your body. Those are just some of the comforting aspects of raindrops. But the rain can sometimes spoil your fun!

It spoiled my Brother Carl's fun once. He left Toronto bursting with excitement as he looked forward to the One-Day International Cricket Match between England and the West Indies. He looked forward to a sunny Queen's Park and the company of his friends Osbert, Ken Mitchell, and our brother Chris. He visualized Brian Lara hitting the ball all the way to Mr. LaCrette's house in River Road. He thought of the fancy footwork and all the "glorious uncertainties" of cricket.

But rain became the inglorious certainty! The rain came and his optimism faded. Rain, which makes farmers laugh and made me smile on Grand Anse Beach, placed huge frowns on the faces of cricket fans that day. The abandoned game—the ultimate fear—was realized.

Rain does not please all of us all of the time. It did not please me the day it *jammed me* by the police station in Sauteurs, St. Patrick's. I spent a few boring hours hiding from the heavy raindrops.

In the meantime, I received a lecture from a resident about the different kinds of rainfall that visited St. Patrick's. I was told about the mountain rain and the rain that comes from the Atlantic Ocean. I was informed that it was the Atlantic rain that had me caged in front of the police station that day.

Finally, the rain ended and the *rainflies* came out. I emerged from my hiding place also and walked into a huge pool of water wearing my best *Sunday shoes*. I made it home before another downpour.

Dem Ants Smart For So

Since I was a little boy, I have been looking at the ants. I started observing them more intensely after I read a passage from the book of Solomon, which advised that we "should go to the ant, consider its ways and be wise."

I then started putting the ants under the microscope. There were so many species of ants in Grenada to study: there were red ants, blacks ants; wood ants which we called *tac tac, flamer,* crazy ants, and various other kinds of ants.

I looked at them and saw how they sometimes traveled in long lines and whenever they *bounced up* each other, they stopped to whisper before moving on. They were unlike some people who thought themselves too good to communicate or say hello as they walked in the street.

I noticed too, that the ants loved to share. They shared their food in the same manner many Grenadian people used to share before selfishness, greed and the love of materialism trickled in.

I never saw an ant try to *backsqueeze ah* piece *ah* bread when the other ants were not looking. If an ant noticed food in its path, it never tried to eat it all by itself. I saw how that ant turned around and disappeared only to reappear in the company of many other ants.

It was always a community affair. Thy put their strength together and dragged the piece of bread to their nest. They reminded me of the people of Grenada who used to come together, pool their resources and help each other put up houses or reap their crops. They were not unlike the people of Gouyave who joined together to pull the nets and then shared the catch.

When the ants were deep down in their holes, they did not have to worry about people crushing them with heavy *water boots.* They could share and eat in safety and comfort.

The ants I looked at were wise enough to store food for a rainy day. A dead grasshopper, for instance, would be dragged to the nest, dissected, some of it eaten, and part stocked away for future days. They were different from some greedy people who lived for the moment and always tried to gobble down everything right away. The ant saved for the tough days.

If an ant stumbled onto a dead ant in its path, it went up to the dead comrade, paused as if paying respect and then moved in a different direction. That spot became a prohibited zone. The ant never acted like *fass people* who always wanted to find out cause and reason for death. The ant took no chances. You kill one of them and the others *split the scene.* They *duffed out* immediately and sought safer grounds.

Now I will tell you about the stinging part. I can't tell which type of ants gave the most painful sting. I know, however, that those little insects can cause *big people* to shed tears.

I remember the occasion I was relaxing under a tree on Bathway Beach. I got a stinging awaking. I was lying down on a black ant's nest and they did not like that. They began to bite. I had to rush and throw myself into the seawater, although I was not ready to bathe.

Red ants stung painfully too. Those ants were especially fond of the *pit latrines.* They assembled on the seats and as soon as you put your *bamsee* there, they were ready for you. The red ants even walked on the clothespins that people used to hang the clothes to dry in the yard. It was wise to always dust the underwear properly before putting it on.

I remember an ant story someone once told about a *badpay* priest. He never paid his tailor for the gowns that were made for him. The tailor became fed up with the priest and decided to teach him a lesson. He made a gown for the priest and let it rest on a *red ants nest* for a considerable time. The priest took the gown without paying and hurriedly put it on to say the mass. The ants went to work immediately. Father cried out in pain,

"Brothers and sisters, the Lord is in my heart, but the devil is in my *arse!*"

While the worshippers were begging *Papa Gawd* for mercy, the priest was begging the ants for compassion. The tailor sat in the back of the church and smiled.

The ants reminded me of bees. They, like bees, chose special spots to sting. Ants, bees and *maribone* love to attack the area above one's eyes. The ant will climb all the way up your entire body just to sting you above your eyes.

They were used to climbing mango and plum trees, but they were not foolish to sting the trees. They saved that for people. Solomon was right, they are wise. They climbed people in the same manner they climbed trees and then PING!—right above the eyelids, they let them have it.

An ant stung me above my right eye once. The eye became swollen. My friend Bosco looked at me and laughed:

"*Bwoy,* in these hard times,

yuh putting on weight?"

After that, my girlfriend asked me to take her to a matinee. I asked her, 'Who me? *Yuh mad, or wha?*"

I told her I was not going anywhere with that swollen eye. But I had to go to school the following Monday. I prayed for the swelling to go down before my schoolmates saw me. That was the kind of thing that school children loved to see.

The ants were so notorious for their sting that they termed an angry man who lived in Tyrrel Street "Red Ants". He was as hot-tempered as the red ants, black ants, *tac tac* and all the *flammer* ants put together.

FISHING TIME

I Remember Mr. Cliff, A Grenadian fisherman

He was a soft-spoken Grenadian and he loved the sea. He was as fond of the sea as my brother Keith. The sea was *his bread and butter,* and whenever the weather permitted, he braved the choppy waters to haul in snapper, butterfish or whatever fish might bite.

His effort was a powerful testament of the Grenadian will to work and, for me, lay to rest the myth that Americans have a monopoly on "rugged independence" and that abiding urge to succeed. West Indian people are hard workers too!

Mr. Cliff allowed me to join him on one of his outings. I always wanted to gain a first hand knowledge of the fisherman's experience and to quell forever my fears of the sea. I grew up hearing stories of squalls and *circle hole,* and of fishermen who never made it back to shore.

I was familiar also with the stories of unfortunate souls who went adrift and drifted all the way into Venezuelan prison cells. Then the politicians had a tough job, diplomatically, trying to wrestle with Venezuelan authorities for the release of the poor fishermen. Nevertheless, I discarded all my fears and boarded the small boat docked in Lagoon Road. I was ready for the trip, or I thought so.

129

We moved out one quiet *foreday* morning. In the stillness of the morn, I had time to ponder. Brother Cliff was not a man of many words, so I was left to my thoughts for long spells. I thought of the fishermen and the risk they took each day. I thought of people complaining about the price of fish. The effort that fishermen made, putting their lives on the line (pardon the pun) to catch the fish was not appreciated by all. Indeed, a fisherman's ordeal can be a trying one.

I even reflected on the time Daniel, a fisherman in Belmont, told me he saw a "marmaid," as he called it. I tried telling him there was no such thing, but that only encouraged him to initiate another conversation about Sea Devils. I gave up and listened. I walked away not knowing for sure if he really believed that such creatures existed.

Mr. Cliff and I headed in the direction of Point Salines. I was hoping that he would throw down anchor and start the ball rolling. I started to worry a bit as land began to fade in the distance. I remembered my Grandma saying, "Seawater have no branch." That was not a consoling thought, when the land began to disappear from view.

To make matters worse, we had no pig on board. *Ole time* fishermen used to carry pigs on their boats. If the boat encountered difficulty and began to sink, all they had to do was throw the pig overboard and then swim in any direction the pig put its nose. Pigs always knew where land was, it was said

Brother Cliff threw down anchor. Another fishing boat whizzed by. I said "Good!" I liked the idea of company nearby, just in case! While he was getting his fishing equipment ready, I took the opportunity to devour a few *Ceylon mangoes* I had carried in a paper bag. Nothing tastes sweeter than mangoes washed in the morning seawater. Nothing is more refreshing than the fresh smell of the morning sea breeze.

I only prayed that the mangoes did not give me *belly works,* or worse, *shittings,* as they were also known to do. A boat parked in the sea was not the ideal place for a bowel disruption. We did not walk with the toilet.

Brother Cliff hooked a butterfish. And then he reeled in a snapper. It was turning out to be fun, until a spoiler appeared.

The sun appeared in all its blazing glory. I was not prepared for that. There was no shelter from the burning heat. I wished for the trees that clothed the beautiful Grand Anse or Bathway. I longed to duck beneath a branch to shade myself from the roasting punishment.

Brother Cliff, so involved in his fishing, did not even notice my discomfort. It was just another working day for him. He had grown accustomed to heat without shade. Fishing was his livelihood and he had to survive, so there was no time to bother with the sun and its scorching rays. He had no time to worry about his peeling back. He fished and he kept hauling them in.

I was happy when we headed home. I went home with my sunburnt back and a great appreciation for the fisherman. That day, I learned to respect the fisherman and to understand that fighting to catch fish is as difficult as fighting the merciless elements.

A Fishing Friendship

He always possessed the urge to fish. It was in his blood and he began casting his line at an early age.

He grew up during a period when fishing was a hobby for many young people in Grenada. Some loved to fish, wile others just observed.

We made our own fishing rods fashioned from the straight branch of the *Bowlie tree*. The *Bowlie* rod was suitable because of its flexibility. Nylon string was used for the fishing line and that came in varying thickness. When a hook was attached to the line, the fishing rod was complete.

He fished near the old Mill in Maran and also off the coast near the rocks in Belmont. He fished next to the Green Bridge close to Queen's Park. The catch always had the familiar local names: *Ca Ca Bari, Grunt, Brim, Long Gyah, Bobby, Shitty,* and the fish called *Tuff Tuff* that no one wanted to eat. He also caught fish known internationally as snapper and butterfish.

He enjoyed fishing, and we, too, grew fond of throwing our lines into the water. One day, we baited our hooks and threw our lines into the sea near the Fire Station on the Carenage, but rain began to fall heavily. We tied our lines to the nearby jetty and sought shelter close to the fire engines.

From our shelter, we observed a line move and we knew a fish had taken the bait. Disregarding the rain, we ran to the jetty and pulled the tightened line. A huge snapper was at the end of my Brother Carl's line. It was big enough to fill a pot for all of us to enjoy.

The fish we caught, or the fish that caught itself, was an exceptional prize for us, but for Lenny, who had mastered the art of fishing, a catch like that was just another haul. He had the patience of Job and nothing deterred him while he was fishing. He was

Santiago in Hemmingway's "The Old Man and the Sea."

When he moved from Grenada to Brooklyn, Lenny brought with him his enthusiasm for fishing. He fathered two boys, bought them fishing rods early in life, and told them about the *bowlie rod* he used for fishing in Grenada. He took them fishing at Canarsie Pier, Far Rockaway and Sheephead's Bay.

He showed them how to hold the rod and when to pull. He also told them how important it was to exercise patience, for one never knew when the fish would bite.

The young boys loved to hear the stories of his fishing days in Grenada while they observed him demonstrating his fishing skills in Brooklyn and Queens.

Lenny also told me stories of his fishing adventures in Brooklyn and invited me to visit his home. One day, I visited, but he was not at home, so I waited. His car soon pulled up and out jumped his two sons; one carrying a fish called fluke. He informed me that they had just returned from a short fishing stint near Far Rockaway.

His son, who held the fish, promptly offered it to me, but I wanted him to keep his worthy prize. He said it was just one of the many fishes that he had caught in recent times so I could have it. Lenny took the fish from his son and gave it to me.

I was elated that a friendship that had blossomed from our boyhood fishing days in Grenada glowed even brighter in full view of his sons who were born in Brooklyn.

Pulling Fish Nets

I saw them as they pulled the fishnets in Gouyave, St. John's. I observed the men and women as they used their powerful muscles to haul in the *big jacks* and all the other fishes that were trapped in the nets.

Whenever one feels inclined to speak about fishing in Grenada, one's mind should automatically go to the Parish of St. John's and to the Lance in particular. Indeed, there are other areas where fishes were caught in considerable quantity, but Gouyave was and is the nerve center of the fishing industry. It remains the fishing pulse of Grenada. It is fitting also, that the big celebration known as "Fisherman's Birthday" held on June 29th each year is celebrated most lavishly in Gouyave.

I was always impressed by the unity displayed when residents of Gouyave got together to pull the fishnets. I used to look on with keen interest as they held on to the ropes and pulled. I saw how the muscles bulge in the shoulders of the strong barebacked men as they tugged and I observed the captain as he stood in a small boat in the sea and directed the entire operation.

The notice for casting the nets sometimes came early and occasionally unexpected. It sometimes came at *foreday* morning. Sharp eyes were always able to spot the disturbance in the sea. They looked and saw the jumping school of fish and they knew that it was time to cast the nets. The loud shout, "Boat cho, boat cho" told the fishermen and women that it was time to throw the nets into the water.

They knew it was the signal that *big jacks* or some other fishes were "beating" in the water. The water became a boiling pot. The wise ones knew from the color of the water what catch was likely. That skill came from the many years of experience observing the water and casting the nets.

The endeavor called for proficiency and knowledge of the art of luring fish into the nets. It took more than a little savvy to know the direction the school of fish was running. The fish could not be allowed to escape.

The divers knew how to *beat the water* to chase the fish into the nets and to prevent them from getting away. It was a combined effort involving those who pulled and those who chased the fish into the waiting trap. It was an art developed to near perfection.

I took note of their sense of purpose. I viewed them as they leaned forward and summoned every ounce of strength. Then they tugged with all their might. Pulling the nets involved discipline, proper timing and common sense. It was hard work, but work made easier by their combined effort. They gave added meaning to the old adage "unity is strength." As they pulled, I heard their chatter.

I looked on as the lively group of people pulled and rattled their mouths off. They shouted, they laughed and teased each other, but they never lost sight of the goal. It was the perfect setting for *ole talk*, *taybae* and the occasional *mamagism*.

They smiled, they joked and they gesticulated. It was the ideal environment for the hearty display of friendly teasing and often *ah good cussin.* Now and then someone gave advice to the men in the small boats and to those swimming around in the water. And the bad words echoed through the air

The reward came after the fish-laden nets were finally pulled to the shore. The nets and the cork attached to them lay in a bundled heap on the sand. The baskets were filled. All those who helped pull, were given a portion of the catch. The captain got his share and those who diligently tugged the ropes were rewarded. It was a practice known as *"djhaley."* That was the sharing part.

Then another day arrived, and it was time for others to pull.

Ye Fishermen!

A bright and sunny day to all the fishermen of Grenada who arise before the crack of dawn and make their way to the ocean to catch the fish that delight Grenadian palates. You risk your lives daily battling the elements—braving the winds and rain to pull in tuna and kingfish.

Your comrades sometimes disappear. Some drift in the wide expanse for days before a rescuing hand appears. There are occasions when your labor produces no gratifying reward. Undaunted, you rise again, gather your equipment and push out to sea one more time. There is always a brighter day!

You deserve our praises and one should think twice before uttering disagreement with the price of your catch. God bless you and keep you strong!

PAPPYSHOW

Ah Once Made Ah Crab Trap

In *dem days,* little boys made tops, *spinning cutters* and crab traps; big men made things like fish pots and *fowl coob.* When some *ah dem* put their fish pots to trap fish by the rocks in Belmont, they always found their fish pots, but sometimes their friends rose early and found the fish before them. They gathered the fish long before the cock even thought about crowing.

I sat down and made *ah* crab trap. *Ah took meh time* and made the thing. *Ah* put energy into it just like *Macmere* Phillip spent time making his mattress. And I felt proud that I had built something myself. It was harder for me to make a *slingingshot* or a *bamboo kite,* but I was able to put a crab trap together with relative ease.

I put some mango skin as bait and *ah* set the crab trap right there by Fatman and *dem,* close to the spot where Angel Harps used to beat the sweet steel pan music.

The whole night I thought of the crab I would catch. I had seen the monster. It was a large, blue crab with massive claws. We used to call the claws the *gundy.* It was a good crab to make *crab back* or the tasty *crab and callaloo.*

The next day, *ah* got up early and jumped over that little spot by Marshall's shop and made my way down to the Wharf. *Yeah, bwoy*! The crab trap was shut. *Ah* said, "Nice!" That was a good sign. My heart raced and I started to rejoice.

I carefully opened the latch and peered in. I had caught *ah* big, fat rat!

Bamboozled by a Lambie Shell

I have always associated the blowing of the *lambie* shell with fish. That connection was so established in my mind that one Labor Day in Brooklyn, I heard the blare of a *lambie* shell and I instinctively turned around and looked for the fish.

Once, while chatting with friends on Herbert Blaize Street in Grenada, I heard the distinctive sound of the *lambie* horn coming from the Carenage. I darted past Mr. Marshall's shop and made my way to the Carenage thinking only of the *big jacks* and snapper I would carry back to Brooklyn. I was hoping to find those super-size Jacks that Mammy used to stuff with ingredients and tie with a string.

I found the man who was blowing the shell near the cigarette factory.

He was selling green bananas!

Fooled by the "Calm" Sea

I stood on an elevation near McDonald College in St. Patrick's and my eyes peered out to sea, beholding the seemingly gentle calm. The picture was comforting to my mind. I wrapped myself in the tranquility of that moment.

But then I was ushered back to reality by a sobering realism. It stemmed from an experience I had years ago. The thought hit me with the force and harshness of a *planass:*

Years before, I had stood near Low Town and experienced a similar tranquility when I looked out to sea. It was also a blissful moment. My mood turned out to be a mirage, an eerie deception.

We pushed out from the mooring, that morning, in out boat. Soon we were greeted by angry waves that battered and tortured us. At times, the upsurges plunged us into deep tidal pits.

Like brave Grenadians, we weathered the monstrous surfs and we reached our destination. We had survived those wicked looking pillars of water that were not observable when we stood on the shore.

I had looked out to sea and was fooled by the seemingly gentleness, spied from afar. The seawater treated me like *ah pappyshow*. I learned a lesson:

Things are not always what they appear to be especially when viewed from a distance.

THE CALL OF THE BEACH

Old Mr. Marryshow on Pandy Beach.

I saw him there,
As he stood,
A man whose youth,
Had faded long.
Old and gray,
With shaking hands,
He stood and gazed,
Straight out to sea,
While his naked feet,
Were gently soothed,
By the rolling tides,
Of Mount Pandy.

There he stood,
On the glittering sand,
Scorched and parched,
By the Grenada sun.
He stood and looked,
Out to sea,

And I wondered what
Thoughts had he.
A mind seemed lost,
A man engulfed,
In a trance-like stare
At the horizon far.

I dare not ask,
He did not tell.
What made him stare?
What gripped his mind?
He had the right
To all his thoughts.

Then suddenly he turned
And looked at me.
And said,
In a soft and quiet voice,
God Bless!

Pandy Beach in the Morning

Pandy Beach summoned early. It was a call I could not easily dismiss. I yearned for the freshness of the morning air. I shook the slumber from my sleepy eyes and headed for the quietness of the beach.

I welcomed the early morning solitude. At the beach, I could sit and bury myself in blissful thoughts before taking a dive in the cool water. There I could be calm and be at peace with myself. There I could sit and reflect like old Mr. Marryshow who stared at the horizon. There I could watch the gentle waves as they bathed the sandy edge. I could do so peacefully before the others came. I could relax and meditate in the serene environment.

I ambled past Mr. Romain's house and ran into another early riser. I stumbled into Roystan, *man on the run.* He had risen to tend the cows he had tied up somewhere in Grand Anse. We found the time for a short chat and then I prepared to *buss the short cut* to the beach.

Roystan, I admired greatly for his individuality. He was and is appropriately termed *man on the run.* As industrious as they come, he makes his living tending his animals, doing landscaping and digging *pit latrine.* He is still a hard worker. He is a hard worker like Budu Beard, the carpenter was before him. Then, he finds the time to attend church

I looked out for the dogs. Dogs rose early too, and they did not have a single qualm about spoiling someone's precious morn. I remembered the days I used to walk on tiptoe to avoid disturbing angry dogs. I gingerly made my way to the beach, afraid to wake man's best friend and sometimes enemy too.

I ran into someone else. Miss Margaret's mother had arisen early. She was preparing to sweep the yard and then to feed the chicks. She was happy to see me:

"Wait, *Doo Doo, ah* have two mangoes for you. They fell from the tree last night."

I took the mangoes and graciously thanked her for them. Mangoes always go well with an early morning swim in Pandy Beach. She has since departed— "may God bless her soul."

I finally reached the sand. Someone else had beaten me to it. He was there to look after his boat and fish net. I had met him before, but I never knew his name. Grenadians can talk to you for years without knowing your name. One's personality shines brighter and is more important than the handle called a name. I watched him as he pushed his boat out to sea.

I sat beneath a tree on Pandy Beach. I watched and listened to the gentle swash of the waves. I sat there and I was at peace with myself.

Reflections at the Beach

I picked up the brown paper bag that lay on the *Morris chair* and began to stuff it with mangoes. I selected two Ceylon mangoes, a mango Rose, two Starch mangoes and I threw in a Beff mango in case that was not enough.

The Beff mango would satisfy anyone and we sometimes called it a *bellyful* mango. I slipped on my *bathing pants* and headed for the nearby Grand Anse beach carrying the mango bag. I took the little shortcut near the spot where Silver Sands Hotel once stood. I often used the steps there to dust off sand from my feet after my sea bath.

It was early morning and the air was fresh. The unmistakable scent of seaweed filled the air. I spotted a *Ko-kee-o- ko* tree at the far end of the beach. A number of beautifully adorned seashells lined the sandy shore. They looked so attractive lying on the sand. One peek at a shell and Mother Nature's unmatched craftsmanship became evident.

The shells were obviously pushed to the shore by the waves that splashed throughout the night. Those were the types of shells the tourists loved. They were often seen on the covers of specially make Spice baskets and ornaments the vendors sold to the visitors.

I carefully chose some of the shells and placed them in the brown paper bag. After picking a spot for the bag, I nestled myself between the roots of a Manchineel tree.

The Manchineel tree, which we pronounced *Mangeleen,* is a dangerous tree. It bears a small green fruit that is poisonous but looks appealing to the eye. A milky substance that oozes from it is known to blister the skin and many people knew it caused blindness. There were stories of tourists who mistakenly took the fruit for an edible delight and subsequently paid the price for their ignorance.

Nevertheless, it was my habit to sit beneath the Manchineel tree and relax before taking *ah header* or *bellyflap* in the water.

I sat there and looked at the sand crabs as they darted in and out of their holes. Some came close to me and stood motionless with their *gundies* ajar and observed me. One slight motion and they all scampered off. I saw how they struggled when caught in the waves. They anchored their legs in the sand for support and waited until the waves retreated.

I stared at them as they cleaned their eyes. I loved looking at the sand crabs. Sometimes I picked them up and held them in my hands.

I never took that chance with the big land crabs that lived in holes or even the reddish ones I used to spot near Glean's jetty in Lagoon Road, which was once called the Mang.

The big land crabs were the ones my sisters, Ros, Monica, Joan, and Valda used for making the appetizing *crab back*. Great patience was needed to remove the meaty parts from the crab.

When one sat down to devour the meal served in the same back of the crab, the taste buds rejoiced.

I remembered the time we had a big *crocus bag* filled with land crabs in our kitchen. Somehow, they all escaped, but we managed to catch a few and to run from some.

We had caught them in Westerhall one rainy night. When heavy rains flooded their holes, they all came out. Sometimes we took a *searchlight* and shined the light right into their eyes. They stopped in their tracks just like the *manicou*. We then picked them up with care. No one wanted his or her finger to be caught in the crab's little *gundy*. The big *gundy* might harmlessly span your wrist, but the little *gundy* was always sure to connect to a finger.

There were a few brave souls who used to push their hands deep into the crab holes and pull up the crabs. I knew a *fella* from River Road who often did that. I still shudder when I reflect on the thought.

As I sat and stared at the sand crabs, I wondered why so many creatures were afraid of humans. I used to see birds perch themselves on top the backs of cows in Woodlands, Happy Hill and Woburn, but I am yet to see a wild bird do the same on a person's back. It is true that "monkey knows which tree to climb." The sand crabs often ran away as soon as someone appeared.

I looked at the bag of mangoes and debated whether I should bathe first and then eat them, or wash them in the seawater and begin to savor their taste. A popular calypso said that "when it comes to eating, when *yuh* eating like *ah* Viking." Exactly what I usually did to mangoes was "eat like a Viking."

A number of black ants had crawled into the bag. I took out the mangoes and dusted the bag before placing it in another spot close to the tree. I did not have the stomach of Moosch, a man who ate anything.

Then I headed for the water. I took my hand and touched the water. I made the sign of the cross, a custom that I grew up with. Making the sign of the cross was an automatic gesture.

The water was cold and whenever that was the case, I stood there and made all kinds of *simi dim*. I jumped around, passed my hands in the water, but was reluctant to plunge in. Sometimes I even tasted the water, but I dreaded the coldness on my back. I stood there and made *ah pappyshow* of myself.

Then I felt it was time to take a *header*. I had played around too long. *Ah big man* like I was should not be afraid of cold water. I dived in and stayed below, holding my breath for sometime. I moved slowly along the bottom, and then I came up and made a little *dog swim*. I wondered why I had wasted that entire time making *ah bobolee* of myself before taking that dive.

I looked into the direction of the tree where I had put the brown paper bag containing the mangoes and shells. The bag was gone!

I knew for sure why the animals did not trust humans!

Nothing Like a Beach Party

Most Grenadians love a beach party. It does not matter whether it takes place at Bathway, Blanco Beach or Grand Anse; it is usually a time of great fun in the sun. It is a wonderful time for family and friends to get together to mingle, play and share a laugh.

But wait! Before one thinks of preparing for the trip to the beach, it is important to find out what type of mood the sea is in. The seawater has a reputation for *tearing tail* at certain times of the year. I have seen the huge waves blast against the walls near Melville Street. I am sure you don't want the rough seas to wash away your pot of *pelau* or *oildown*. Just the thought of that happening can make a grown person cry. There are times of the year when the sea is extremely rough; no one should think of a beach party then!

The sea doesn't seem to like the Christmas season. Fishermen then have to look out and gauge the state of the water outside the Lance or Low Town before venturing out. You ever went down in a hole in the sea? It can be a frightening experience.

Easter is a much gentler time and therefore a more popular occasion for the famed beach party. The sea probably remains calm out of respect for St. Peter and those disciples who were fishermen. At Easter, therefore, we get a break to frolic and have fun on the beach.

The buses and cars pull up close to the sand and the people unload those big pots filled with mouth-watering Grenadian food. When you see all that food, you know heaven arrive on Earth!

A big cookout on the beach is fun, but some of us prefer to cook the food at home and carry it to the beach. One does not have to wait to eat. You eat any time. When the food is cooking on the beach, you have to peep to see when it is ready each time you take a *duck* in the water.

Talk about *ducking*—that was very popular once! I used to stand on the Wharf and see the big boys *ducking* all the smaller ones. You are in the water wading smoothly along and then someone unexpectedly shoves your head into the water. They *duck* you and you drink some seawater. Then you feel like drinking some pipe water or a Red Spot soft drink.

The beach party provides fun for all. Some go to the beach party to drink rum and play cards and dominoes. They don't even bother to bring their *bathing suits*. Playing cards with the *fellas* is their idea of a beach party. Their feet won't even see the sea.

After a drink or two, some lie in the sand and fall asleep, shifting occasionally when a *big horse fly* stings their nose. One must watch out for those flies. One bit me once on a beach in Carriacou. I still think I am feeling the sting sometimes.

There are those who like to dance to calypso and reggae on the beach. Others just sit there and *maco* the women walking about in their sexy bikinis. Some keep peeping at the pot nonstop. There are those who do all of the above.

We like to play cricket and football on the beach. We can recklessly dive on the sand and take catches we can't take on the hard grassy cricket ground. We snatch the ball in a more spectacular way than the professional cricketers do.

Play is halted occasionally when the wave appears, but as soon as it recedes, it is back to *bat and ball*. If we forget to carry the bats, we can always improvise and grab a couple coconut bats from the nearby trees. The coconut tree will save the day.

We do all of that and keep our eyes on the pot There are always those who do not wait to eat. While you are playing *bat and ball*, they might forget that you also, could get hungry and gobble down your share. It's easy for them to forget you as they plunge into the delicious rice and peas.

If you spot them digging into the pot with a big pot spoon and pulling up the chicken legs, it is a signal for you to put the bat down.

You put the bat down faster if it's some breadfruit, *callaloo* or pig's tail from an *oildown* pot. That can disappear fast!

You take a sip of rum punch and watch the children play. Children always enjoy themselves on the beach. It is the perfect atmosphere for them. They run on the sand and play with their ball. They play in sweet innocence.

The young ladies, too, play their volleyball or engage in braiding hair and *ole talking.* The ole-timers crack jokes and drink their *grog.*

You then look to the horizon and are captivated by the fading sunset. It is time to pack for the journey back home. All good things must come to an end, but there will be another beach party. It was always wise to check and see if the drivers were sober before leaving. There will be another one as long as *Papa God* and the waves allow.

CRICKET, FOOTBALL & HORSE RACING

Voop

For those of you who are fortunate to be visiting Grenada for a cricket match, "Have a wonderful time!"

Cricket, *bat and ball*, call it what you like, but don't call it boring. You will have a nice time, not only because you will see world-class batsmen hitting sixes, but it will also be a great time for you to *bounce up* that fellow who used to *rap* you behind your head in school. And that long time *ting!*

Making the trip alone? *Ah doh* want you to end up in divorce court, so be careful! It will be a time when people who have not seen you *in* such a long time will shout:

"*Aye, bwoy, yuh here?*"

Then you can answer:

"*Nah, bro, ah* still in Brooklyn!"

But you can still have a nice time even if you are not in Grenada to see the game.

You can see cricket on the Dish Network. Here is how I hope to make it enjoyable:

I am going to visit my four friends. I will be seeing the game for free. I will walk with a Grenadian breakfast to share with my friends.

What will I carry? *Easy man, easy*! Fried bakes, fishcakes and *cocoa tea.* I will show them the foods that make Grenadians so strong that we could lift *ah bundle ah wood* with no effort. Every time Devon Smith hits a four, I will put a fried bake in my mouth.

Watching cricket in the morning on TV is not too hard. The difficult part is when the first inning is over and there is a lunch break. The temptation is to indulge in a heavy meal. I must have my lunch break too, just like the cricketers.

After that, sleep will arrest me like a Grenadian policeman. A full belly, tired eyes and *ah* strong rum will make the TV look at me instead of me viewing the fancy strokes the batsmen make.

But I think I have the solution. Every time I doze off, I will drink some hot *cocoa tea.* It is not proper for me to visit my friend's house and fall asleep. If I intend to sleep, I should stay in me *dam* bed!

Papa God, hold the rain! Let the match begin.

Cricket Memories

A few years ago, I went to see the World Cup cricket match between South Africa and the West Indies. It was carried live on television. I was glad I went; not because the *fellas* cooked up a big pot of curried shrimp and rice, but, heck, that too was incentive enough!

Anyway, I was fortunate to see Brian Lara in good form at the wicket and that brought back some very fond memories I have about cricket. Some of them are deeply imprinted on my mind, never to be erased. I am sure that you, too, have some memories perpetually engraved somewhere in your thoughts.

I thought of the man called Gordon Greenidge. He used to hit the ball with such venom as if he wanted to *buss* up the leather. He struck the ball as if he had utter disdain for leather. How can one forget him and his *Bajan* partner, the reliable Desmond Haynes?

Those *fellas* used to make fast bowlers *number one* and probably *number two* in their flannel pants. No one can tell me that those guys did not eat *bluggoe* and *fig* imported from Grenada. That is the only explanation for the vicious strokes and the power behind their shots.

And that tall lamppost they called Clive Lloyd! One step and he was already half-way down the pitch. You had to be a sprinter to keep up with him. I don't know how poor Kalicharran did it!

Remember what Lloyd did to Bedi, the Indian spinner? He back drove a ball and *buss* up the poor Indian man's hand.

There were two spinners from Trinidad called Inshan Ali and Jumadeen. They were fondly referred to as the "spin twins." Pick up the Express newspaper and all you read about was "the spin twins!"

Papayo! Lloyd held their *backside* in Bourda and he hit

Jumadeen so hard the commentator said Lloyd sent the ball in the country. I would not be surprised if they are still looking for the ball

Speaking of commentators! Remember Raffe Knowles? The problem with him was that he used to broadcast both cricket and horse racing. Sometimes, in the claw of excitement, he forgot which game he was announcing. Once, a fielder was chasing the ball—Mr. Knowles took him for a horse and his commentary shifted to the description of a horse race in progress. He caught himself, but not before we had a good laugh.

I was fortunate to see Viv "Smoking Joe" Richards bat at Queen's Park, Grenada in a match that featured Combined Islands against Guyana. Richards had to be good in geometry, the way he bi-sected the field that day. He sent back the Guyanese bowlers toting *ah bundle ah fours* all the way to Georgetown.

That took place in the same Queen's Park where our very own Joe Gibbs bamboozled some star Australian batsmen. Yes, *sah*! Then Joe went and drank *ah* rum with his friends.

This brings me to a batsman called Nurse. That was one angry batsman. He got so *vex* in the wicket once that he first *buss* the ball, then he *buss* his pads. Finally, he *buss* his pants seat. *Doh ask me* what caused that one.

Picture the man called Basil Butcher! You could not get him out on a Saturday at all! That was when butchers made their money and he made runs. He made runs on one end of the wicket while his partner, Rohan, was falling on his *bam bam* and hitting massive sixes.

I never saw the great Sir Gary Sobers in action, but I remember that partnership he put up with his cousin Holford in England. It was a feat that almost sent English cricket pundits staring mad. Those little West Indians boys were out of place. When England thought they had the match in the bag, those two *Bajans* came and spoil the whole thing!

That Sobers was *something else*! He would open the bowling and when you think you got rid of him, it was the *chinaman*, or *back of the hand* stuff in *yuh tail*!

It was once believed that the young Bernard Julien was maturing into the next Gary Sobers. He was still maturing the last time I heard about him!

Ah still vex with Holding and Roberts for what they did to the Indian cricket team at Sabina Park, Jamaica. It was *pace like fire*. After five wickets down and the ball knocking down the Indians, they surrendered. They declared and lost the match. *Ah* never heard of a team declaring and lose in cricket. They later said that they did so to save their players from injuries. Roberts and Holding were bowling as if they were possessed that day.

The Indians had a batsman who terrorized the West Indians while he was at the crease. His name was Gavaska and he was such a thorn in the side of the West Indies team that Lord Relator, the *calypsonian*, made up a song about him:

"They even try with Uton Dowe,
But ah sure they sorry
They bring him now.
It was Gavaska, the real master,
Just like a wall,
They couldn't out Gavaska at all."

One cannot omit the fearless Roy Fredericks. I will never forget that 169 he made against Australia in opposition to the fireballs Thompson and Lillie. I sat next to my little radio in Grenada and rejoiced when he had those Australians running all over the field.

The Australian bowlers were so fast that once, one of them knocked Rowe's stumps out of the ground with a ball that "not even God could have played." Fredericks stood up the way Devon

Smith, the Grenadian cricketer, might stand up against fast bowlers one day.

There were batsmen who were able to entertain the crowds. Colin Milburn of England was one such individual. He had no time to waste at the crease. He did not remain there *poking* all day. If the first ball was a wayward one, it was promptly dispatched to the boundary. First ball bad, first ball six!

Now to the county champs! A county champ is a cricketer who will *blade yuh tail* in the small matches, but when the big day comes on the test ground, he fails.

One of the biggest county champs the West Indies ever saw was the Jamaican Eastern McMorris. The *Bajan* Peter Lashley and Maurice Foster of Jamaica were not far behind. Are there any county champs on the current West Indies team? Bring back Sherwin Williams and you will see *wha ah talking 'bout.*

Yes, sah! West Indies had some good cricketers! Some were born in the wrong time—like Ervin Shillingford of Dominica. *But ah still tink* they messed him up! The West Indies selectors waited until he was almost over the hill to give him a break. *Wha yuh* expect? He was a Small Island boy.

Now, back to my curried shrimp and rice my Guyanese friends, Joe and Michael, cooked. What ah curry!

A Cricket Match Was a Serious Thing

Those *fellas* were serious—dead serious! The younger guys like us were only able to lay claim to Marryshow pasture after the bigger boys, (like Cow, Phantom, Smeko and Foxhead) who attended the Grenada Boys' Secondary School, found interest elsewhere. Still, we learned from them the discipline and organizational skill it took to make a cricket match worthwhile and interesting.

The discipline we diligently employed when we prepared the cricket pitch. We rolled the ground with a huge iron roller and we cut the grass in preparation for our test match. We all played a role in getting the field ready. We took the time and exercised great patience as we sought to bring the field up to our desired standard. We exercised patience and discipline that recent West Indies cricket teams lacked.

When Tyrrel Street played Green Street, it was more serious than a test match. We felt a sense of fulfillment and pride in our effort, and the time and the pain we took to roll the pitch, clear the grass, and prepare for our battle. That was OUR time and no one could deny us our chance to bat, bowl or break a glass window or two with the ball.

When small kids like us played *out-ah-man* with the bigger boys in Tanteen, the only thing we were allowed to do was field. Any of us who took a brilliant catch would get a compliment from the big *fellas,* but that was all.

Our job was to field the ball that big boys were too lazy to run after. I caught the ball once and it was my time to bat, but a big *fella* looked at me and said, "Georgiana boy, *gimme* that bat." I had no choice, but to hand over the bat to him.

We even had our commentators. Lew Smith never played, but he got his radio practice right there on Park Lane.

157

Justin "Crowe" McBournie played for Green Street and he was quite collected then. He collected the ball when one made a bad shot. He did so with superb agility.

Who could forget that wonderful setting on a Sunday morning? I can still picture the yellow buttercups waving gleefully in the gentle breeze. The *bee bush* added to the already colorful scene. Marryshow pasture was a picturesque sight then, and the beauty still glows in my thoughts.

And the game!

When we played cricket, we forgot the nearby *damsel tree*, its branches lowered because of the load. We had no time for governor plums or the tasty mango. It was *bat and ball*. When someone pulled a ball all the way down to Marshall's shop, youthful eyes found that ball before one could have uttered—*Geeze am bread*!

Sometimes, in the midst of an exciting cricket match, a mother came bulldozing her way to the field of play and dragged her embarrassed son away. He probably was guilty of leaving the *wares* unwashed and finding himself on the field of play. All his good friends would laugh at him. Best friends are always the ones who laugh at you if your angry *mooma* dragged you away from a game of cricket.

Nothing stopped our cricket matches. Though players like "Hardo" used to knock down the stumps when he was out, it was all fun, pure fun! It was fun at a time when children were allowed to savor their innocence and when respect and discipline ranked high on the scale of things.

The supporters were always present to stand by the *damsel tree* and shout, "Run, run, run," and then "stay, stay, stay!" They did so because at times the ball went down a slope and the batsmen running between the wickets were unable to see where the ball went. The supporters played an important role.

We played our cricket and we had our fun. Then we went

home to do our homework because we did not want to feel the weight of the teachers' belts the next day.

By the way, I am talking about *winball cricket,* and Charlie Hood, Ben's brother, was a great spinner of the ball.

I Was There!

I was there when Mello went down. Big, strong and powerful Mello, the proud owner of a thunderous right foot, suddenly hit the grass in Queen's Park. My heart bled and I shed a tear when he lost a leg. I felt the pain that pierced his leg. Then he had to hang up his football boots. The referee was there too, but on that day, it was God's call. I sat in Queen's Park Grand Stand and saw it all

I was also there to witness the keen football battle between St. John's Sports and Hurricanes. I looked on as the exuberant crowd crept in. I saw them assemble like religious zealots to witness the rivalry that had festered, ripened and was ready to explode.

I saw the eager feet pace restlessly as eyes bulged with uneasy anticipation. I saw the excitement grow as the ball was centered. I was there to witness a passionate people engulfed by a popular sport bash in an afternoon of nervous excitement. I looked on as young men faced each other on the green grass in Cuthbert Peters Park.

I was also there to observe the spectacle when colorful crowds *ram-crammed* Tanteen to behold the contest played out at Old Trafford. They came from the north and various points to take in the fancy footwork or the enthusiastic display or they just simply came to *buss ah lime.* They came after their daily toil was over.

I recall the lively women selling snow cone, *tambran balls,* and all the goodies that energized the cheering and spirited crowd. It was a worthwhile moment in Grenada's history. The love people had for the football game was always good to see. When Yankeeman scored a goal, the deafening roar raced all the way up Lowthers Lane.

I was there when Big Bear stood like a log in the middle of Tanteen to referee a soft shoe football match. He stood like a lamp-post while his two eyes roamed the field. Running around was for other referees like Bogo or Plug, not for him. Big Bear anchored himself in a chosen spot on the field and did all his officiating from there.

Credit must, however, be given to Big Bear as he helped organize what came to be known as the soft-shoes competition. The match-up often pitted powerful teams like Dazzlers and Point against each other. The team from the Point, St. George's, sometimes used small fishing boats for transport to the Tanteen football field for the game. They arrived for the games like soldiers preparing for battle.

When the Sunday morning game was over, and Kennedy LaCrette had taken his numerous corner kicks with his bare foot, the footballers then dug up the energy for further first divisional work at Queen's Park. Was it the Vienna or leaven bread, or the *bluggoe and saltfish,* which nourished the sinews for such extended football work?

I was there when Atoms football team took on Dauntless. I saw when Big Chow butt someone's *brogues.* I saw the long powerful shots that Big Dog took.

Emotion peaked during such encounters and got even hotter if the referee had the nerve to call a questionable last minute penalty.

I was also there when a referee from Surinam *jooked* Grenada football all the way to an unprecedented pinnacle. All of the Windward Islands shuddered at the thought of meeting the Spice Boys. They still speak in glowing terms of Ashley George, Marques, Alister Telesford, Paul Roberts and Harbin.

They speak about those *fellas* just the way people talk about the excellent football skills of Shalrie Joseph and Jason Roberts today.

Springs Football Fever

In Springs, too, football fever raged. The ardent crowd gathered, just like the other crowds that assembled at Old Trafford and in Victoria, to see the beautiful game.

They came from Belmont and Grand Anse. From Woodlands and Morne Jaloux they came. They flocked the sidelines of Springs pasture to observe the intense rivalry between the competing teams. Some entered the grassy field from the bottom.

They walked past the house that had the big star on top of it. The big Gairy political emblem was there for all to see. They *buss* shortcut near the house where Daddy-O lived. Some stood close to the top road and observed from above, as they sipped cold Carib beer bought from the nearby shop.

They cheered when Cafe Bull blocked Matty. They ducked when Bismarck sent the ball flying in their direction.

They applauded when Red Ants scored for Springs. Red Ants always knew how to find the net and he made it hard for teams to defeat Springs in Springs. Yet, they desperately tried.

When Bowen headed in the ball for Morne Jaloux, the Morne Jaloux posse erupted like Mount St. Helens. They looked on inquisitively as Ghatts gave his team a pep talk.

The Transunit crowd from lower Belmont was present to urge on Debellotte, Cox, Ray and the Vesprey boys. Compere Tig and Punce stood by the goal post and issued instructions to their squad while Back and Neck grumbled as his Grand Anse team got *ah bag ah goals*.

While young men gallantly tackled each other on the field of play, another young man moved among the crowd. He moved with his tray of *Skinup*. He loudly demanded, "Buy the *Skinup*!" The people watched the game and they sucked his *Skinup*.

Valours came out to play and Grogay was ready to run. Valours was the team of brothers. I played on that team as well as my brothers, Chris and Carl. Grogay ran the field as if an Energizer battery powered him.

When his brother, Goday, kicked the ball over the goal post, he promised to drop him from the team for the next match. After the game, they headed for Pandy Beach to take a dip. As they passed Islander Gap, old Mr. Redhead, sitting in his verandah, looked at them and smiled.

The atmosphere was electrifying and magnetic. It pulled Skyie (Redhead) away from bending wire for his *Mas costume.* It dragged Bosco and the Belmont *panmen* away from their steel pans. School children found a nice little spot to clap and cheer after the afternoon bell had sounded. Even the bus drivers slowed down to watch the artistic footwork. They all took in the action.

Back then, it was always a wonderful Springs affair.

Horse Racing

I was never a betting man. The reason is, *ah* was always afraid to lose. If *ah* lose ten dollars *ah* ready to cry crocodile tears. And I would think about it for years.

I take a chance *once in ah blue moon* while playing the Lotto in Brooklyn, especially when I dream the numbers. The only problem is that I always dream the wrong numbers. I am always dead wrong!

When I play the scratch game, I mostly lose. The last one I played, my numbers had to add up to one hundred in order to win a prize. I scratched the prize first. It was $50, 000. I said to myself. "*Oh Gawd, ah lose!*"

If the prize is big, you know you lose already. The first number I scratched was fifty. *Ah* said "good!" The rest of the numbers added up to a grand total of twenty. I got seventy out of a hundred. That's what I used to get in Geography during my secondary school days. That's my luck!

I am fond of horse racing. We had horse racing in Grenada once. Seamoon and Queen's Parks were famed Grenadian race-tracks. Busloads of people used to leave St. George's and head for Seamoon. Busloads used to return with sad faces after they lost money betting on horses.

They were horses that were so swift they used to send them overseas to race. A popular horse was Bamboo Flower, owned by one of the Branches from Gouyave.

Another horse, called Carlos, was perhaps the most outstanding Grenadian racehorse. A speedster called Four White Foot used to gallop like a plane right there in Queen's Park.

As a boy, I used to get on a wooden broomstick and ride just like a jockey on top of Four White Foot. Four White Foot was my hero.

Sometimes you went to the track, but didn't see horse racing at all. There were some *smart men* near the racetracks waiting for you and your few dollars. They used to spread money on the ground and you purchased rings to throw and cover an area to win a prize. You will be pitching those rings for the whole day and all they covered were ten-cent pieces. People like me used to keep flinging the rings and losing, and the *smart men* kept laughing and winning.

Horse racing is but a memory in Grenada. Gone are the days of the stables in Queen's Park and Seamoon. Few people remember the names of the jockeys who rode the horses.

Jamaicans take their horse racing seriously. Grenadians had that fervor, once, when the tracks existed. I don't even see Grenadians these days riding horses that are running on TV, but Jamaicans do that.

Visit an Off Track Betting location in Brooklyn and you would see Jamaicans *caning horses* with an invisible whip. They bend their backs like the jockeys and whip the horses they see on the television.

Some of them walk with notebooks and ponder over them as if they are preparing for the bar examination. And *dem fellas* know the horse's mother, father, how much race it won and lose—everything!

If a horse wins, it is *"Irie."* If the horse loses, it is *Rassclat*!

CHANTS, GAMES, PASTIMES & OTHER CHILDHOOD PLAY

Yesterday

Yesterday was an exciting day for many of us. We were so full of vitality. We had so much energy that we chased the *rainflies* when they came out after the tropical downpour. Sometimes the heavy rain confined us to the house and restricted our freedom to run around or play games. We sang a song to chase the rain away:

"Rain, rain, go away,

Come again another day"

There were times when Mother Nature seemed uncertain, and the sun and rain appeared at the same time. On such occasions, we joked that the devil and his wife were fighting.

There were occasions, also, when we welcomed the heavy rainfall because it gave us the opportunity to bathe in the torrential showers. We jumped and played in the rain until the thunder and lightning sent us dashing inside the house.

Yesterday, we played a little game called "Ship Sail." We placed grains of roasted corn in our hands and made *ah cuff*. Someone then had to guess the number of grains in our clenched fists, and if the guess was correct, that person got the corn

Some children were great at the guessing game, but others were frequent losers. *Ah fella,* nicknamed Lord Hungry, used to lose all the time. We had a little jingle for that game:

"Ship sail

Sail fast

How many men on deck?"

Each grain of corn represented a person. As we played the game, we learned to count at the same time.

We played another game with a tiny piece of paper stuck to the fingernails on each of our index fingers. The objective was to hide the paper that was on those fingers. We quickly pressed the index fingers down with the thumbs to hide the paper and, at the same time, ejected the middle fingers that had no paper on them. Then we pushed out the index fingers again and hid the middle fingers.

It was a trick game and the hope was that the extremely quick movement of the fingers would fool the onlookers into believing there were no interchanging of the fingers. We had our little tune for that also:

"Two little blackbirds sitting on a wall,

One name Peter, one name Paul

Fly away Peter, fly away Paul

Come back Peter, come back Paul."

Yesterday, we found the time to play many interesting games. We were good at the Hula Hoop, and we sometimes *wined* to the ground and came back up with the hula hoop swinging around our waist. We also played *hopscotch, O'Grady Say, Pinchy Pinchy, Rounders,* and a game called Jacks.

Yesterday, we looked for the little sand turtles in the soft dirt below the house and we sometimes put an ant on their nests to draw them out. We enjoyed playing hide and seek in the tall grass that grew in the pastures and at Fort George. At Christmas, we used the toy guns to play *bow bow* or stick em up. However, we never ended up killing anyone.

Yesterday, our parents flogged us for taking out the buttons from our shirts and pants to play a game called *Button Tips*. We even took the buttons from our church clothes and school uniform. Then some of us got blows with a coconut broom or the leather belt. We swept the yard with the coconut broom and we got *ah cutarse* with the same coconut broom.

Yesterday, we cried when our friends teased us, and that encouraged them to tease us more:
"Cry cry baby, one ah one, ah dumpling,
Take off your shoes and run up the mountain."
Those who cried too much were dubbed cry *cry cry babies.*

Yesterday, our Sunday dinner was something we looked forward to. *Sunday food* was special. Not too many children wanted to eat everyday foods like bluggoe, *dasheen* and *fig* on Sunday.

Sunday meal was the occasion for foods like stewed beef and chicken, and the tasty rice and pigeon peas. The *callaloo* was an appetizing side dish. We had our lettuce, carrots and sweet pepper too.

We were always on the lookout for those who were bent on grabbing the meat from our plates. My bigger brother, George, once caught me with a common trick. He whispered, "Look, *ah blackbird!*"

I looked and my meat was gone. It was always the meat they took. No one bothered to take the yams, pumpkin or sweet potatoes.

Yesterday, we fought for the *bun bun* that was left in the pot after the *pelau* was cooked. Everyone wanted the tasty *bun bun* that was left in the bottom of the iron pot.

Yesterday, it was customary for us to leave some food in the plate after eating. That was called good table manners. We ate our food and left a little piece of meat in the plate. We also placed the knife into the teeth of the fork to signal that we had finished eating.

These days, many people clean their plates as dry as a sun-scorched plum seed. They have long forgotten all those table manners *ting*.

Yesterday, we said our grace before our meals:
"We thank thee lord for the world so sweet,
We thank thee for the food we eat,
We thank thee for the birds that sing,
We thank thee Lord for everything."
And when it was our bedtime we said another prayer:
"Now I lay me down to sleep,
I pray the Lord my soul to keep,
If I should die before I wake,
I pray the Lord my soul to take.

In my little bed I lie,
Heavenly Father, hear my cry.
Lord protect me through this night
And bring me safe till morning light."

Or songs to put us to bed:

"Now the day is over,
Night is drawing nigh,
Shadows of the evening
Streak across the sky."

At Christmastime we sang:

"Christmas is coming the goose is getting fat.

Please put a penny in an old man's hat.

If you haven't got a penny, a ha'penny would do.

If you haven't got a ha'penny, then God bless you."

Yesterday, we were bitten by bed bugs. We slept on the fiber mattress and bedbugs used to *galavant* on the fiber mattress. They were also fond of the *Macintosh* the babies slept on.

And when someone *pee pee on* the mattress, the bed bugs were happier. Then the mattress was placed in the hot sun to be dried.

Sometimes the bed bugs made their way to the benches at school. Those who were not bitten on the mattress at home did not escape the bite on the school bench. That enabled some students to remain alert during the boring History and Geography classes.

Yesterday Grandma told us *Nansi Stories.* We sometimes sat in the moonlight and listened to the stories. Some of the stories were handed down from generation to generation, but others were impromptu tales made up as we sat under the trees.

Many of our elders spoke patois and were able to mix in some French words in the stories. There were stories of Jumbie, Soucoyant and other frightening tales. Many of the stories were so scary that the sight of a bluggoe leaf dancing in the wind at night sent us scampering into the house.

Other stories were tales of Brer Anansi, Brer Rabbit, Compere Ziah and Compere Tig. Some tales had their roots in Africa. The storyteller usually began with the words, "Tim Tim." When "Tim Tim" was said someone answered *Bashe*. Then the story began. Yesterday, we ran into the house after going to the movies to see Christopher Lee, Vincent Price and Peter Cushing play their Dracula roles in the horror movies. The movie called the Gorgon was a big hit.

Yesterday our eyes were sharp. When Granny called us to thread a needle, it was one, two, three and it was done. There were times we had to leave the cricket and football games to thread the needle or wash the *wares*. We did not always do so willingly.

Yesterday, our parents sometimes spoke to us in parables. They quoted the parables from the Bible, as well as local expressions to get the point across. Examples of those saying were:

Is come, *yuh* coming

Study *yuh* head

The longest rope has an end

Monkey say cool breeze, baboon say wait a while

What sweet is goat mouth does be sour in its *bam bam*

Crappo smoke *yuh* pipe

When goat *mess* ready to roll any slight breeze would do

Play with dogie, dogie will lick *yuh* mouth

Monkey knows what tree to climb

Where horse reach, donkey does reach

Cow horn never too heavy for its head

You will never miss the water till the well runs dry

Respect yourself

Who have cocoa in sun must look for rain

You will never see the day Pompey lick Caesar

One day one day congote'

One day for watchman, one day

for thief

Learning is better than silver and gold

They spoke to us, and at times we had to pause to decipher the message they wanted to convey. If you placed your hands on a costly piece of furniture or glassware, a parent might calmly remark, "*Dat ting* cost a lot of money, you know." We then knew we had to be careful. When we pushed them to their limits they angrily shouted, "Jesus, Mary and Joseph!"

Yesterday, we used a little tin container to sell our guava cheese and other goodies to help out our parents. The little tin container was important and its content helped put a little bread and butter on the table. To many parents it was a necessity.

The little containers, that held the *tambran balls*, fudge, sugar cake, guava cheese and pineapple tarts, were tucked into the schoolbag and carried to school. When the recess bell rang, it was time to pull out the container and make the sale. Not every school child had the patience to wait for the break time to munch on the cocoa fudge or guava cheese. The sale sometimes occurred while the teacher was talking about meandering rivers, the circulatory system, or the Maroons of Jamaica. While some students were busy taking notes, others were eagerly eating cocoa fudge or slipping a five or ten- cent piece below the desk to purchase a sugar cake.

The teacher sometimes saw the transaction and threatened to confiscate the little container. No conscientious schoolchild wanted that to happen.

With each purchase of a groundnut sweetie, a mammy or granny became more equipped to purchase a tin of corn beef or a pound of rice.

When the little change was taken home after school, mammy counted it and smiled. She was gratified that her little son or daughter was playing a significant role in ensuring that the enticing aroma continued to rise from the pot on the coals.

Yesterday was a time when every cent counted. The demands were many:

School uniforms had to be purchased. School fees had to be paid on time. It was necessary to have proper Sunday wear to attend church.

Many parents therefore found themselves in a constant struggle to provide for their children. They therefore used their abilities to make various appetizing snacks to sell.

Parents like Ma Rubes went to the schools to sell the goodies. She built a close relationship with the students.

There was another woman named Miss Eve who became famous for the tasty *nut sweetie* she sold near to Mother Rose School in St. George's. Miss Gertie was noted for her brand of candy known as *Nigger Boy Sweetie.*

Women like Miss Nella and Miss Melina sold peppermint *sweetie and groundnut* near Empire cinema. I remember Miss Pearl selling oranges on *Old Year's* night.

Yesterday, we did not have the luxury of videotapes, playstations, and televisions. We did not have the technological advances that make life so much easier today.

We had hard work, togetherness and the moonlight. And yes, we had sorrows and disappointments too! The moonlight is still with us, but the Nansi stories are fading fast.

In those days, we played with little toy soldiers we got from the United States. We used to make them fight each other. One of the toy soldiers looked just like *me compere* Joey.

The girls used to play with dolls whose eyes were as blue as the Tempe soap or the *blue* we used to put in our clothes. Then the "Black is Beautiful" slogan took root and black dolls appeared in the stores. People went window-shopping at Christmastime to see the black and brown dolls in the stores. The fantastic thing about window-shopping was that even though some people were as broke as cockroaches, they window-shopped and found some pleasure in doing that.

Charles, the Teacher

Charles made all kind of kites. He made *flex kites* and he made *bamboo kites.*

He made other things too!

When Depo and *dem* graduated from making and flying the small *cocorico* kite, they ambled over to Marryshow pasture to seek Charles and his kite-making skills.

It was kite season! Anybody ever *sling your kite?* A kite would be sailing elegantly in the wind only to be taken down by a stone attached to a piece of string. Some pranksters used to put razor blades in the tail of their kite to cut the string of other kites, then hid somewhere and have a good *belly laugh.*

The *cororico* was the simplest of kites. We made cocoa leaves fly like *dem Ligaroo* in Grand Anse. One just had to find a good dried cocoa leaf, punch two fine holes somewhere near the middle, and get something light to use for a tail. Then the *cocorico* was ready to sail in the wind.

We made *cocorico* and we made *Coolie kites.* That very easy to make and those of us with less professional skill than Charles were able to craft the *Coolie kites* effortlessly.

Many of us, however, opted for the fancy and brilliantly colored *flex kites.* Some preferred the *bamboo kite* with the *mad bull* that enabled it to sing all day. While the *bamboo kites* were singing in the air, the engines of the wooden buses like Teresa B, Monkey Toe and Labor Reward were singing in the streets. Fatty Derek was teaching us how to sing in Palmer School.

Music was everywhere! The *bamboo kite* sang all day until someone got fed up with the singing and put a razor blade in the tail of his kite to cut the string.

Some of the kites were pretty, pretty, pretty, but caught their *nen nen* to fly. The wind would blow stronger than Hurricane Ivan could, but all the kite did was *butt, butt, butt*.

When the big bamboo kites started to *butt,* everyone had to clear the way. Make room!

Finally succeeding in getting the kite into the air, someone was waiting with a stone attached to a string to sling it. Frustration got the better of you and you decided to forget the kite and make a *spinning cutter.*

Charles did not have to teach us how to make a *spinner cutter.* All we needed was a *crown cork* or the cover of a condense milk can. We took a stone and flatted the *crown cork* or tin cover. Then we punched a hole in the middle. Next, we passed a piece of string through the hole and we were ready to spin the *spinning cutter.* That was a dangerous pastime and one had to be extremely careful because those things were as sharp as the razor blade they put in the tail of the kites.

We *slacked our kites* and we played with our *spinning cutters,* and when we got tired of that, we went to look for Charles again.

We sought Charles' help to make a top. The harder the wood, the better the top, but the tougher it was to be made. *Fellas* like Charles make tops with ease. He made tops while Macmere Phillip was fashioning the most comfortable coconut fiber mattresses.

Charles even painted the tops before spinning them in the road. The tops would fall asleep in the road for long spells. They stood in a spot in the road and went to bed. They slept while standing up like the drunken men near Marshall's shop.

While the tops slept, we looked for the crook of a tree to make a *slinging shot.* A *slinging shot* was useful to hit those mangoes on Teresita's tree that the hand could not reach.

We played with our tops and we used our *slinging shot* to knock down Teresita and O'Gilvie's mangoes.

Once again, we looked for Charles. Charles knew where the best *Bowlie* rods were. We used the bowlie branch to make our fishing rod, and then we headed for the wharf to catch a grunt, snapper or *cacabari.*

We got tired of fishing so we asked Charles for a *ballswheel* and he showed us how to make a cart or scooter. The cart was important as it was used to transport groceries and tools for our parents.

Charles took time from his busy schedule to show us how to use a piece of rubber and wood to make scooters. He warned us to be on the look out for Black Church and Boraggy on their police motor bikes. He told us to exercise care when we were in the street.

Charles was more than a teacher. He was an inspiration.

The good *ole* days!

STYLE, SCHOOL CLOTHES, HAIR CUTS & KEEPING CLEAN

Jooking Shirts, Stiff Uniforms and Rolled Up Skirts

School children claimed that Miss Wallace used to take a broomstick and *jook* down the shirts. No school child wanted to be caught wearing Miss Wallace's *jook down shirt*. It was as bad as wearing a *dog muzzle shoe,* or pants made with flour bags. It was as bad as going to school wearing a *hula hoop slipper.* But it was better than wearing patched pants or pants that left a hole in the *backside* exposed for all Grenadians to *maco.*

Children in Grenada today don't know too much about patched pants. Back then children who wore patched pants were in style. An amusing sight was seeing someone wearing khaki pants with a black patch. When one's mother could not find the right cloth to make a patch, any type of material was used.

We used to take a ripe breadfruit and grease the bottom of a board and skate down the hills. We ended up with pants devoid of posterior. We often skated in our school clothes, ripped our pants and reaped our parents' anger. It was then time for the dreaded patch.

Some kids just wore the pants with no patch at all. They walked around with their *bamsee* exposed.

In those days, people used to put starch in clothes. The starch made the Presentation College boys look like the sailors who played in the Belmont Carnival band. They resembled the sailors who walked on the Wharf when the battle ships were tied up on the pier.

Did you starch your white shirt today? When Presentation College boys wore the white shirt and white pants, starching the shirt gave it a very stiff appearance.

To make the material nice and stiff, some people even added *candle spum* saved from the graves on All Saint's night. The coal pot iron removed all creases.

How about putting some *blue* in your clothes? When you *dun* that, wash the clothes with Tempe blue soap. A Grenadian Tempe soap gives a better wash than *Breeze.*

Meanwhile, some GBSS boys complained when they were laughed at as they wore the *dog bed* gray pants to school. School children said the material was suitable for dogs to sleep on.

Then bell-bottom pants hit the scene in the 1970's and that made some headmasters very angry. Everybody had grown accustomed to the *gun mouth* or double-barrel pants. That was the standard wear.

One wore a *gun mouth* pants and was contented. *Gun mouth* was what we knew. Even the priest wore *gun mouth pants* under the gown.

Soon there was a competition to see who could wear the biggest bell-bottom. The bell-bottom was matched with the platform shoes. If a gun mouth or bell-bottom pants was too short, one was accused of *flooding.* Someone was sure to ask, "*Wha'* river *yuh* crossing?"

Another kind of pants was called the *fat pants*. Children today wear the *fat pants* eagerly, but "yesterday" they were not favored. Back then, even the *scrutch* had to be in the right place. Today, the *scrutch* is as long as those the traffic police used to wear.

The girls of St John's Christian Secondary School were forced to wear the long skirt. They adopted the roll up and the roll down method. The skirts were down below the knees when the students were at school, and they were rolled up when the bus reached Gouyave or St. George's after the afternoon dismissal bell rang.

The girls hated the idea of wearing the long skirts at a time when the mini-skirts and hot pants were the style. A long skirt was transformed into a mini skirt every school day. They rolled the skirt up so other children would not laugh.

Do you wonder what clothes school children are laughing at today? Do you remember the saying,

"What is joke for school children is death for *crappo*."

Ah George Otway

Ah George Otway was the swiftest bath a Grenadian could take. People in Sauteurs, a parish in the far north of Grenada, called such a bath a *Western*. When they were very late for school or work, the George Otway came in very handy. They hit the shower and were out before one could have uttered *coonumoonu*. They then used the bathtowel to wipe off the *soapfroth* that remained on their backs. Some people just ducked themselves in the seawater and *called that George*.

The water that flowed through the pipes used to cut off regularly. You were lucky if you got *ah George Otway*. You are singing a calypso and soaping your skin and suddenly—water gone!

People got around water stopping by heading for Pandy Beach, the Lance and other beaches for their bath. They were forced to leave the salt water on their skin if the pipe water did not come back in time for them to rinse.

There were times when the rain fell hard and in the midst of the downpour, the water stopped. *Dat* always puzzled me. How could *water go* when so much rain was falling?

People jumped into the yard and bathe in the rain. A rain bath was always a pleasant experience. The water could be collected in a *lard pan* and poured over the head. Some of the water could be used to wash the mud from your feet or to wash the mangoes that fell from the trees while you are bathing in the rain.

We knew about hot water bath before we left for cold climates. When the sun was extremely hot, all we had to do was turn on the pipe and feel the hot water run down our backs. It never lasted long, though, but we bathe in the hot water until it turned cold on us.

Barbers, Trims Afros and White Wigs

Grenadian *fellas* were always particular about the type of hair-cut they received. If you were a barber and you gave a man a bad trim, it was unlikely that he would put his *bamsee* on your barber chair again.

A barber chair was sometimes a big stone in the yard or the root of a mango tree. *Fellas* used to sit there and get *all kinds ah trim.* Others went by Morriset, Reds or Cutie, and sat on a real barber chair, and relaxed while the barbers turned them around.

Those who could not afford the chair ended up by Mr. Marshall, and then complained how he *chang chang* their heads.

School children loved to see *ah fella* with *ah chang chang head.* It was very easy to *chang chang* someone's head. You just passed the scissors anywhere. You cut a little here, a lot there and clean all the hair over there. The head then looked like a lawn after Nahoo finished passing *ah cutlass* on it.

A barber's job was never easy. There were people who wanted a particular *muff* in front of their heads and if the barber cut off the *muff,* it was *ruction* in the place.

There were those who preferred a *willopeak* and the barber had to be careful to use the razor properly to give the man his *willowpeak.*

Sideburns had to be trimmed properly. You gave a man *ah high rounds* and he *squinged up his face* like Muffin when she took *ah eights ah strong rum.*

And if *ah fella* ended up with razor bumps behind his head he blamed the rusty razor that some barbers were too *cheap* to replace.

A quality trim was therefore essential. That was more impor-tant if you did not want to hear your friends tell you that you had a *jail bud trim* or asked if you killed priest or which barber you beat up for the haircut.

I wanted a quality trim once. It was called a continental trim and it was the style then. I sat under Tanty Agnes' house in Tyrrel Street and let *ah fella* go to work on *meh head.* He told me that he was good on the continental trim. I believed him. *Mamayo*!

When the man was finished with me, I looked in the mirror. I nearly *bawled.* The so-called barber made valleys, winding roads, *all kind ah ting in meh head.*

Mammy Georgiana pulled out *ah belt and ah got ah good continental cutarse*! And to make matters worse, I had to face my fellow students at Schaper School. *Lawd!* I prayed for a miracle to make the hair grow back quickly. I decided to wear a hat that resembled the one that Hardfoot always kept on his head.

Then the Afro came in during the 1970's and everybody forgot the continental trim and the other fancy trims. Everybody wanted an Afro. Even the women started growing some big Afros.

Barbers began to *ketch their backside* to make *ah* dollar. All *dem* people wanted was *ah touch up* or *ah rounds.*

The barbers were no *pappyut.* They had to survive. They started charging the same price once you sat on the chair, the big stone or the mango root. One barber in Gouyave charged more when he had to trim people who were almost bald. He charged more when he had to waste time to look for the hair.

Many people tried hard to grow the Afro. They had all the beautiful women plait their hair every day, but the Afros were only *coming to come,* but never came. They did all kinds of things to make their hair grow. They washed it with *cochoneel.* They covered it with the woolen hat called *tam,* but they had no luck. Meanwhile, the *douglas* had Afros that almost reached the roof.

Many parents, teachers and headmasters hated the Afro. They hated it just as the barbers, but they hated it for a different reason. They believed it was a sign of rebellion. The parents and headmasters, therefore, sent the students to the barbers and the barbers laughed. The barbers with their big Afros laughed.

It was a different time! The colonial period had ended and Grenada became independent in 1974.

However, judges in Grenada still dressed as if Colonialism was just beginning.

Have you ever seen them with the white wigs on their heads?

FILL YUH BELLY

Smell Now! Grenadian Bread!

I sat in the class and silently smiled when the professor declared, "The French, they loooooove bread!" He went on to say that the French ate bread with almost every meal. Other students laughed because of the way he emphasized the word "love." I smiled because he helped resurrect some old and distant, but pleasant, memories.

I remembered the *leaven bread* that was a regular part of our diet. I recalled other types of bread too. The Vienna bread came to mind and that famous homemade bread that Mammy used to bake.

Even the prisoners made appetizing bread up on Richmond Hill. That was the bread people who ended up in the hospital used to eat. Some people did not know they could make bread until they ended up in prison. They made bread and cut down huge mahogany trees on the Hill.

The *leaven bread* was made with fermented dough. Small children received one *leaven bread.* The portion increased with maturity. By the time they started attending secondary school, they were munching on one-and-a-half *leaven bread.*

When times were rough, it was bread and Kool-Aid. By graduation, they graduated to two-*leaven bread*. When they started to work, they had the choice of putting aside the bread for *fig and saltfish* in the morning. Some people still prefer that.

If you want to know how much Grenadians love bread, ask Tony who used to sell in Braithwaite's shop on the Wharf. People used to stand in line to buy hot bread and butter, bread and pig snout, or bread and salami. They used to get it wrapped up in brown paper to eat up as they watched the movie in Empire.

I will never forget the man who sold bread and *saltfish souse* on the Carenage. He pulled a crowd also. Raphael, my school friend, made up a song about him:

"Sorrel sweet like sugar,

Mauby bitter like gall,

Ginger beer burning like pepper,

But bread and *saltfish* soft like sponge."

Bread *went well* with almost anything. Bread and fishcake anyone? I knew a student who came to Schaper School with bread and *keg butter*. I once saw his anger when he discovered that someone stole his bread and hid his container in a hole in the wall. I thought he was going to end up in the *crazy house.*

The next day he came with more bread and *keg butter,* and warned his friends not to eat it if anyone offered it to them.

Someone later said he had put *sandbox* or something like that in the bread and butter. *Sandbox* can send you to the toilet for hours.

I knew a man in Belmont who used to eat bread and pepper sauce. He ate bread and the pepper sauce Miss Margaret made.

Try to steal someone's bread and Christmas ham and see how fast that person will call La Qua or Otway to bury you.

There is no enticing smell like the smell of bread baking in the ovens of Grenada. Get up one *foreday* morning and walk past

Homemade or Ideal bakery and take a deep breath! Immediately you see real significance in the verse, "Give us this day our daily bread."

Inhale the smell of bread baking in Grand Roy and you will be tempted to drop anchor right there. You just sit there and savor the fragrance.

We have a rich baking tradition—a legacy left by baking icons like Prax, Specky, Miss Molly, Wilfred, Flash and Mr. Thomas, who almost put Blue Danube *out of the runnings or* the "bakings."

Ah, now, to the homemade bread! That bread taste good even when it is stale. One little piece and you are good to go.

Any woman will tell you that nothing is better than a good Grenadian loaf. It is better than a Guyana plantain or the plantain that Brer Anansi gave his children.

As Sparrow would say, "So satisfying." It tastes good because it is made with love. Indeed, it is kneaded with Grenadian affection.

A man called Allan is known here in Brooklyn for his famous bread. He makes very tasty bread. West Indian people line up in the cold to buy his bread on Sunday mornings.

Some Grenadians stand in line too. They line up just the way we used to line up at Palmer School to be flogged. Every time I spot them, I feel like pulling them aside and inquire:

"*Wha* happen to the bread *yuh* mammy used to bake?"

Me Grenadian Mammy Made All ah Dat!

Potato stew, plum stew, damsel stew, tambran stew, golden apple stew, guava cheese, guava jam, cocoa fudge, stuff fudge, sugar cake, nut sweetie, ground nut sugar cake, coconut tart, coconut bun, hot cross buns, fried bakes, Johnny bakes, pineapple tart, stuff jacks, conkee, tambran ball, snow ice, milk block, soursop ice cream, soursop block, coo coo, cornmeal porridge, cornmeal dumpling, turnover, fried breadfruit, gospo juice, passionfruit juice, soursop juice, lime juice, grapefruit juice, sea moss, mauby, ginger beer, sorrel, dried pea soup, cow foot soup, breadfruit soup, split pea soup, callaloo soup, fish brawf, stewed tatou, lambie waters, fish cake, oildown, steam jacks, cook-up rice crab back, tania log, stewed beef, stewed chicken foot, blood pudden, bread pudden, potato pudden, banana fritters, pound plantain, fontay, christmas cake, pound cake, ginger sweetie, nut sweetie, bread, fried plantain, peppersauce, banana fritters, cocoa tea, bush tea, corned jacks and then . . . . . .

Ah big dose *ah* senna pod or castor oils to send us flying into the latrine.

The Coal Pot, the Hand Grinder, the Food Carrier

Never knock the coal pot. Don't say anything bad about that old warrior. The coal pot was the Titanic, indeed the Bismarck, taking your mammy or granny through the roughest waters! It stood fast, before the gas and electric stove gave it a well-deserved rest. The old reliable coal pot stood firm like Mount Zion.

Perhaps you used to run and hide when your mother called you to fan the coal pot. One had to fan the thing so the coals would light. If you dropped a little bit of kerosene on the coals that helped a bit, and then you fanned less. But when one was in the mood to play with marbles, kick football, or fly kite, it was discomforting to fan the coal pot.

We fanned the coal pot to roast our corn. I tried roasting corn on a gas stove on several occasions. The corn always smelled like gas. Nothing is better than a coal-pot-roasted corn.

The coal pot was a hero during the time of the iron comb. When the ladies put the iron comb on the coal pot, the thing got hot, hot, hot. And it did the job. Well, that was if they got it on their hair before it got cold. It got hot and then cooled quickly— so timing had to be just right.

Today, one can plug in an electric clothes iron and bingo! Not so with the coal pot. The heavy iron was placed on the coal pot to get hot and then it was used to smooth out the wrinkles from the skirt or khaki pants. When that was done, all the creases disappeared. Today, our electric iron gives us more creases than ten cricket pitches.

Don't get burned with an iron or coal pot. It will be a trophy to remember for the rest of your days. A coal pot once fried a spot on my right shin. The mark is still there—a little mark in memory of the coal pot.

The coal pot had a section called the arch. That was where all the ashes went. One could scrape out the ashes, then take some flour, and roll a dumpling, and place it within the arch.

The arch was useful for roasting sweet potatoes and ripe *bluggoe* too. Have you ever eaten a coal-pot-roasted ripe *bluggoe?*

For the coal pot to work, one had to have coals. A man called George Beard used to dig coal pits all over Belmont. For some reason, some of the coals were hard to ignite. That was true especially when the wood used to make the coal was not suitable. One would fan until the hands gave up and the coal would not light.

Give praise to our mothers who had to fight with the coals as they hurried to prepare their children's lunch before they came home from school during the midday recess. It was not an easy task. But they fought and conquered.

Yes, the coal pot was the Titanic.

Yes, the coal pot was the Bismarck.

And, yes, all praise to our parents and grandparents who struggled with the coal pot!

We used a hand mill to grind peppers to make the sauce used to spice up our *oildown.* The same mill, we also used, to grind our corn to make our cornmeal dumpling, *asham, coo coo* and *conkee.* That mill we also used to grind our fruits for our black Christmas cake. *Ah,* not to forget grinding our cocoa.

Grinding is no fun. When our right hand gets tired, we employ the left hand to carry on. Then it's back to the right hand. But that was yesterday!

Today, we put a plug into a socket and sit back and wait.

Those were the days of the food carrier. Some students attended school with carriers that had three stands. One stand was for dumpling, another for yams, and the other for a piece of stewed fowl.

A student's carrier once fell in the middle of the market as he jumped from a wooden bus and two cooked green bananas and a piece of pig's snout jumped out. He kept on walking with his head held high as though nothing happened. He used to boast that he ate only beef and chicken. He was lucky school children had not seen him.

Talking Soup, Grenadian Soup!

Nothing could please some Grenadians more than a nice hot bowl of Spice Island soup. In fact, some have a special day in the week set aside for pouring soup *down the hatch.*

One fellow I know refused to talk to his wife for a whole week because she failed to make him his favorite cow foot soup. The man had already set his mind on the yam, dumpling and *dasheen* swimming around in the soup only to be sadly disappointed.

You talk about nightmare? Well, he had *soupmare* that night.

To make it worse, she told him, "If *yuh* like so much soup, why the hell *yuh din* get up and make it for *yuh blastid self?*"

I reflect on the time when a group of us were invited to gobble down some pig's tail soup at a friend's house. The food was well prepared and very appetizing, certainly indicative of Grenadian culinary talent. After everyone there had eaten, one *bol'* Grenadian belched, then stretched, and turned to the host and said:

"Food taste nice, but next time make sure *yuh put ah piece ah* pig snout in it."

Now, after consuming all that food, he had the nerve to talk about pig snout. What a *bol' face* Grenadian! *Yuh tink* we easy?

I never liked breadfruit soup or pumpkin soup. They say that pumpkin soup is very good for you, but all I do is eat the meat and *provisions* and leave the soup alone.

Not so with dry peas soup. I will *clean dat up* anytime. I am still kicking myself for the time I threw away a whole bowl of peas soup in Woodlands, St George's. A *maribone* flew right into the bowl and immediately my appetite vanished.

I still dream of that bowl of soup and all that salt beef, sweet potatoes and yam that decorated it. I *shuddah* just pulled the *maribone* out, but when you are young, you think differently.

That soup tasted better than the corn soup Pressureman and

dem usually make on Utica Avenue in Brooklyn.

I still don't know how the cow head soup the boys made in Calliste a few years ago tasted. I had just jumped off an American Airline flight at Point Salines Airport, and was immediately greeted with the invitation to nourish bones terrorized by the merciless New York winter.

Ah said to myself, "Cow head?" *Nah bwoy,* I went looking for *fish brawf.*

When last *yuh* had a turtle soup? A turtle soup will make a dead turtle raise its head. Turtle soup is better than Viagra. It can even stiffen the waters of Niagara,

Turtle have its season in Grenada. If you embark on a turtle diet, your mate will only smile when turtle is in season. And then you will have to run back to good *ole* reliable *tania log, sea moss,* and *boise bande.*

There are people who compare chicken soup to penicillin. All *ah* know is that it can drive away a cold fast.

Yuh ever drank *ah* hot soup that made *yuh* sweat? I sweat so much in Grenada once, that someone by the market in St. George's asked me if I was defrosting. *Yuh* sweat more than if you were digging *bush yam* in Birchgrove when you drink *dat* hot soup. People who *tief bush yam tief* so fast they have no time to sweat. I am not referring to them.

And now to you ladies! *Yuh* want to *doo* a man? Nothing is better than *callaloo soup.* He will never what you put in *dey* to *doo* him. Don't give the man lentil soup or goat head soup. And if *yuh* give him Chinese wonton soup, you have no chance of *dooing* him. *Yuh* can't hold a Grenadian man with that. *Joke yuh making*!

Finally, remember it is *ah* soup you are preparing so don't make the *water long, long, long.* And remember too, it's not porridge. It can't be too thick. It has to be just right. A perfect mouth-watering Grenadian soup!

Put in a little pepper sauce you purchase from the man on the Carenage and enjoy your soup! You are then ready to *drogue ah bag ah nutmeg. Waters for the back*! *Yeah man. Waters for the back*!

To all my Grenadian, Caribbean, and other friends, have a happy soup day.

Jane, *yuh* cooking?

Ice Cream, Snow Cones And Other Delights

I will take you back; way back to the time Franco made the best ice cream in town. Nicks made a tasty ice cream too.

The cone shell was made close to the spot on Melville Street where one exited Sendall tunnel. Many people used to dart through that tunnel, especially when a big truck rumbled behind. Every one was afraid of the big *Janet truck* thundering its way through that narrow underpass. Sometimes one had to *squinge up* against the wall to allow the big trucks sufficient room to pass.

When students could not afford the ice cream, they bought the crispy cone shell and *called that George.*

Those were the days of the popular snow cone. Who called that thing 'snow cone' in tropical Grenada?

There were lots of appetizing goodies and it was difficult to choose from the nut sweetie, sugar cake, guava cheese, cocoa fudge, *tambran balls*, and the other locally made mouth pleasers.

Ye Farmers!

We *hauled cutlass* and we dug *bush yam* until we hand got corn. *Ah tell yuh,* it was *big maco jumbie yam ah* talking 'bout. Yam big like *hengman. Doh* ask me how *tief* used to go away with that!

I asked *meh compere* and he replied angrily, "*Bwoy,* please ask me about things *dat* I know about."

Anyway, we dug the yam and sweet potato—not the one Dan Quayle spelled with an E at the end. We ate *Irish potato.* Once, I asked a Korean man in a Brooklyn food market to sell me a bag of *Irish potato* and he looked at me as though I dropped from Mars. But that was what we knew—*Irish potato.* Some words just stuck in the brain. I still say naught instead of zero

You farmers who rise to till the soil are a mighty pillar of our society. You bend your backs in dedicated struggle to dig the yams, *dasheen* and potatoes and then transport them to the Market .You pick the peas that we enjoy in our green pea soup. You teach us that despite the stigma of slavery, the fork could be elevated to an emblem of pride and productivity. There is dignity attached to cultivating the ground. Our young people must know that!

May the seeds you sow continue to blossom.

MUSIC IN WE BLOOD

They Labored Hard

They labored hard, long hours spent,
The perfect tune their minds were bent,
Musical charm from pans arose,
I stood on the wharf in awe I froze.

Spellbound, entrapped by sound of steel,
And deep within the rhythm feel,
Sweet tenor pan rang through the air,
Touched by bass, I shed a tear.

Again and again, the same song they played,
The bandleader's mind not quickly swayed,
The notes were struck, a rightful ring,
Melodious pan that night did sing.

And then there was a touching scene,
The bandleader smiled, a sudden beam,
For Angel Harps had knocked a chord,
Harmonious note, hard work's reward.

The Mas We Knew

Grenada Carnival was always a colorful and enjoyable affair. It still is, but the days of the big costumed bands of the 1960's are gone!

We used to stand and stare in awe as the wonderfully clad masqueraders happily danced on the streets. The mind-boggling headpieces and the creative art of the wire benders always thrilled us. The names Away, John Bruno, Patterson, and Ken Sylvester will always be remembered for their ability to portray historical *mas* that brought buccaneers, pirates and even Julius Caesar back to life. We remember George Croney for his contribution to the growth of the steel pan music in Grenada.

Carnival was a serious affair that sent people searching all over Belmont and Springs for sheepskin or bulls' horns to play in the Viking band.

My earliest recollection of Carnival was the occasion I stood with my mother and brothers in a little spot near the Health Center on Melville Street. I looked on in amazement as wild Indians with their fancy feathers formed a circle and hopped around like the Hopi and Apache Indians of North America.

I also saw the *Jab Jab* with his red tongue, horn and little black box. I heard that Jab Jab chant:
"Who lay we lambay,
Who lay we la,
Ah want *ah* penny,
To pay me passage,
To go back to hell,
And *ah* hungry like hell.

The *Jab Jab* walked around frightening little children. Some of them had posies on their heads, chains around their waists, and snakes around their necks. The *Jab Jab* used to stray long distances from the bacchanal with his little dolly in the black box asking people to put *ah* change in the box to see what was inside. A snake sometimes lay coiled up in the box.

While the *jab jab* did his thing, the *shortknee* with his mirrors and powder was raising his feet high in the air and attracting attention.

Those were the days of the mud masks. I can still remember shaping the clay or mud to create a very gruesome face. We used newspapers to plaster onto the mud face before putting the mask to dry in the sun. When the mask was dried, we separated it form the mud and painted it. There was *ah fella* we called Mud Mask who did not have to wear *ah* mask at all.

Carnival was excitement; indeed, great fun. The *ole mas* was a spectacle many looked forward to. It was the platform for the ingenious and creative mind.

A few years ago, I saw my friend Café Bull portray a banana tree on the Carenage and his impressive talent amazed me. I often marveled at the fun the masqueraders were able to poke at the politicians and other people in the society during the *Jourvert* celebration. Some of the slogans were into the realm of what Grenadians termed *commonness*, but Carnival always had a touch of that.

It was not unusual then for someone to play Ivan Wood. Ivan Wood was a popular clothing store in St. George's. All one needed was *ah* big piece *ah* wood to portray Ivan Wood.

Similarly, Jonas Browne (ooops! Jon arse Browne) was easy to play. All *ah fella* had to do was paint his *bam bam* brown.

If you wanted to make people laugh like they *caught ah glad,* it was good to play "The Police force." All that called for was for someone to dress like *ah* police and sit down on a *poe* and keep bawling" urgggggggggggggh!" It was never a good idea to force too hard for reasons that were obvious.

A baldheaded man with lines drawn on his head and a newspaper in his hand was a good example of the headline news.

Some of the best *ole mas* portrayals with the placards and all took place in Gouyave. A man ran around with a lighted torch playing Herbert Blaize.

An energetic young man with a hose spraying water on a gate played Watergate.

Ah fella put *ah* bowl on his face and his cardboard sign reminded us that "Gouyave people *bowl face.*"

Another pretended he was marking words on a tire. He played McIntyre .

And one must not forget the man with the wheelbarrow filled with grass. He was pushing grass.

Truly, the *ole mas* was geared to make people think and laugh at the same time.

The thrill was the big *mas bands* on Market Hill. Market Hill was once decked with cobbled stones just like Cooper Hill. The stones originated from the rivers. Then they paved it. The paved hill made it easier for the revelers to do their stuff on Carnival Monday.

I remember the big Carnival bands on Market Hill and their kaleidoscopic display. I can still visualize the spectacularly attired masqueraders as they pranced and swayed in the full embrace of the afternoon sun. Their arrival on the top of the hill was perfectly timed to allow the sun to bring out the magnificent sparkle of satin, shiny beads and candlefloss.

The crowds lined the sides of the hill and some stood at the bottom, but all anxiously awaited the men, women and children in the big *mas bands.*

They waited on "Flag Wavers of Sienna" and the many colors. They looked on as a huge wooden guillotine on wheels from the band, "The French Revolution" made its way down Market Hill.

They observed the slaves in the band "Fall of the Roman Empire" as they struggled with a chariot on Market Hill.

The crowds noted the drunken sailors in their spotless white *leggo* to the infectious sounds of the steel drums. They saw the sailors put their hands around each other and sway from one side of Market Hill to the other. And they witnessed the excitement on the faces on the Zulu warriors clad in their African garb holding their shields and spears as they frolicked on Market Hill.

On Carnival Tuesday night the tempo heated up. The sound of steel echoed throughout the St. George's capital. Melville Street and the area near BuyRite supermarket were *ram-crammed* with men and women in tight embrace. They danced, they wined and *cawayed* as panmen pounded the tenor pan like the devil in rage. Some people calmly *chipped* to the beat. The *chip* was a slow graceful movement with the feet keeping perfect harmony with the music.

As the night wore on, a few tired panmen left the stands that carried the pans and joined the jump-up. It was time for them to squeeze the remaining juice from the Carnival before the Carnival curtain folded.

Can't Catch Us with Music

I stood in the elevator on the job humming an old Country and Western tune made popular by Charlie Pride. A woman asked me how I knew that song.

I had to go back to Grenada and the days when we knew all kinds of songs and music. We liked our reggae and our calypso, but we could also tell you that the song playing on the radio was "Maggie May" sung by Rod Stewart, or we could tell you who it was that sang "Rainy Night in Georgia." We knew the vibes of Sam Cooke and Ray Charles.

Yes, Miss, you could not catch us with music at all. Funny thing, we still keeping pace—we could tell you about Beenieman and the songs that Mariah Carey sings. *Bwoy,* we *ain't* easy where songs and music is concerned!

We sang from *Ring-Around-ah-Roses* to "*Gimme* me the Bum Bum, Audrie," and then we hit *dem* with –

"Me en want no bone, g*ee* me flesh alone, if *yuh saltfish* hard and boney, you *ent* talking to me."

We slowed it down with "Stealing Love on the Side." We used to listen to Indian music by a *fella* called Mukesh when we tuned in to 610-Radio. We remember Auntie Kaye asking children, "And what are you going to sing dear?"

Oh, yes! Grenadians grew up with all kinds of songs and music. We had music to make you wine; music to help you dine; and, most of all, music to make you *grind. Yuh* ever *grind?*

We had music to make you perspire and La Qua, the undertaker, played music when you expired.

These days we hear of music to make you bump and wine, but some of us only wanted to *grind.* We sang more reggae than the *fellas* from Jamaica! And we knew how to dance to the music, too!

You remember the rock steady? *Bwoy,* that was *ah kind ah*

dance. Some people who started to rock after a couple of drinks became very unsteady and then somebody had to get them steady. That was their rock steady!

I stood on the Wharf one night and watched my cousin Keith Bridgeman and some ladies do the rock steady in a place next to Cable and Wireless. Then I went and tried it. They even used to dance the rock steady in the GBSS auditorium. A place on the Carenage opened called the "Cubby Hole." I had just mastered the rock steady.

Something new arrived on the scene. *Ah whole set ah* Jamaican Roys came—I Roy, U Roy and a *fella* called Big Youth.

A guy nicknamed Casa—long dead—learned all the Big Youth songs. He had a way of shaking his head while he *rapped the vibes*.

In those days you were nothing if you could not *skank*. Rastamen were the biggest *skankers* and when they smoked their *tampee,* you had to clear the way. They carried big radios on their shoulders blasting "War in ah Babylon!" They were raising their feet high and *skanking* all over Grenada.

Ah bunch ah bike fellas—Akala and *dem*—were big time *skankers*. They rode all the way to Gouyave and *skanked* in front of Chessman shop. They nearly knocked down the old man Pat Tat while *skanking.*

Purcell put a jukebox in a shop in Florida. St. John's so the Rastamen could *skank* while *ole timers* drank their *grog* and wondered what the hell those *youngsters* were doing.

That song you hear playing, madam is by a Haitian group called Tabou Combo. And that one is *ah* waltz. We even danced to the *Cassian* music at graduation ball. All wheel and no balance, heel and toe, one two one, one two one, one one-one. *Dat ole man dey* is doing the fox trot. *Dat* one is dancing to the *Bajan spooge. Yuh tink* we easy?

Now, let me sing an Ajamu calypso song for you!

Years Ago, I Heard The Shango Drums

I tossed and turned in restless agony as the incessant beat of rhythmical drums echoed through the silent night. Drumbeats ignited the will and re-established the bond with ancestors long past. Drums, drums and more drums!

Drums like the Big Drums of Carriacou. Drums that came alive in the dead of night and awoke the soul. Drums, drums and more drums! Drums that could not be stilled.

Drums that spoke with brilliant clarity, too profound to define. Drums that tugged at my yearning soul and lifted me from my slumber by its constant beckoning.

I could rest no more.

Myriad spirits dwelled within the beat. Countless divine animating influences undimmed by horrors of the Trans-Atlantic plight spoke to me of unearthly rhythms that sprang from my motherland.

I rose to the call and followed the rugged path to the spot in Lagoon Road. I made my way to the talking drums.

At last my soul was at rest.

Years ago, I heard the *Shango* drums.

I heard the Wail.

I heard the wail
Heart gripping lament,
In the song,
The folk rhythm,
From Africa,
That touched Grenada.

I heard the wail,
And something stirred,
From deep within,
The spirit woke,
And grabbed the hands,
Of the ancestors.

I heard the wail,
And my soul reached out,
Crossed the passage,
One more time.

I heard the wail,
The mournful cry,
Still in the voices,
And in the drums,
That yet connect,
After the separation.

I heard the wail
And I woke once more.
I sprung to life,
And found myself,
In Africa,
Once again.

West Indian Party

You can hardly find a Grenadian or West Indian who doesn't like a good party. We crave the fun and we like the *jam session.* We groove and grind to the sound of reggae, calypso and, sometimes, even to a bottle and spoon.

At times, we hold onto our women so tight that *breeze cyan pass.* We move and we groove and often *wine* down to the floor. Music is in our blood and the gyrating hips one sees on Carnival day is a testimony to our musical inclination.

We are, however, not easy to please and I am often discomforted when I see people giving the DJs a rough time while the music play.

It is not an easy thing to play music that will please everybody. Like food, people have different tastes. Some DJs, however, bring trouble onto themselves.

Many West Indian men leave their women at home and attend the party alone. The DJ ends up playing to a group of men and very few women. Some Grenadians call that a *bullpen* or a *male box* party.

The DJ gets the crowd angry when he plays a soft, slow jam like "Stealing Love on the Side" in such a situation. Now tell me, where are the women to steal love on the side with in a *bull pen party*?

Some uninvited men end up stealing a bottle of beer on the side.

I was invited to a party once and, when I got there, I was happy to see that the place was crammed, but the men and women were sitting.

The only man *wine-ing* was the DJ. I don't know if he was drunk or what. But he was dancing up a storm while the people were grumbling. He was playing music he liked and, perhaps, was saying to himself, "Who the hell want to dance, dance, *ah doh care!*"

Music in yuh wire!

I do at times feel sorry for the DJs. People are fond of disturbing them. They will come up with requests for songs that some DJs never heard of. Some even ask for Jim Reeves, the Louvin Brothers or songs one hears in church.

Others ask for songs that people have not even made yet and, if the DJ don't play the song, he or she gets a *cussing.* They call for *soca*, request reggae, but there are those who dance to anything.

It is a known fact that many Guyanese love old, slow music. They love the "oldie-goldie" music just the way they cherish old cars.

A Jamaican might get annoyed if the DJ is too preoccupied with Trinidad *soca* music. If you find yourself in a *Trini* party, you might have to dance *soca* until your shoes wear out.

Grenadians? We dance to any *dam* thing. When we get nice, you can even bring the salsa and the twist. Come with the electric slide, and we will dance to that too.

I almost put my friends in big trouble at a Guyanese party one night. They asked us to play the music and we were happy to do so.

We did not expect the Guyanese present to call for ten slow songs in a row. It was a good thing we had some King Curtis and Percy Sledge albums.

I tried to help. I dug into the record pile and came up with "Sylvie's Mother." They almost killed me when that song began to play. "Take that *so and so* Sylvie's mother off!" Needless to say, they did not invite us to play again.

I went to a Jamaican party once. When I got there the place was dark, music was blasting, but I could not see anyone.

I was about to leave, but then I realized the dancing was really taking place against the walls while the middle of the hall was empty. Everyone was *grinding* against the wall.

Not everybody goes to a party to dance. I know a man who goes to parties to eat. He likes to go to the parties where he is sure to get *oildown,* jerk pork and pig foot souse to eat.

He told me he likes the pig so much that the only thing in a pig he never ate is the grunt. That was only because he was never able to catch the grunt.

There are people go to parties to stand outside. Some end up by the bar and stay there. They go from the bar to the toilet and back, especially after consuming the free beers. Others just stand in a party and *maco.* They stand there and *scope the scene.*

Some are like the wind-up toys we got at Christmas time. They wind themselves up to dance, and they don't stop until the last song plays. They don't even need a partner and most times they wear out the DJ with their non-stop dancing.

Finally, there are the people who do not like to leave a party. A DJ got so exhausted once when he saw it was 9:00 a. m., and the people were still dancing as if the party just started. He put on the burial song "Nearer My God to Me. They started *wine-ing* to that song too. He gave up the ghost!

IN THE PIT

Saturday Afternoon at the Empire Cinema

Empire Cinema stood close to the Phoenix cigarette factory on the Carenage. People went to the movies regularly then. There were those who saw almost every film that reached Grenada. Many people were able to do so because they received what was known as *ah pass* to enter the theater. Big Bear and a *fella* nicknamed Saltfish used to give *passes*.

The big shot people went to Balcony, the smaller shots went to House, and the no-shots *called it George* in Pit.

If the *picture buss,* those who congregated in pit erupted first. They hated when the picture was disrupted. "Miss Parsaud, *yuh muddah arse! Haul yuh so and so,*" they usually shouted. They vented their anger, not even knowing if Miss Parsaud, who owned Empire Cinema, was present.

A film that was cut in the midst of heated action was serious cause for angry shouts and *bad words.* Those were the days of the gun-toting heroes and villains like Fernando Sancho, Pecos, Django and the bad Wild West.

People also flocked to see war movies like "To Hell and Back," "None, But the Brave," and "The Thin Red Line."

Those same people now sit in the comfort of their homes and see those movies on television.

It was extremely difficult to get a ticket to see such films on Christmas Eve night or *Old Year's night* when all the buses from other parishes jammed the Carenage. It was easier if someone threw a *Jun Jun* into the crowd and people scattered.

A *Jun Jun* was a mixture of ingredients like rotten eggs or stale pee. When the crowd was thick and *ram-crammed* for the midnight show, the *Jun Jun* came raining down. It was always well prepared to disturb one's sense of smell.

We on the Screen

Sidney Poitier and some other black actors appeared on the silver screen in the Empire, Reno and Deluxe theaters. Every black man on the screen looked like somebody in Mt. Rich, Belmont, River Road, or St. Paul's.

People looked at the screen and *bawled out* –

"Look, look!

Dat is Black Boy's brother!"

"*Bonjay!*

Look at Tall Boy!"

When Chinese Movies Hit Grenada

Yeah bwoy! They packed up Clint Eastwood and John Wayne, and all you heard was Chin Seng, Wang Yu and Shoalin Masters.

All the war movies took a back seat. The James Bond movies too! If you were Grenadian and not riding the pine in Empire or Regal you were probably listening to a sermon in the Berean, Open Bible or Gospel Hall churches. For when those Chinese movies rocked Grenada, they astounded many people also

Those Kung Fu and Shoalin movies were different. The old men were the greatest fighters and some, like the drunken masters, fought harder when totally intoxicated.

A Chinese man or woman warrior would stay on the ground and fly into a twenty-foot tree like a helicopter. One man would defeat an entire army. Spears were grabbed with teeth. The impossible was done, and people loved it. You would see a man train for two-thirds of a movie and then fight for the remaining one-third to avenge his parent's death.

Some of the movies were in Chinese with the English translations at the bottom of the screen. There was a fancy term for that called subtitles. But we did not mind; we were accustomed to sitting in the Catholic Church and listening to an entire mass said in Latin.

All we wanted to see was action and action, from start to finish. It was not surprising when a bad flu hit Grenada around the same time the Chinese movies struck; it was said that people caught the "Wang Yu."

A Kung Fu movie sometimes started with fighting and for the rest of the movie was just that, fight and more fight. Sometimes we did not even know what they were fighting for. All we wanted to know was Silver Fox was there beating up the other masters of Kung Fu. And if there was no fight, the movie was no good and everyone would complain afterwards.

Then the other craze came—the Kung Fu schools. I was in Florida (Grenada) one time, next to St. Paul's shop. While the juke-box belted out reggae and the *fellas* were *skanking* to the song "Ride *yuh* donkey," others were practicing their Karate and Kung Fu.

Ah fella called Chicken and another named Johnny, who became Prime Minister Gairy's bodyguard, were talented martial arts men in Grenada at the time.

Me? I only went to Regal and Empire and saw men kick up men. That was until they introduced women fighters kicking up both men and women. One woman would beat a restaurant full of men. And when the big crook heard of it, he would send some top crooks to challenge her. By that time, she joined with the star and beat up all the crooks.

We sat in Pit and watched *all ah dat* and then we went home to practice our Kung Fu, ate our bakes and *saltfish,* and drank our *bush tea.*

These days when I walk down Flatbush Avenue in Brooklyn, I sometimes see all those Kung Fu movies on cassette tape, selling for three dollars or so.

I remember the time I used to spend sixty cents for a seat in House, back in Grenada, to see the Kung Fu fights and then leave the cinema wondering *what the hell* the big fight was all about.

HOLIDAY LIGHTS

All Saint's Night

It was always fascinating to stand at the top of Cemetery Hill and observe the fiery flutter of candles dancing on top the numerous graves on All Saint's night.

It was a time when those who were normally afraid to set foot in the cemetery forgot their fears and found themselves among the dearly, and not so dearly, departed. No one was afraid of spirits or *Jumbie* on that night and people outnumbered all the spirits and ghosts on All Saint's night on Cemetery Hill.

It was the time when school children were free to visit the cemetery and *buss ah lime* in the light. Those, who could not make it to the gravesides, lit candles on their doorsteps. While people in the United States observe Halloween, Grenadians celebrate All Saint's night.

On All Saint's night the various lanterns and their exquisite designs were evident. Most children knew how to make a lantern. They were gifted with their hands and fashioned lanterns with the same admirable skill they used to make tops, wooden boats and kites.

They are still gifted today, but do not devote much time to

making things like lanterns. The *Bowlie lantern* was prominent on All Saint's night. That lantern was crafted from the fruit of the *Calabash* tree. Good care was exercised when the internal part of the *bowlie* was removed because if it broke the lantern could not be made.

Those who did not have the patience to make the *bowlie* lantern settled for one made with Milo or Ovaltine cans. Holes were punched into the can so that air got in to keep the candle inside glowing.

All Saint's night on Cemetery Hill was a festival of lights; the darker the night, the more brilliant the shine of the candles. That was one night when the light of the moon was an unwelcome guest. Children eagerly looked forward to the night of November first.

Spicy Christmas

It was the night before Christmas and the wooden *Morris chairs* were a glittering dark brown. The floor was a mirror; glowing brighter than the glassy marble we used to *pitch* in the backyard. Hours of sand-papering and polishing had left elbows and hands aching. What the heck! It was Christmas and Granny and Mammy wanted the place to look good.

The sorrel and ginger beer were already made. Grandma was beating the ingredients to make the black cake in a large bowl.

Watch out! Somebody was always willing to fight for the bowl. The batter was as tasty as the baked product, and greedy eyes were watching.

And the ham! You leave out the ham and you leave out Christmas. Something salt must pass in your mouth, according to Chalkdust, the *calypsonian*. It is hard to separate ham from a Grenadian Christmas. Even some Rastas, who hated pork, used to hide and *tear lash in the ham.*

There was one hell of a big tree on the Esplanade. It bore a yellow fruit that looked like a berry. There was another one in Tanteen. I am sure there were more in other places in Grenada.

People used to wrap boxes with gift paper (Christmas paper) and tie them up on the tree on the Esplanade. As a child, the temptation was always to *jook* down one of those boxes to see what was inside, or to hope that one would fall. That tree bore abundantly, but people were afraid to eat the fruit.

A friend once told me: "The *blastid* thing must be good to eat! It's man *dat* make rules about what is good and not good to eat."

Ah said, "You go ahead and tell me how it taste."

We had another tree. That was the real Christmas tree, and it gave us the smell of Christmas. It put us in the right Christmas mood. That was the tree we decorated and put a car or other toy beneath it.

We were fond of the little twenty-five cent gun that used to *buss shots.* Sometimes you bought a roll of shots and the thing would *buss* only a few.

On the night before Christmas, we took out our starlight and lighted it.

Some children sent up rockets in the Market Square and made policemen get vex, vex, vex.

Grandma used to get annoyed if we lighted the starlight in the house, "*Allyuh* want to burn down the house?"

By the day before Christmas, the cards were supposed to have arrived from America, Canada or England. Great Aunt Sylvia never failed to send the cards.

The Christmas cards were always pretty with snowflakes and Jack Frost on the outside. Forget the outside; we wanted to see what was inside! That was our Christmas money.

The words were good too. Words like "Chestnuts roasting on an open fire." We were accustomed to roasting breadfruit and corn. We did not bother too much with the chestnut thing.

On the night before Christmas, carols were everywhere. The Belmont *steelband* took to the streets days before, and young men and women *wined* to the song "O Christmas Tree."

The Parang, in Spanish, came through loud and clear from 610-Radio, and we were thrilled with the voice of the Moonlight Serenaders.

At Christmas Eve, there was the big midnight show at Empire with Big Bear standing near the door to Pit, telling people the show sold out.

"What! Time to pelt *ah Jun Jun, Bwoy!*" *All ah dat* was Christmas.

At Christmas, nobody smoked *Phoenix any end cigarettes.* Everybody puffed the expensive Solent and 555's.

They drank a red wine from Guyana which, if you drank on the night before Christmas, you were sure to think the yard was your bed. Even if they passed a piece of pork by your nose you would not wake.

Christmas was and is love. Love in Sauteurs. Love in Grand Mal. Love in Victoria. Love all over Grenada and the Caribbean.

If, however, you are away from Grenada, if you are in Brooklyn, find some people from Mt. Moritz. Try to locate a man called Mr. Charlie Simon or his son Jude. They will really show you what Christmas was and is!

Not Me and White Christmas

First let me say that *ah* can't sing the song entitled "*Ah* never see *ah* White Christmas" anymore. *Ah* saw so many White Christmases, *ah* started believing in *Father Christmas*. One time *ah* even began looking for Rudolph, the red nose reindeer.

Ah remember one December, when snow fell so hard and the ice was very slippery, *ah* fell on me *bam bam* right in the middle of Church Avenue in Brooklyn. *Dam, good for me!*

Doh gee me no White Christmas! *Dat* good for Santa Claus. *Gee me ah hot sun Christmas* that could burn me *tail* like it does burn *dem* grapes on Grand Anse beach.

Doh gee me no White Christmas! Gee me ah Mong Mong Christmas. *Gee me ah* River Road Christmas. *Gee me ah* Christmas where *ah* could stand on the Carenage and listen to Angel Harps pan on the truck as it goes around. *Gee me ah* Belmont Christmas.

Ah want ah Christmas where *ah* could lie down under *ah* mango tree and fall asleep. If *ah do dat* here in Brooklyn, *dey go* mug me *backside.* Gee me *ah* Mount Rich Christmas!

Ah want *ah* Christmas where *ah* could go down by Fantasia nightclub and walk out on the beach when *ah get nice, nice, nice.* Then *ah* go look up in the sky and try to spot the stars *dem* three wise men followed. *Yuh* can't see *dat* here; all you see is gray skies.

Ah want to take a deep breath by the beach and suck in some of that fresh sea breeze. *Ah doh care* if *ah stump me toe* on an *orman* tree in the dark.

Ah want *ah* Christmas where *ah* could relax with a little radio under a breadfruit tree. Then *ah* go listen to Jacob Miller wishing everybody a "merry ice-mas" and Sparrow singing. "There is no place like home for the holiday."

Ah want to be home to smell bread baking by Homemade or

Ideal bakery and to drink *ah* beer by Blue Danube.

Gee me ah Christmas where *ah* could drink *ah* coconut water with *dem* boys by the Grand Anse Post Office. A Christmas where ah could visit me *ole* time friends in Florida, Grand Roy and Gouyave.

We could talk about the *ole* time days when guys used to skank to I-Roy, U-Roy and *all ah dem* other Jamaican Roys. *Dem* boys used to shout out words like "Lion" and "*Ah till yuh*" just like Big Youth.

Gee me ah Christmas where *ah* could see someone who remembers the time me and Rex fought in Tanteen pasture and the time *me muddah* gave me ah good *cutarse.*

Yes, *me* friend! *Gee me ah* Grenadian Christmas. *Ah* hot sun Christmas. *Gee me ah* Christmas where *ah* could look around and see *me* friends who come in from Canada, Washington, England and Trinidad. Then, *ah fella* go watch me and say, "*Wha go on* dey Carl?"

Then *ah* go tell him, "Carl is *me* brother in Toronto. I'm Wendell!"

Christmas in the Cold

It was Christmas morning and it was extremely frigid outside, too cold for man or beast. It was the type of coldness that reduced the steaming radiator to simply an ornament in the corner of the room. I ran the words of John Keats' poem over and over in my head:

"St. Agnes Eve.
Ah bitter chill it was,
The owl for all his feathers was a-cold.
The hare limp'd trembling through the frozen grass
And silent the flock in wooly fold."

When I studied that poem at the St. John's Christian Secondary School in Grenada, I did not have the slightest idea of the true implication of those words. But then, I experienced the cold in Brooklyn and the words took on real significance.

It felt colder because I was a long distance from the Christmas I knew. I was away from the *Parang* and Daddy-O playing the carols on his cuatro on Christmas morning. I could not hear the sound of the Angel Harps or Belmont steel drums. It was a different type of Christmas.

The ham was already cooked. Sticks of cloves protruded like spikes from it. It was ready to be served. The sorrel and ginger beer were tucked away in the refrigerator.

Colored lights blinked from the Christmas tree I had set up in a corner of the living room. A glowing silver star was at the top and the beautiful array of fancy decorations made the Christmas tree an attractive sight. I sat and listened as an old tune, "Christmas Bells are Ringing," played on the nearby record player.

While I sat buried in my thoughts, the doorbell rang and sunshine rushed in. My brother Charlie and his merry band of friends had arrived and suddenly it did not feel so cold. They had braved the freezing temperature to wish me a merry Christmas.

Before the words "Happy Christmas" was uttered, someone shouted:

"Bring out the rum!"

Another asked:

"*Whey* the ham? *Doh backsqueeze, it*'s Christmas"

One of the things we learned in Grenada was to always prepare for the Christmas season. In fact, our scoutmaster advised us to be prepared for everything. That meant having all the goodies ready in case someone dropped in on Christmas day. I was happy that I had made ready all that food, drinks and music to entertain my friends.

A spontaneous party started. A few of my neighbors joined the fun. *Ah fella* snatched *ah* piece of ham from my son's plate and started to *wine* to the song "Feliz Navidad." Someone called for a Christmas *calypso* by the *calypsonian* Singing Francine. Another asked for Kitchener's "Drink ah Rum on ah Christmas Morning." Someone wanted to hear an Ajamu *Parang song.*

A friend of mine called Lloyd, wearing a heavy winter coat, danced till he fell on the floor. The Caribbean warmth drove away the wrath of Old Man Winter and Frosty the Snowman.

I was happy that despite the finger-numbing, wintry weather and my longing for the Christmas I knew, my brother and his Caribbean friends took the time to visit me and put a spark into my Christmas.

This Thing Called Ham

There is the ham that is sold in a white bag and there is the other bigger, heavier ham that comes from Virginia. The heavier ham is the one that might be too big for the pot you have, so you have to figure out a method to boil out the salt.

You might ask the butcher to cut it in half and leave the other half for the New Year—if you could wait that long. Many of us can't take that torture! If you have a *lard pan* then you could boil a very big ham.

Taking out the salt can be difficult, but you want to be sure you leave in some salt, for a saltless ham is no ham at all. A saltless ham might be better for you if you have high blood pressure, but who cares about pressure when there is ham to eat?

When you start eating ham, you cannot stop. The urge is always there to pick at the tempting thing.

Even as a child, every time your mother was not looking, you would pick the ham. Sometimes, you pick out too big a piece that she would miss, so you had to put back piece. And after a while you pick that piece again. It was like *tiefing* condensed milk—you had to go slow.

Reminding you, if you visit a house and they tell you to cut a piece a ham, always remember don't *junk* the ham! There is nothing worse than *junking* a ham. It makes people believe that you want Christmas to be done quick.

You see, when ham done, Christmas done too!

I saw how vexed a *fella* got one Christmas morn when somebody started *junking* his ham. He did not say anything then, but *ah* noticed him in the corner watching *ko-kee-eyed*. Later, he complained how the man was *junking* his ham. And the man was not even Grenadian!

This salt ham is special. If you want to know how special,

wait until Christmas Day. When your friends visit, offer them a piece of the packaged ham you pick up in the grocery and see how fast they run! "Who the hell yuh giving *dat*?" they will inquire.

And then the ham bone—you don't throw that away! You collect some green peas and make a pea soup, leaving room in the pot for the ham bone

Yuh put *yuh* ham to soak yet?

ROYALTY IN QUEEN'S PARK

The Queen's Visit

This time *ah go* start with Queen's Park!

I will begin with the very same Queen's Park where Australia in recent times showed the West Indies how West Indians used to play cricket during the Sobers and Lloyd era.

I remember Queen's Park, where I stood in the blinding sun and got a brutal chastising, just to see the Queen and the Duke of Edinburgh.

We had no choice. They made schoolchildren stand up in the blazing sun, in our freshly pressed khaki pants or well-tailored skirts, to see the Queen smile and wave at us. Some students waved and while they waved they fainted in the hot sun.

We polished our shoes as if we were in the police force. *Ah could* still hear Palmer's voice shouting: "Blue shirt, khaki pants, navy blue socks and blacks shoes." *All ah dat* we had to put on to see the Queen of Britain.

The Queen's visit was so important that Lord Kitchener, the calypsonian sang "The Queen and the Duke coming."

Which Grenadian will stand up today and take a *cut-tail* from the sun just to see the Queen wave? Kitchener could sing until he falls on the ground.

I will never again stand in the hot sun while the Queen drives around in a limousine with Prince Phillip! Not even if they put King Cobra on *me* back! She was driving around in limousine and I was waving as if Christ had returned. *Nah!*

After that, I resembled a sunburned sea grape from Grand Anse beach. Cricketers bowl from the River end or the Darbeau end in Queen's Park, but the sun was bowling from all ends and above our heads that day.

When we were finished saluting the Queen and the Union Jack, they gave us a choice of a Fanta or Red Spot *sweet drink* to *cool out.*

We had to "take that and cool it!"

THE MIGHTY
HURRICANES

Hurricane Janet

The rain came down in thunderous might,
Huge billows leaped right into sight,
Sturdy roots no anchor be,
The massive trees washed out to sea.

The wind its voice an eerie sound,
The fury heard for miles around,
Rivers from their banks o'erflow,
Destruction and a mighty blow.

The pier no longer could withstand,
The constant blast, the furious band,
The trees in bloom, the harvest full,
Shattered by the raging bull.

O Janet! We remember thee,
True monster from the distant sea,
Our spirit though you failed to shake,
Despite the horror left in your wake.

A Mind of Its Own

Nobody could tell me that hurricanes don't think like humans. They even have eyes. Hurricane Janet had twenty-twenty vision. It stayed way out in the Atlantic and spotted poor little Grenada and decided to knock down all the nutmeg and banana trees. It destroyed the trees and the island took years to catch itself.

Ivan, the Terrible, was worse and Grenadians will remember Ivan even more than Janet.

I studied a hurricane called Kyle once. I saw its birth on the Weather Channel. I watched its development closely.

It was born just like those babies who sprung to life at the Colony Hospital in St. George's. It was first a low pressure system, turned into a depression, and then became a tropical storm.

The thing was changing form just like the undertaker who changed into a sardine can back in the days of old Mr. La Qua. There were those who believed it was La Qua who turned himself into a sardine can.

Then Kyle became a hurricane. A hurricane has no mercy. Janet washed away a family in St. Patrick's. It knocked down the Pier in St. George's, and sent coconuts floating in the streets of Grenada. I can't think of many Grenadians who called their children Janet after that monstrous experience. It turned Melville Street into a part of the Caribbean Sea.

People still tremble when they hear the name Janet. They tremble more when the name Ivan pops up.

One never knows for sure where a hurricane will end up. The hurricane always knows. The weather forecasters only guess, and many times the guess is dead wrong!

Let's take Kyle for example. It was a hurricane heading north into the Atlantic and they told us that it only threatened maritime interests. That's a fancy term that concerns boats that pass the shipping lanes.

Kyle decided not to pursue that northward route and suddenly changed its mind and started going south. Then it moved southwest, due west, and then west-southwest. It was confusing people just like some of the English books that were meant to *bamboose* Grenadians. While the meteorologists were looking at its eyewall, its eyeball knew exactly which island or land it was looking at. Kyle finally went to the United States.

A hurricane is like a person. It thinks!

Do you remember Hurricane Mitch? Hurricane Mitch confused everybody. It was going this way and then that way, and then this way again. The poor individuals on the boat called the Phantom thought they could out-run Mitch, but Mitch changed its mind and slammed them with all its might. Then it put a licking on the people of Central America.

You have to take a hurricane seriously. Do you ever notice how they sometimes stand up, pause, and then decide *whose tail to buss*? That stationary mode is just a time-out for them to think.

They take a time-out like the basketball players. They think like the students who sit the GCE and CXC examinations. While the geography students study about winding rivers, the hurricane plays with peoples' minds while meandering out there in the Atlantic. The best thing to do is follow my old scout master's advice and "Be Prepared."

Next time you hear that a hurricane is moving east remember it can change its mind and move west. Remember too, it could be looking at you!

Hurricane Ivan Ah Want to Talk to You!

Ivan, you wretch, you son of *ah* gun, you good for nothing scamp!

Now tell me something: *Ah big maco Jumbie* monster like you chose poor little Grenada to make all *yuh commess* and *ruction?*

You lick down mango trees, *fat pork trees, bluggoe trees, gospo trees;* all kind *ah* trees. *Dem fellas* cried when you pelt down the *bob bon day* trees.

Yuh ha cuss! You wiped out all the *zootie,* stinging nettles and *purgatay. Manicou* had to run for cover. *Dem* stray dogs on the beach hauled *dey* tail from the sand. Even the *Zandolee* had to dash away and hide in *ah* hole.

There were no bushes left to sting Grenadians on their *bam bam.* Not even the *sandbox* tree you left to gee *dem shittings.* You left no tree for people to hide and *mess* when they got loose bowels. *Lawd,* Ivan, you *din* have to do that.

After you passed, the people had to *ketch dey rass* to make *ah panquaye.* You mash up so much roofs they called you Roofus. You removed all the roofs so people could look up in the sky and see *dem* stars. *Yuh* put so much pressure on *dem,* they saw stars. They moved around in *ah* daze as if they had *lite. Starlite*!

You ring up *dem* galvanize like clothes. People could not even find their clothespins. You knocked down all the remaining *pit latrines.* People had to *number two* in the open air.

You even break up the Stadium in Queen's Park. You *doh* even like sports. You *bugger* you!

You put *dem* big trees in the middle of the road so no motor car could pass. Not even *ah* donkey cart *cuddah* pass. You put *dem* trees *dey* for Grenadian men to force and lift and get the embarrassing *ma koo koo.* You loved *dat, eh,* Ivan? No roofs on *dem fellas* heads and big *ma koo koo* for them to *drogue. Dey* dragged big wood in the road, strained themselves and got the *ma koo koo.*

You made it easier for Grenadians to peep. You heard the calypsonian singing about "Grenadians peeping" so you pelt down all *dem* trees to make Grenadians peep even more. *They din* need spying glass.

People, who used to *ketch dey nen nen* to *maco* in Willis, *cuddah* peep from all up *dey* and see who drinking rum in River Road. They could see who bathing by the river under the Green Bridge. You turned the Spice paradise into *ah* peeping paradise. Some people never knew they had neighbors till you lick down *dem* trees behind their houses.

O, *Gawd,* Ivan, why you did *dat?*

After you made your mischief, the people overseas were generous and they sent *all kinda tings,* including smoke herrings, *saltfish* and pig snout to Grenada. They also received an abundance of beans. *Dem tings* came from Trinidad, America, Canada, England and various other places.

But the Grenada people had to wait till the breadfruit trees grew back so *dey* could make *dey* favorite *oildown.* You knew how Grenadians loved their *oildown.*

It was imported beans you wanted *dem* to eat so *dey* could walk and *leggo* wind *ah* hundred and fifty miles per hour like the winds you had. You *din* have to do *dat* Ivan, you too damn *worthliss!*

You lucky *ah din ketch* you. It was two *planass ah wuddah* put in *yuh backside!*

The Old Morris Chair

The old *Morris chair* is gone! Ivan destroyed it. It was swept away by the cruel hand of the raging tempest. The *Morris chair* is gone, but the memories remain.

For *donkey years,* we sat on our little chair near the window and observed the gleaming stars in the Spice Island sky. We relaxed in comfort and saw the moon in its full splendor as it stood in majestic pose high above the Anglican Church.

Through the years, we established a deep affection for that *Morris chair.* It was our seat of comfort. It was the chair we sat on as we ploughed deep into the schoolbooks in earnest preparation for our various school examinations.

We often sat there and spied through the window and noted the huge ships as they propelled their way out of the St. George's harbor. We marveled at the frosty waves left in their wake. We stared as the disturbed water splashed against the small boats that danced in the harbor.

We sat on that chair and peered at Fort George and saw the *flamboyant* trees clothed in their fiery red robes. We smiled as the branches waved in the evening breeze. And yes, we sat on that *Morris chair* and sipped our cocoa tea, *mauby* and sometimes a Carib beer.

Then Hurricane Ivan came and the *Morris chair* was gone.

We loved that chair. At Christmastime, we used to polish it until we saw the reflection of our faces in the gleaming mahogany. And we noted the contended smile on Grandma's face. From time to time, the cushions were replaced, but the wooden structure remained through the years. It was as "constant as the northern star."

Then Ivan came and it disappeared.

Our favorite *Morris chair* survived Hurricane Janet and the weight of many a heavy *bam bam* but Ivan took it away. It provided a resting-place for the little baby who comfortably lay there and drank from his tiny bottle. Grandma sat on that chair and combed the children's hair.

We reclined in ease and watched as the *fowl cock* perched itself high atop the sugar apple tree as night approached. We saw the bird use its fluttering feathers to stabilize itself on a swaying branch. We looked on, as it settled itself for its nocturnal slumber. Then the darkness enveloped the neighborhood.

We cannot forget that chair. We will forever cherish its memory and the thought of sitting there and listening to the restless *crappo* as it constantly croaked in the banana stool behind the house.

The powerful winds of the forceful storm swept away our favorite chair, but not the valued memories that are embedded in our minds.

The Morris chair is gone. One day, however, I will sit on another chair in the same spot. I will look through the window and the stars will shine.

FIRES, DEATHS &
SPIRITS OF THE NIGHT

Fires

Back then, Frenchy store burned down. Before that fire, during the 1950's, there was a big one at sea when the tourist liner, Bianca C, caught fire. Grenadians in small boats rushed to the aid of the tourists.

The Italian government was so pleased with the heroic deeds of Grenadians that they donated a stature as a symbol of their gratitude. That stature was initially placed near Pandy Beach and anyone standing on the Carenage easily spotted its outstretched hands.

The young people loved fires. Some loved it better if it was the school that went up in smoke. It meant more time to *pitch marbles, stone mangoes* or fly kites. Palmer School burnt also, but soon another one was built. Education was priority and schools were rebuilt in haste.

Back then *ah* Frenchy *fella* died and they put him in a grave that looked just like a house on Cemetery Hill. It happened around the same time President John F. Kennedy was assassinated.

Spirits of the Night

Those were the days of the *Loupgaroux* or *Ligaroo,* the *Soucoyant* and the *La Diablesse* or female devil.

Grenadian folklore speaks of an individual called Doctor Ojas who met a *La Diablesse* by the Rocks near Tanteen and was captivated by her sweet talk. He began chatting with the woman in the dark, and got the shock of his life when he looked down and saw her cow foot. He took off with such a speed that the wind he made killed two of Miss Cinty's chickens. The *La Diablesse* shouted "You lucky, *ah wuddah* break *yuh gadamn* neck." Poor Ojas ended up trembling like a leaf in his house. He was so disoriented that he washed his face with *bay rum* instead of water.

The *Loupgaroux* was a tough word to say. Grenadians got tired of pronouncing that hard French word so most of them just said *Ligaroo. Ligaroos* used to suck people's blood every night.

People said that Nahoo and Zoon were notorious Ligaroos. Some women used to wake up with big red marks on their skin and knew for sure that a *Ligaroo* had paid a visit. The marks were more easily seen on light skinned women.

There was a notable difference between a *Ligaroo* and a plane. The *Ligaroo* did not have to taxi before take off. He took off like a UFO. As time progressed, some *Ligaroos* got so lazy that they started riding motorbikes or driving cars. They had acquired a level of sophistication and were too lazy to fly. *Ligaroos* even marched each year in the Queen's Birthday Parade.

People started taking action against the *Ligaroo.* Some nailed a horseshoe over the door to keep them out. They placed a bowl of rice or sand in front the door to force the evil, nocturnal intruder to count every grain before daylight. That was a sure way to trap a *Ligaroo.*

Then there were those who slept with their *clothes before*

behind. It was said that doing that kept *Ligaroos* away. People also placed garlic in front of their doorsteps or placed a cross there.

Back then thieves thrived on the superstitious. Every vessel needed a soul and it was believed that little boys were sacrificed to protect the boat. That was not a comforting thought for anyone who passed those boats that were docked on the wharf.

Cocoa thieves scared people too. They placed a coffin right in the middle of the road near the cocoa trees. People were terrified to pass in that area so the cocoa thieves stole the cocoa with ease and comfort.

My mind races back with more speed than the Volkswagen car Mama Aird sold was capable of. Yes, *sah*!

In those days we believed all *kinda tings*. And that's cool. Like the Irish people and their Leprechauns and the Guyanese who spoke of the "Oldhigue" and "Firerass"(our Ligaroo), we too, had our myths that sent us scampering into the house on a dark night or just stirred our imagination.

I still smile when I pass by the Rocks above the Fire Station. I smile because I remember the mythical tales, not only about the *Crebo* and its crown, but also about Daddy Ojas and the Lajablaisse, and La Qua and the sardine can. I still think about the story of the *fowlcock*, which stood above the dead man's picture in St. Paul's. Busloads of people visited the house hoping to see the *fowlcock* staring at the man's picture..

I can't recall ever seeing a *Crebo*, but I used to look for them while I *jooked* down cocoa from the small cocoa trees in Morne Jaloux. I looked for them to *duff out* in case I saw one.

Remember the words *"Duff out"*? That came from the period when *fellas* used to look at you and greet you with the term "Mankind" or simply "Maaaan!" Everyone knew that the *Crebo* loved damp spots and it was believed that they used to *galavant* in the cocoa leaves.

As I picked the cocoa, I looked around whenever I heard a rustling of the dried leaves. Sometimes the disturbance was caused by the slither of a small snake, and the snake and I would run from each other.

The size of a snake never mattered to me; a snake was a snake! I kept a small dried piece *ah* wood nearby because they told me that if the *Crebo* grabbed onto my leg, all I had to do was break the stick and fool the *Crebo* into thinking it had broken my leg. It was then supposed to release its hold. Yeah right!

I also heard the stories about the *Crebo* nursing the breast of the young mother and of the crowns the *Crebos* wore on their heads. I had dreams of finding a crown, but I never wanted to find *ah Crebo. Nah*!

Like the Greeks, we too have our mythology!

Graves, Coffins and Funerals

Nowadays, a great part of Cemetery Hill in St. George's is lined with these new types of graves that look like a big box above ground. They resemble houses and some have spaces waiting, for the husband or wife, when they eventually *kick the bucket*.

Back then, someone got a hole in the mud, which was dug up to put someone else, after a number of years. We often saw bits of bones when the gravediggers dug up the old graves. Families are now ensuring that their loved ones remain encased forever.

Do you realize that no one wants to be buried in a coffin these days? Everyone wants a big casket. People eat the cheapest food and save money to be buried in the most expensive casket. There are those who act as if they want to be the richest individuals in the grave.

Today, one can even obtain a picture of the tree that produced the casket. One can get information on the type of wood, the age of the wood, and the hardness or softness of the wood used to make the casket. When you leave the funeral home, you have so much knowledge you are ready to open your own funeral agency.

Many Grenadians are afraid of that type of work. That does not include a friend of mine living in New York who is making a killing in the field. The last time I saw him he told me that business was good, but he needs some more work from Grenadians. I am not dying to tell my Grenadian friends what he said!

These days, there is a happening at the funeral called *happy hour* in Grenada. If you can't afford a happy hour, postpone your death.

You have to save up enough money for the people to enjoy the rum, goat meat, and rice and peas that make the happy hour worthwhile. People don't want to waste their precious time to attend a happy hour if there is not enough food and drinks.

It is different from the *ole time days* when people had a couple bottles of rum, and sang "Come Holy Ghost." Now, it's big *fete* and as soon as one dies, they begin assembling at the home for the happy hour.

It is not unusual for people to attend without even knowing who *kick the bucket*. They are often more concerned with the beers submerged in the buckets of ice.

SORROW & LOSS

Goodbye Dear Mother

One last farewell, one final hymn,
Our grieving hearts today will sing,
But deep within our spirits cling,
Holding fast, the joys still ring.

And off to yonder's open door,
A new abode, a glorious shore,
Though sad and mournful to the core,
Her charm we'll feel for evermore.

Her children's eyes in sorrow cry,
The flower gone but did not die,
And when our hands we wave goodbye,
A pleasant smile from in the sky.

A kind woman who tried her best,
Obeyed the call and passed the test,
A peaceful night, a quiet rest,
Goodbye dear Mom God richly Bless.

A Talk about the Island Queen

"Not even Lucy's straw hat!"

Those were the somber words my Great-Grandmother uttered in the wake of a terrible disaster that occurred on the seas, August 5, 1944, somewhere between Grenada and St. Vincent.

I journeyed to the Bronx on Wednesday, 18th August 2004, to meet with my Great-Aunt Sylvia to get some details concerning the disappearance of the Island Queen, one of two boats that left Grenada on that sad day in 1944, during the Second World War.

The Island Queen had left Grenada on an excursion loaded with the children of some of Grenada's prominent citizens.

I grew up hearing stories of the Island Queen. One of the stories that floated around was that the boat had a German engine and a British submarine torpedoed it. Aunt Sylvia told me that she had heard of that too, but the confusing part about that story was that nothing from the boat washed up to shore in either Grenada or St. Vincent.

Nothing was found; not even Lucy's straw hat was recovered!

Another theory pointed to the submarine volcano, Kick Em' Jenny, which lurks off the northern part of Grenada. Some believed that the Island Queen was swallowed up by the turbulent waves in the sea above the volcano. My Great-Aunt was also familiar with that story, but she kept insisting that there was no firm evidence about what really happened on that day.

The other boat that had left Grenada, the Providence Mark, made it safely to St. Vincent, and those on that boat were shocked when the Island Queen, which was supposed to get there an hour earlier, had not docked.

Aunt Sylvia then related the saddest part of the story. I saw the grief in her eyes as she told me of the loss of her brother, Hyacinth, and her sister, Lucy.

She related how Lucy had taken her nephew, Dunbar, into her arms, and said, "Come, kiss Mama goodbye, you might never see Mama again."

Lucy always called herself Mama when she took the little boy into her arms. Her words proved prophetic.

And then there was the story of Hyacinth. Hyacinth, originally, could not get passage on the Island Queen because it had reached its capacity.

A bigshot, named S. A. Francis, was gambling somewhere and was winning when they told him that the boat was about to leave. He said, "Let the boat go!"

His seat therefore became available and Hyacinth was the unfortunate soul who got it. He hurriedly packed a few things in a suitcase and boarded the boat. No one has seen him since!

Aunt Sylvia referred to the great jubilation that existed as Hyacinth and Lucy joined the others and boarded the Island Queen for the trip. The happy group packed their harmonicas, guitars and other musical instruments, hoping to entertain themselves on the trip. Whatever music they played became their requiem.

She told me of the sadness that overcame my Great-Grandma. She joined the parents of the lost children in daily vigil by the Pier at Melville Street as they looked for signs of the Island Queen. There were periods of hope when someone thought they saw the boat approaching, but the hope always turned out to be false. Many parents, on hearing of a sighting, would rush to the shore, only to be sadly disappointed.

According to Aunt Sylvia many pots were burnt while people stood by peering into the Caribbean Sea.

I left her with a saddened heart. I still do not know what happened to my Grandfather Hyacinth on that mysterious day. Many years have gone by since the disaster and the truth is yet to be known.

Aunt Sylvia related the sorrow that visited the parents and families of those who were lost. A few parents lost more than two children.

The gruesome evidence that would write the final chapter of the Island Queen is perhaps buried somewhere beneath the Caribbean Sea.

Remembering My Brother Keith.

He loved to dive,
Beneath the tides,
In his underworld,
The deep blue sea,
Off Point Salines,
Where choppy froth,
Lured his brave,
Adventurous soul.

And danger lurked,
With each descent,
Each fish he spiked,
A chance he took.
For years he plunged,
And often gained,
Until one plunge,
Was not the same.

One final dip,
One deadly dive,
Life's precious dreams,
Just faded by.
Down he went,
In the tidal rage,
To dive no more.
The sea he loved
Had called him home.

Better Late Than Never

Well! me *bwoy, ah see* you finally making the trip back home! They say better late than never, and I am sad to see it's so late for you. Anyway, home is always home, dead or alive, but I think most of us prefer to be home alive.

It would have been nice for you to go home and sleep in an old house and feel the rain as it pounded on the rooftop. Put your head down to sleep, and it feels better than a "rainy night in Georgia." You listen to the *crappo* singing in the banana stool behind the house.

When you wake up in the morning, you don't have to reach for a winter coat. You stare through the window and count *rainflies* like you used to do as a child while growing up in St. Paul's.

How relaxing it would have been for you to stand by the fort and delve in the quiet surroundings! You could have sat in the little Summerhouse there and relax. Wouldn't it have been nice to savor the aroma of the nutmegs and mace in St. Patrick's?

Yes, you *shuddah* go home occasionally and eat *ah oildown, ah* fresh fish *brawf,* and a pea soup with some big dumplings floating in it. When you bite into them, you smile with satisfaction. That is the kind of dumplings your mammy used to make. Remember *dat?*

You could have climbed a Ceylon mango tree for *ole* time sake, and pick some cashews from the cashew tree.

Drink one of those big *waternuts*—there is a song that promised, "It's good for your daughter."

You break a sugar apple in half and you put all the seeds in your mouth at once. That is living, pal, that is living!

But the Maker already gave you the signal and you answered his call.

You missed getting up early in the morning and going down

by the bay. Look good. See *dem* people pulling the fishnets? You could have joined them. Get that feel once again.

Those are fresh fish. You could put them right in the pot. Eat them and wake up those bones long ravished by the brutal cold. Those fish will never see ice.

When you drink the *brawf yuh* could *pull ah good iron*. You could put a bag of yams on your head and walk from River Road to the Carenage, *fuss yuh strong*.

Go down to Grand Anse beach before the morning *fowl cock* crows! *Fowl cock* used to crow in Grenada early in the morning, but these days, *fowl cocks* crowing all night.

At Grand Anse you will meet old-timers ducking themselves in the water and chatting. You can see them at Levera Beach and Bathway too.

They are soldiers away from the battlefield. They served their time in the snow, and now they are fortunate to salvage some of the spice before *Basil* calls them home like he called you.

You could have enjoyed that comforting experience, but now they will have to sing a hymn for you as they put you in the sod. They will say a prayer for you too.

For forty years you missed all of this. You missed Fisherman's birthday on the Lance. You missed all those sweet mangoes from Victoria. You missed the quietness of Grand Etang. You missed Regatta in Carriacou and listening to the sound of the Big Drums.

They say that friendship is golden and there is ample joy in a reunion. It was your choice to stay away and I respect that. I wish you had made the trip before. I wished you had visited even if it was for two weeks.

I will put two *golden apples* and a *sapodilla* on your grave my friend. I remember how much you loved those fruits!

Ma Rubes Remembered

She was a good woman, an exceptional Grenadian and a wonderful mother. She was also my mother's best friend. They knew each other for years and like seeds well sown, their association blossomed into a remarkable friendship.

They had a bond that took them to the market together early on Saturday mornings to purchase the fruits and vegetables and to *brango* with friends. And when one was spotted, people knew it was time to look for the other. It was a friendship that was rekindled in the great beyond.

Their relationship prompted the one who woke first on mornings to call the other, and then the both of them thanked God for another day. Theirs was a friendship that started in the days when Grenadians lit the *masanto* and kerosene lamp, and it became a strengthened chord when they turned on the switch. Their friendship existed since the days of Teresita and *Tanty* Faithy.

It is very easy for one to be attracted to a person who bountifully radiates human warmth. It is natural to feel comfortable in the company of one who communicates with a simplicity that reaches the dept of the soul. It is soothing to sit on a verandah and *ole talk*, and feel relaxed in the company of one who genuinely appreciates people. Ma Rubes was a special woman!

I see her still. I picture her as she briskly made her way across the Carenage. I remember the occasion we left a funeral at Cemetery Hill and walked to the Market Square. I had returned to Grenada to attend a funeral and she was doing what she often did—attending funerals.

We had a wonderful chat, one that felt good in the refreshing sea breeze as we passed Melville Street.

I remember the time I visited her and she showed me the

many hats she had. She told me of her many cherished friends in America, Trinidad, Canada, England and other places. Her friends always gave her hats so she had no shortage of hats to attend the funerals. She was proud of her collection, and as she showed them to me she tried on a few. She asked me how they looked.

I think of the time that I decided to pay her a surprise visit. I had landed in Grenada, but she was not aware of that. I rose early one morning and decided to walk all the way to her house, which was about three miles from where I lived. I smiled as I thought of the expression she would have on her face when she saw me.

I vividly recall walking up to steps to her house and knocking gently on the door. She opened the door and almost fell over a chair in excitement when she saw me. Happiness radiated from her face.

I felt relaxed and at home and very much at ease in her company. She had so many stories to tell me about my mother, and she told me how much she missed her dear departed friend, Georgiana. We made an arrangement to visit my mother's grave.

We did so a few days later. We walked up to the grave. It was a hot, sunny day, and I recall how the sweat dripped from my forehead. Ma Rubes bent over and started clearing the bush and shrubs that were beginning to cover the grave. As she pulled the bushes, she uttered comforting words to my mother,

"Georgie, we can't let this bush cover your headstone!"

I helped her clear the bush while she pointed out all the nearby graves and told me who were buried there. She showed me where Hardfoot was buried, and she pointed to the spot where Peter lay. Then it was time for us to leave.

I will always remember her for the wonderful chat we had under a plum tree near her house in Frequente. The tree was laden with tempting looking plums. She told me of the dreadful mealy bug which destroyed many of the plums and other fruits years ago. The blight was gone and the trees produced bountifully again.

I recall how I filled a paper bag with some of the juicy plums and took to Grand Anse beach where I sat and ate them.

She is gone, but her memory will forever be etched in the minds of Grenadians who knew her. They will always remember her talented hands, which produced some of the best *tambran balls* one could have asked for.

Her jovial personality will always be remembered, and the care and dedication she displayed in bringing up her children should always be an example for many to emulate.

AH GOING BACK

Ah Going Back

Ah going back,
To the sixties time,
Big seventies *lime*.
Back to Clancy Island,
Leggo Beast band,
Hear music blast,
That time done past.
Then to BBC,
To breeze and spree,
And ride donkey,
And feel so free.

Ah going back,
Big *fete* back then,
In the Lion's Den,
Pan in yuh wire,
The place on fire,
Nice *people for so!*

Just pay at the door.

Ah going back,
To Black Experience Band,
Harmony with brass,
Magnificent Six,
Children got licks,
Fish on the Wharf,
And big *mas* scene,
Down Market Hill,
We had our fill.

Ah going back,
To Carriacou Sparrow,
Pamela's dance troupe,
Crow on radio,
And Auntie Kay,
Talking in style,
Was worth the while.

Ah going back,
To sit down in class,
But not end up last,
Back to *China Town*,
Stew fish and rice,
Tasted so nice.

Ah going back,
To the wooden bus,
To play hide and seek,
Then stone mango,
And dance *shango*.

Ah going back,
To kick *ah* ball,
And *buss ah* fall,
To drink *bush tea,*
Dive in the sea,
To take *ah* drive,
In *ah* Hillman car,
And *ah* Bedford bus,
Then walk in dust.

Ah going back,
To put me food,
An *ah carrier,*
And dance the *ska,*
To climb *ah* hill,
And ground to till.

Ah going back,
To wear Afro,
An sport *cornrow,*
To wear shirt jac,
And walk bare back,
And watch me girl,
In short hot pants,
Ah feel so good
Ah want to dance.

Ah going back,
To sing in church,
And watch moonlight,
That shines so bright.

Then to the river stone,
To relax alone.

Ah going back,
To the political jam,
The place *ram-cram,*
To take *ah* walk.
In the cool night wind,
The joys it bring.

Ah going back
To do limbo,
But *mess in Poe?*
Eh Eh
No more!

Marryshow pasture

An image lingers in the mind,
Still undimmed by flow of time,
The buttercups in breeze did sway,
A yellow delight that sunny day.

Beauty in its glory found,
Full-robed branches did surround,
The grass-paved soil engaged my sight,
As bees on petals did alight.

Embraced by that compelling feel,
Strong link to nature tightly seal,
My soul absorbed the view around,
Unruffled stage, hardly a sound.

To Marryshow pasture again I go,
Scenic spot I came to know,
Nestled deep within my brain,
Lodged inside the view the same.

I Sat on Those Steps and Spoke to My Son

One more time, I sat on those steps, the concrete steps worn and battered by the agents of erosion.

I spoke to my son. I told him of the time I sat there, near Malou's house, and prayed for the sun to dry my clothes. I could not go home wet. I related the harsh lesson I learned when I was a boy.

I did not seek my mother's permission when I sneaked out to the Carenage and stood on the jetty in front of the Fire Station, and observed my friends taking *headers* in the water. Some took *belly flaps.*

I had not yet perfected the art of "swimiology," a term I picked up from the famed Justin "Crowe" McBournie.

Then something unfortunate happened. Someone accidentally clipped my leg and I was in the water and struggling. I went down once and I went down again.

It was hopeless until a hand grabbed me. The hand would not let me drown. I was dragged to the safety of the jetty where I emptied my stomach. I was saved—and saved by one of my Carenage friends.

Today, I still probe my mind to find the one responsible for extending my life. Wherever you are, thank you!

I got up from the step and pointed out to my son, the area where we used to *pitch marbles.* I wondered how so many of us fitted into that miniature spot behind Malou's house.

I showed him the location where Peter *zupped* someone's marble and the spot where I used to chase *fireflies.* I pointed out to the area where the *morocoy* used to walk slowly.

I took him to the exact location where Hardfoot's hat fell off. That was one of the few times his hat left his head.

I pointed out the little space where Yankeeman and I nearly fought over a marble. I had traveled from Brooklyn with some marbles and pretty soon all his new found friends were *pitching marbles* on Cooper Hill. They did so for hours in the hot sun. Their play discounted the myth that children these days have no interest in *pitching* marbles or enjoying such pastimes.

Next, I showed him the spot where the Baron of Tyrrel Street dwelled. When Red Ants was angry, school children did not venture near his house. Some had to *foot it up* the short cut to Green Street to escape his boiling wrath.

Once I tried to be respectful and greeted him as "Mr. Red Ants," but that angered him more. He threw a piece of iron behind me and luckily it missed.

In retrospect, I wonder if school children were not responsible for turning Red Ants into a sour *gospo.* They teased him all the time.

I showed him Tyrrel Street and explained how essential it was for us to *scope the scene* before walking to school. We had to make sure there were no *bull cows* on the road traveling to their slaughter in Melville Street. You spot a cow and you had to break the Olympic record to get to school. And that depended on you not slipping in the soft excrement the animals were fond of leaving in the middle of the road.

I showed him where we played road tennis in front of Mr. Moore's house at the bottom of Cooper Hill. We had to stop each time a car approached to let it pass.

I pointed out the Guide's Hut, and I told him of the time a man called Kennedy came with a big bamboo kite, and everyone who had a small flex kite kept it grounded. Then we went to Long Drain and I told him how we used to pass there on our way to kick football at Old Trafford.

I had to include the spot known to us as Bikini Beach. That

was our Grand Anse! After playing football in Tanteen on Sundays, it was off to Bikini Beach for a pleasant dive.

I informed him about the dip that cooled the banging we took while playing football in the rain in Tanteen Pasture. We always had the field to ourselves if the stevedores were not playing against sailors from the ships docked on the Pier.

I took him to the Wharf and showed him the little area where the Cubby Hole once stood. The Cubby Hole was a nice little dance spot where people moved to the captivating sounds of reggae and calypso.

Then I told him of the time Gairy reconstructed the Carenage into a beach during the Easter Water Parade.

I gave him some details about China Town and the big spark it was. It was the entertaining pulse of St. George's at one time.

I showed him the gate where Leon used to pass and enter the Pier to liberate some groceries and other stuff, until they got fed up with his stealing and banned him. I still don't how he escaped with those heavy barrels of salt beef.

I told him about Mr. Marshall, the kind shopkeeper, who trusted us when we could not afford to buy. I took him to Canash hill and showed him where Palmer school once stood. I stressed how important it was for us to adhere to the rules of the school.

I related stories of the love that existed among neighbors and the joy we experienced at Christmastime.

Yes, I told my son:
About life on Cooper Hill
And life on the Wharf
And Park Lane
And Green Street
And buttercups
And *shack shack*

And of my cousin Shampoo
And Bugs
And Depo
And he will tell his son
When I am gone!

.

Tell Dem Young People Dat!

So *yuh* foot sprain *eh?* Well, rub the *dam* thing with *ah corn hux*, Canadian healing oil, mentholated spirits and then some soft candle. You will be ready for the next football game. Nothing beats *ah corn hux*!

So you got wet in the rain? Well, it's time to soak your head with Limacol—"the freshness of a breeze in a bottle." You could even try some Alcolado. If that don't work, try soaking your head with *bay rum,* and tie a cloth around it like the Visagoth used to do while he sat on the mango stool. Then you could drink a Phensic or Cafenol, and if that still don't work, rub the thing with *ah* soft candle again.

So you feel you are getting a cold, a bellyache, a headache, or any other kind of ache? Well, you better don't let granny know because it's the castor oil in *yuh backside.* Castor oil was the remedy for every ailment. Just threaten a child who pretended to be sick in order to duck school with a dose of castor oil, and he or she was out the door with the books in a flash.

Well, you tell your father you want a new pair of shoes. Look out! The footwear might be a rubber slipper, *washicong,* or *Jim boots.* You go to school with a rubber slipper and you became a laughing stock.

Jim boots with pegs was acceptable, but for heaven's sake, don't take off the *Jim boots* in the house. The smell would wake the dead. Please put them outside so people can sleep.

You bathe with carbolic soap, and someone was sure to ask you what kind of perfume you are wearing.

You skate down the hill and you put a nice hole in your khaki pants! A black patch might stop up that hole. When cloth is scarce, you might even walk with your with your behind outside. Nothing was better than a cold, cold white *Red Spot.* A cold *Solo* was gratifying too.

Eat a *conkee* wrapped in *bluggoe leaf* and then *wash dat* down with some *gospo juice. Gospo* juice will open your appetite; open your appetite to drink *ah callaloo* soup.

And you feel like *pelting ah iron?* Make sure the rubber doesn't *buss*! Use *ah* Tinex condom!

A RETURN TRIP

Ah Reach

Ah reach!
Papayo! Ah touch down,
Ah back in the Spice,
Reacquainted once more,
With the smell of Nutmeg,
Cinnamon and clove.

Ah the smell!
Ah feel sea breeze,
On me smiling face,
I am refreshed.
Ah ready
For the bachannal.

Ah hear *ah pan,*
The sound of steel.
Ah hear *ah* beat,
The *soca* sweet.

Mamayo!
It's carnival time,
*Ma*s and *commess,*
Wine if yuh wine-ing,
Leh me back me shirt.

Ah reach!
Time to awaken,
These sleeping legs.
Time to shake the fog,
The smog and snow,
That choked the mind,
In the other clime.
Time to *shake ah leg,*
To jump and prance.
Yuh hear dem?
Yuh see dem?
Gee me room *compere*
Ah reach!

Shitty Was Himself Again

Shitty was himself again!

For a few memorable hours on Carnival *Jourvert* morning, he was no longer the crazy person that cursed people and caused disturbances all over the town. He was the Shitty of old, knocking the steel rim with vigor and passion, and, at the same time, knocking away the madness that made people run away from him. The behavior that had lent justification to the unflattering opinion of him was not evident on Carnival *Jourvert* morning.

I looked at him and I marveled. He was once again transformed into the classic steel man of yore. He displayed the traditional poise and stance. He was back into a time when seasoned steel men like Mafu lighted up the Carenage with the spirited percussion.

Shitty was back in his prime and once more, found himself in the familiar setting that he knew so well. He was a soldier—still at the battlefield, long after his comrades had kicked the bucket or laid up their arms.

His face glowed as he pounded feverishly on the steel rim. He glanced in my direction and smiled, and I returned the smile. He was the conventional *masman* sucking in the rich beat of the steel pan. The captivating music was the catalyst that lifted the veil of madness from him on Carnival Monday morning.

He kept perfect step. He was no outsider that morning. He belonged to the frolicking crowd.

There were those whose actions seemed out of touch that morning and, yes, there were others who jumped and danced and acted as though they had run away from the crazy house.

But Shitty was a sane man among them and he was an instructor in the art of steel beating. He was the Shitty of old while the steelband played and he pounded the steel!

271

Daddy-O in "Pink Ah Form!"

I heard the sound—that very familiar sound—and I knew he was close.

I was reacquainted with vibes I had heard before. The strum of the cuatro grew louder. I raised my head and beheld the coconut hat. I saw the spectacular coconut hat adorned with beautiful Spice Isle flowers. He played and he sang. He sang and I smiled. And the tourists looked on in awe.

I saw the fancy footwork, and I was absolutely sure it was Daddy-O. Yes, it was the legendary Daddy-O himself. He had endured. He had weathered the elements, and his strings too, had stood the test of time. Daddy-O was as lively as a cricket.

He gracefully leaped forward as he sang and then he stylishly *backed backed.* Then he sprung around like a figure skater in the heat of contest.

Years of rehearsal had perfected his style and he moved with polish and the smoothness of a well-oiled machine.

Daddy-O was doing his thing on Grand Anse Beach.

Miss Olive Spoke about Bush Tea

I met Miss Olive as she stood in front of her house and she recognized me immediately. She had grown old, but her steps were still sprightly. She looked at me, smiled, called my name and asked me when I had arrived. I told her that I had landed the previous Saturday night, and it so nice and relaxing to be home again.

Something caught my eye. Right before me was a healthy-looking plant. I asked her if that was *Santa Maria* and she said yes. It was the special *Santa Maria* that my mother used to make *bush tea* when I was a child growing up not very far from the hill where Miss Olive lived.

My question paved the way for a lengthy discussion with Miss Olive on *bush tea*. She showed me the other plants that freely grew around her house.

She pointed out b*ig thyme* and *ven ven."* She grabbed a leaf called *black sage* and asked me to smell it. My nostrils quickly recognized the scent.

Miss Olive was versed on the names of the plants and their medical benefits. She knew that *wormgrass* was good for people who had worms. She told me how valuable *fever grass* was for lowering the temperatures of children when fever attacked. She referred to *Coolie paw paw* or caraili as a great medicine for cooling the body and for treating diabetes.

She called all the plants by the old local names she knew so well. She spoke about *jumpup and kiss me* , *man better man, christmas bush,* and *shado beni.* She referred to *zeba pique, water cressels* and *old maid.*

She knew the bush that was good for clearing up scars on the skin and the plant called *jiggerbush* that was vital when the bowels became loose. She spoke about *lemon grass* and *sugar dish.* She mentioned *soursop* leaves that were used to wean babies from breastfeeding, and she told me how important cinnamon tea, lime leaf and mint were for getting rid of gas in the stomach.

She spoke and I listened, and I lamented the fact that old people like Miss Olive and Miss Judith Bain, with their wisdom, were becoming so rare in Grenada. Those knowledgeable people were fading just like the *patois language* that declined from the lips of Grenadians.

She spoke about the times doctors used to seek out the elderly people for remedies when their medicines proved futile. Many of the old people were good *bush doctors* and they made use of simple everyday things like limes and honey to chase the common cold away. They had a cure for many ailments and the medicine grew right in the backyard.

I listened to her, absorbing all the information she was giving me. Then I coughed, and she told me to wait a moment. She went into her house and emerged with a small paper bag. She told me that if I get the cold, I could boil some of the bush in the bag and drink it with a little honey.

She then asked me to see her before I returned to America. She would have another package of bush for me.

DREAMING FROM A DISTANCE

Ole Talk in Prospect Park

It was an unusually cool July morning in Brooklyn. The type of morning that made it difficult for me to resist nature's tug, I decided to take a stroll in nearby Prospect Park.

A good morning it was for a walk in the park because the air was fresh, the trees were well-clothed in a healthy green, and the ducks waddled peacefully on the tranquil lake, I have always had a special fondness for lakes

During my stroll, I *bounced* up two Grenadian friends I had not seen in ages. They had awakened early for their morning jog. We heartily greeted each other and immediately started chatting about the unusual coolness.

As we spoke, I pulled out from my pocket a sheet of paper on which I had written the opening lines of a poem. It was a poem about *rounders,* a popular game we played as children in Grenada. I joked that it was a good morning for *rounders,* teasing their brains to see if they still remembered that sport. They both recalled that game and we laughed as we reflected on other forms of childhood entertainment.

The conversation soon switched to *bamboo bussing* in Grenada. *Bamboo bussing* was once a popular pastime among children. Some of the knots were removed from the bamboo rod, and kerosene was poured into the groove. The bamboo rod was then lit.

All the children became excited as the blasts went off. One of my two friends recalled the time he lost his eyebrows when he got too close to the fireworks. He laughed, but I was sure he had found no amusement when that occurred years ago.

The conversation turned to the many beatings they had received from their parents when it was discovered that they had stolen the kerosene from the lamps and stoves to use for *bamboo bussing.*

One of the two men made reference to the time his father sent him to buy kerosene, but before giving him the money, he spat on the pavement and warned him to return with the kerosene before the spit dried.

Failure to do so meant a good cut *backside.*

He had to run the two miles or so to the store and back before the sun dried the spit. There was no time for him to *skylark.*

There was a time he played a game of marbles with his friends, and someone told him that his father was looking for him—with a belt. It was always easy to guess why your father would look for you. He scampered home to avoid a public flogging. All children hated such a humiliating spectacle.

We spoke of the times a young man had to peep to see if a young woman's father was nearby before attempting to speak to her. Fathers and mothers were very protective of their daughters. Fathers, especially, knew the tricks they themselves employed as youths, so they were a step or two ahead of any scheme the young man tried.

We walked and we talked. The *ole talk* seemed more worthwhile than our jog, which had turned into a walk.

We spoke about climbing trees and picking mangoes. We revisited the coconut trees and recalled how unsafe it was to hold on to the first branch when one climbed to the top of that tree—the first branch was always the one that tended to loosen easily. It was safer to grab a stronger, inner branch for support.

We spoke about the sweet sugar apples that we grabbed from the trees before the birds and blacks ants got them.

We revisited the days we used to sit by the transistor radio and listened as the English commentators broadcast the cricket matches. The battery-operated transistor radio often proved more reliable than those powered by electricity.

Sometimes, in the midst of an important game, the coverage would cease due to the dreaded electrical power failure.

At night, when the electricity failed, we lit the reliable kerosene lamp or a candle.

We kept on walking and the *ole talk* kept flowing. We dug up memories of old strict schoolteachers, and we recalled the bright and not so brilliant students.

We spoke about the small sweet Starch mango. I told them about the time a crab grabbed my little finger in its *gundy*.

The *bush tea* that our mothers used to give us to drink was a topic of its own.

One friend mentioned the big, yellow, school buses that came to Grenada during Prime Minister Gairy's time. Many people thought that they were too big for the narrow roads, but the drivers handled them with great expertise.

Then someone mentioned the prison trucks that were used to transport the prisoners all over the country and people used to shout - *jail bud!* - when they spotted the prisoners.

We walked around the park twice. We got some good exercise and some welcomed laughter from the *brango*.

Then one of my friends asked: *"yuh remember when fellas used to take belly flaps in Miami Beach near Melville Street?"*

That was a topic for another walk around the park at another time.

Two Elderly Men Reflect

The two retired Grenadian men sat down to their favorite game of dominoes. They had long hung up their working boots, so their sought to liven their days by an occasional gathering for some *brango* and an exciting game of cards.

It was many years since they left the Isle of Spice, but the memories of their time spent there still lingered in their minds. The years of residing in the cold did not did not cloud the thoughts they harbored of the place of their birth.

They were always eager to hear of developments, not only in Grenada, but the entire Caribbean. Occasionally, they made the trip home for some relaxation and to meet friends and family who were still alive.

They played their game and their minds journeyed back into time. They pulled back memories of a time they once knew so well.

I sat on a chair and observed as they knocked the dominoes on the table, sporadically pausing to take a drink of strong rum from a bottle that lay on it. I sat there and paid heed to the voices of experience.

When they left Grenada in the 1950's, the island was still a British Crown Colony. The donkey cart was a method of transportation and the Queen's Birthday Parade was a yearly celebration. Those Grenadians, who served in the World Wars, marched in the parade and proudly displayed their medals. In those days, only the bigshots drove the few motor cars that rumbled on the streets.

They recalled the happy feeling they experienced when they were fortunate to get a lift in a car owned by an estate owner or some other well-to-do person. They mentioned how favored they felt when they rode in the cars. The *drop* was sometimes a reward for climbing a coconut tree and picking coconuts for the owner of the vehicles or for doing some other work.

One of the two friends, Bogart, had journeyed to England and the other, Cecil, initially settled in Harlem before residing in Brooklyn. They met again, two jovial souls, whose minds were active, and who, at times, seemed to possess the energy of the great Grenadian footballer called Peter Punder.

I listened to them as they resurrected ancient happenings of their days in the Spice Isle. The stories were many and varied, and followed no set order or pattern. It was a little of this and a little of that, but the *ole talk* was never dull.

They played their cards, drank their rum and mentioned whatever came to mind. They brought up stories of the film shows that were shown in the Market Square in St. George's, mixed with memories of *torching crabs* on the rainy Grenadian nights.

They spoke of the popular fishing site in Palmiste, known as the Dig, where *manicou* and *tatou* were also caught. Bogart had such a good memory; he even recalled the name of his favorite dog that traveled with him on his hunting trips.

I laughed when they spoke of the coconut fiber mattress that was not only used for sleeping, but for hiding money.

And yes, they spoke of the *social women* who used to *cut style* on men they felt were beneath their class. Cecil recalled a certain woman bluntly telling a man, "You are not in my category."

They remembered the time when all the fathers asked the men who were interested in their daughters the famous question: "What is your intention?"

They brought to life stories of the old estates in Grenada, and recalled the rich estate owner called Nyack who once owned many acres of land in Grenada. The huge estate Great Houses were discussed and particular mention was made of a certain estate owner from Britain. Grenadians called him "Shorttaylor" and he lived in St John's many years ago. I listened as they related how he brought all his English customs with him. He never failed to have his maid make him his favorite cup of tea, and she had to ring a bell to let him know when dinner was served. He arrived for his meal dressed up in his jacket and tie, as if he was headed for church.

I learned of the time in Grenada when the banks hired only light-skinned people. It was a period when skin color and class went a long way in deciding one's prominence in the society. Cecil noted that although conditions were improved, the playing field was still not a level one.

I gave ear as topics on the lighter side were brought up. Occasionally, I asked for an explanation of a matter, but it was satisfying to just sit there and listen.

I was amused when a big argument broke out over whether or not a dentist should be called a doctor. Cecil shouted that since anyone can pull out a tooth, he was not inclined to refer to a dentist as a doctor.

The trivial *ole talk* continued as Bogart recalled the time he was an overseer on an estate, and he caught a man stealing water grass. He wanted to *leggo two planass on the man*, but he let him go with a stern warning not to steal again.

They spoke of *ah fella* from Grenada who went to live in California. He often visited them in Brooklyn, and always came dressed up like a cowboy. He wore the tall cowboy shoes and a hat like John Wayne used to wear.

He was a great talker, but much of what he said had to be taken with a grain of salt. They recalled his tale about the time he fought in Vietnam, and blazed his way out of an ambush. He told them that story, although he never served in the military. He filled their ears with tall and imagined tales of his combat heroics.

He told them of the time he removed all the nuts and bolts

from a car in Grenada, and everyone wondered how he was going to put the car together again. He boasted how quickly he did so, and with one turn of the switch, the car started.

While they played their game, I was occasionally asked to check on a pot of curried goat and rice that was cooking on the stove. I would do so quickly, but hurried back to hear more *ole talk*, and to answer questions about events that took place in Grenada after they left.

Their references were many. They pointed out the struggles of Grenadian immigrants, and the plight of those who went to Aruba to work in the oil refineries. They spoke of their mistrust of politicians everywhere, and the many schemes that man used to con his fellowmen.

Then they brought up the topic of their old age and their lives in the United States. Cecil said that he once thought of going back to Grenada to live, but since he had "one foot in the grave and the other on a banana peel" it was too late for him. He made reference to his constant battle with the dreaded *sugar*. They mentioned the medication they had to take for their ailments that were more readily available in Brooklyn than in the Caribbean.

The chat ended when they were tired with their card game. It was time to save the rest of the *brango* for another day.

Rattie and His Trumpet

I met Rattie again. I stumbled into the famed Grenadian musician at a summer picnic at Asbury Park in New Jersey. It was Rattie—much older then—but the same Rattie, who for years thrilled many Grenadians with the delightful sound of his trumpet.

It was he who possessed the broad smile and caused great laughter when he belched out those hilarious jokes. Rattie had not forgotten his trumpet in Grenada and, on that picnic day, we were again lucky to savor his musical talent.

A typical summer bus ride, it was, that involved family and friends who opted for a pleasant day of fun and enjoyment in the park. What a welcome break from the bustle and strain of everyday life in Brooklyn!

It was the appropriate time to seek escape from hard work that sapped the energy. How we yearned for the freedom of the outdoors. What a good opportunity to be reacquainted with old friends, to share a laugh or two, and engage in the type of *ole talk* that evoked nostalgic delight.

Our outing was a wonderful occasion for heart-lifting associations with people not seen in *donkey years.* One never knew who would pop up on these bus rides. It was even possible to meet that guy who stole your marbles in school.

Fun-loving Caribbean people had the chance to pack their cricket bats, footballs and volleyballs in the buses for some friendly sporting encounter. And, indeed, it was the time for old-timers to see if they remembered how to play cricket or to kick a football,

We loaded our barbecue equipment and the seasoned meats necessary to satisfy the bellies that would constantly call for gratification during the day. We were also careful to load the *rum punch and mauby.* Then we boarded the bus at Eastern Parkway and other points, and headed for New Jersey.

Something marvelous and unexpected happened that day!

In the coolness of the afternoon, after much of the games and running around the park, the people had settled down in little groups everywhere. Some were playing cards or dominoes, or just lazing about. Some were listening to their favorite calypso, blasting from their radios. Others were sampling the various mouthwatering Caribbean delights that lined the many tables.

It was then that I saw Rattie. I saw his trumpet, too, and I also heard his laughter. He was seated near a tree, engaged in a lively chat with a number of people.

Suddenly he raised his trumpet to his lips. He began to play a richly flavored, jumpy Caribbean rendition of Neil Diamond's "Sweet Caroline."

A small crowd gathered around him, drawn by the magnetic pull of his jovial sound. The crowd grew bigger as the catchy tone arrested more attention.

Some began to beat their pots with spoons. A young man began to strum his guitar, and someone else began to pound on a drum. More people gathered and onlookers began to smile or inquisitively peered at the sudden happenings.

Then a procession started, and it quickly turned into a Caribbean style *jump up.*

Rattie played and his music echoed throughout the park. The veins in his neck swelled, as he vigorously forced air into his trumpet. The people moved and danced while Rattie played.

The hastily assembled pot and spoon percussion provided the lively backup. It was an impromptu Caribbean Carnival dance at Asbury Park, New Jersey.

Around and around they went in a tireless motion. Rattie played on, as the hip-swinging people followed his shiny trumpet. It was the crowning moment of the picnic. Rattie went to Asbury Park and he brought the Caribbean with him!

THE SPIRIT LIVES

I Felt the Spirit

Once again I felt the spirit. It bubbled within. The spiritual tide hit me with more force than hurricane Ivan's ferocious winds. I felt the spirit and I was elated because I knew that in times when the flesh is weak, the spirit can be powerful.

The spirit is the ingredient that will always lift us from the havoc wrought by disasters. The spirit will give us hope. I felt the spirit, which in the past, enabled us to forge a pleasant relationship with each other, and throughout the years, helped cultivate that affable unity among us.

Indeed, there were times when political chaos raised its ugly head, but we must let that remain in the past. The clarion call goes out for unity.

Our Spice Isle is wounded and bruised, and as one people, we must struggle to help it rise from its dilapidated state.

I felt the spirit of the headmaster R. O. Palmer who always encouraged his students to strive to do their very best. He taught us to pursue excellence at all times because nothing, but the best was good enough. He encouraged us to memorize the famous words by Longfellow:

"The heights of great men reached and kept were not attained by sudden flight, but they, while their companions slept, were toiling upwards in the night."

He urged us to strike the iron while it was hot, in order to obtain the best result. He told us to "strike with all our might." In times of national disaster, we have to assist with all our might.

I felt the spirit of the scoutmasters and guide leaders who taught all the young men and women how to handle themselves in difficult situations. We learned to tie knots, climbed mountains, and to perform helpful deeds in the community. We were also encouraged to hold the hands of the old and feeble, as they crossed the streets. We were beseeched to respect our elders and those who failed to do so felt the wrath of teachers and parents. We learned to give a helping hand when the need arose. We knew love.

I felt the spirit when I reflected on Miss Cinty, Tyrone's mother, who often shared her Sunday lunch with the neighbors. She called all the neighborhood children to her house for a spirited celebration on Christmas Day. Such generosity was prevalent among neighbors.

I remembered the chicken feet that Miss Teresita stewed so well, and as she bit into the mouth-watering gummy part, she used to poke her head out her window and shout,

"*Ah ha*! Georgiana!

Christ is the answer!

Gumarrre!"

The *gumare* was the gluey part of the stewed chicken feet. The term "Christ is the Answer" was borrowed from a popular revival that was once held at the Market Hill Pentecostal church.

I felt the spirit when I heard about the togetherness that existed, especially in the rural parts of Grenada after Hurricane Ivan struck.

People came together with their strong motivation to help. It was refreshing to hear that the *maroon spirit* lived. I was thrilled when I heard of the young men from Florida who put back the roof on Errol's mother's house after Ivan knocked it off. Many Grenadians in years past used to pool their strength and expertise to help each other construct houses and clear land.

They pounded nails into roofs and feasted on *oildown,* rice and peas and foods that were prepared for the occasion.

It was the same spark, which moved within the pioneers who traveled to England in the 1950's and 60's, and who sent for their families and friends.

It was the spirit that motivated Mr. Rush to offer lodging to a Grenadian he did not know who had just stepped off the plane at JFK International Airport. We must keep such warmth alive.

I felt the spirit that energized strong community figures as Pa Ferdie, "Shuff" Peters of Gouyave, Ben Roberts, Willie Redhead and also sport personalities like Big Bear, Roy St. John and "Papa Plug."

Those were some of our respected salt of the earth. They fostered a tight kinship among Grenadians when they mobilized people to work or play together. We need that spirit today.

Unity must never take a holiday. Throughout the various parishes, there are good-hearted people. Community spirit never fails and people who lend their energies to advance the welfare of their fellowmen must always be acknowledged. Lift them up high!

I felt the spirit when I thought of parents who woke their children early in the morning so that they could tie their goats and sheep before heading off to school. That called for discipline. The children looked after their animals and had time to help their parents with household chores, and still found time to do their homework.

I felt the spirit and I was reminded of the time my brother

Chris and I planted corn in Belmont. It was hard work forking the ground, but the joy came when we got some corn to roast on the *coal pot*. The soil is our hope. The hurricane will always devastate the crops, but we must plant again, and again, and again.

We must maintain the spirit that in the past urged people to help out at the fair, harvest or garden party. We must keep the spirit that makes it easy to say good day to our neighbor. We must revive the old tradition that spurred out grandparents to visit and feed those who live in the homes for the aged and the mentally challenged.

We must preserve the spirit of charity and friendship.

FINAL PLEA

Teach Me, Granny, Teach Me

Teach me Granny teach me,
Connect me to your past!
Cherished mores of yesterday,
The values that should last.
For I can only be myself,
And proud of whence I came,
Not swept by every wind of change,
Or called by other name.

Tell me of the *shango* dance,
Sky Red, and *canboulay*;
Black sage, *big thyme* and *lemon grass*,
Respect you showed in class.

Tell me of the *Ligaroo*,
Maypole and *jooking board*,
And days expensive fancy food,
You hardly could afford.

Tell me of the *pan cup,*
The *blue* you put in clothes,
The grater and the *swizzle stick,*
Tell me before you doze.

Tell me of the sucking leech,
Drew blood from poisoned spot,
Your skill in making Christmas cake,
And O! That nice fried bake.

Tell me of the slate you used,
To write your name in school,
"Ring around the roses"
The times you played the fool.

Tell me of the *sou sou,*
You joined to pay the rent,
And that good for nothing Grand Pa
Who gave you not a cent.

Tell me how you sat and knit,
The vests for newly born,
And all the yummy food you made
With just a pound of corn.

Tell me of the stories
Told under mango tree,
Kerosene lamp that shed the light
So every one could see.

Tell me of the concerts, the fair, and harvest ripe
And what you gave the children

When little bellies gripe.

Tell me all those things, Granny,
Before you say goodbye,
And I will tell my little ones,
When you are in the sky.

Don't Neglect Your Past

A people who ignores the past,
True concepts then will never last,
Know the road from where you came,
Cut not that cord for wealth or fame.

Stay grounded in the cultural flow,
Tested things you came to know,
Despise not what grandparents taught,
Reflect and think and don't be bought.

Don't be wrapped in every thing,
Strange ideas that they will fling.
Cling close to that you always know,
Time tested ones parents bestow.

This is no campaign against change,
That you keep in worthwhile range,
What lifts the soul one feels the most,
It's true! this is no idle boast.

To children, you must pass it on,
Ideas that will make them strong,
And help them always to be free,
Of false baggage not meant to be.

About the Author

Anthony W. DeRiggs, a.k.a. Wendell, was born in St. George's Grenada. He attended the St. George's Catholic Boys' School and the St. John's Christian Secondary School. He taught for a number of years at the latter school. In 1978, he left Grenada and settled in Brooklyn, U.S.A. He holds a BA in History from Brooklyn College. The book,"Recollections of an Island Man" is his first published book. He also intends to publish his collection of poems entitled "Poetic Island Reminiscences."

Acknowledgements

I want to thank all those who encouraged me to write this book. Their inspiration made my work easier. I cannot list all the names here but I want to especially mention the following family members, friends and co-workers:

Sandra DeRiggs, Chris DeRiggs, Carl DeRiggs, Charles DeRiggs, Victoria DeRiggs, Dr. Basil Marryshow, Ben Hood, Charlie Hood, Tyrone Scipio, Error Alexis, Judy Campbell, Mary Beare, Stephanie Burns, Joy Rathan, Monica Phillip, Valda Browne, Anthony Howard, Sue Patrice, Michael Samuel, Lincoln Samuel, Jeffrey Williams, Marcia Braveboy, Joe Cozier, Rosemarie Noel Clarke, Alinda Pinto, Dr. Anthony Henry, Germaine Pope, Patricia Self, Judy Loriano, Herman Hall, Stanley Hagley, Grace Barriteau, Felix Cordero, Joan Pedersen, Heather Smith, Yvonne Phillip, Katherine Theodore, Phillip David, Jeanette Fitzgerald, Lee Bagley, Jonathan Gabriel, Helene Ajello, Vernon Louison, Jerry Grant, Anthony Louison, Alene Lewis, Auldris Alman Murray, Angela Armbrust, Asif Islam and Lennard Fleming.

I am grateful to the people from the Spiceislander Talkshop. They provided me with the energy that propelled me to tackle this work. A warm thank you to the following:

Lavandula, Brian, Recs, NJtony, Kesri, Spiceislander, Comrade, Spanisheyes, Aim, Ackee, Vanilla, PI, Shabbaz, Snow, Depo, Stinking toe, Bathway, Vin-su, Sue, CT, Jane, Corporal Naught, Bakes and fishcakes, Maudos, Tagwa, Snow, Don, Aileen, Spider, Mote, Slice, Cityman, Vanilla, Judy, and all the wonderful people of the Spiceislander Talkshop.

I must also thank Bigdrumnation.org for featuring my poems and stories and for answering my questions. My appreciation goes out to Everybody's Magazine for highlighting my story in the October 2005 issue. Thanks all!

GLOSSARY

Ah	"Substitute for I, of"
Ah bag ah goals	Many goals
Ah bunch ah fellas	A group of boys or men
Ah cutarse	A flogging
Ah doh care	I don't care
Ah doh like dat	I don't like that
Ah doh noe	I don't know
Ah drink up	"A meeting of friends where they cook, eat, drink and engage in casual talk."
Ah ent cutting no grass	I am not cutting any grass.
Ah get nice	I feel good. (sometimes after consuming alcohol.)
Ah go bring you up	I will file a law suit against you. I will take you to court.
Ah hate dat	I hate that
Ah kind ah dance	A particular type of dance
Ah leggo ah big one	I pass loud wind
Ah make ah ting	I perform an act (without great skill).
Ah pass	A free entry into the cinema
Ah put so much licks on the mango	I eagerly devoured the mango
Ah rounds	"A neat shaving of the hair on the sides, back and front of one's head."
Ah still vex	I am still annoyed

Ah tell yuh	I am assuring you
Ah took me time	I moved at my leisure.
Ah touch up	"Not a complete haircut, just the cutting of the hair to give it a neat appearance."
Ah used to clean up the mangoes	It was my habit to eat all the mangoes
Ah wuddah	I would have
Air condition transportation	Wooden buses with numerous side openings for ventilation.
All ah dat	All of that
All skin teeth is no laugh	Not every laugh is genuine.
Allyuh	"You all, all of you, a group"
Allyuh doh see	All of you don't see
Aloooo there	Hello there
Asham	Snack made with grounded parched corn with sugar added. A must on All Saints night.
Bacchanal	"Noise and confusion, big party, scandal"
Back and neck chicken.	Back and neck chicken parts that were packaged and sold.
Back back	"To go backwards, reverse"
Back of the hand stuff	A method of bowling in the cricket game.
Backside	One's posterior part
Backsqueeze	To keep back all or a portion of something
Bad as crab	Very bad
Bad pay people	People who borrow money but don't pay back
Bad talk	To speak ill of people usually in their absence.
Bad words	Obscene language
Badjohn	A neighborhood bully.
Bahoe	"A far place, the most remote part of the country. The residence of foolish people."
Bajan	Barbadian
Balla-hoo	Small slender fish with a long narrow snout.

Ballswheel	Automobile bering
Bam bam	"One's posterior part, one's butt"
Bamboo	A plant of the grass family which grows up to forty feet or more.
Bamboo bussing	Noise that results when kerosene is placed in the bamboo rod and ignited .
Bamboo kite	A kite made from the bamboo plant
Bambooze	"Mesmerize, confuse with words, bamboozle"
Bamsee	"One's posterior part, butt, one's bottom"
Barring	Blocking one's view
Basil	Death
Basil calls	Death summons
Bat and ball	A term for the cricket game.
Bathing suit	Swimwear
Bawl out	"To shout out loud sometimes because of fear, anger or surprise."
Bayrum	Type of alcohol that people use to rub their joints. Some drink it. The bayrum leaf known botanically as Laurus nobilis is brewed with the rum.
Bazodee	"Confused, stupefied."
Bee bush	A vine that grows widespread in Grenada. It produces a pink flower that attracts bees.
Before behind	To wear the front part of a garment where the back should be.
Belly laugh	A very hearty laugh
Bellyflap	Diving into the water with the belly hitting the surface.
Bellyworks	Abnormal stomach cramps leading to diarrhea
Betche	Bitch
Big belly	"Pot belly, large stomach"
Big Jack	Fish of the Jack family that is usually caught in a net.
Big lime	"Big hangout, large gathering at a party or other event."
Big maco jumbie yam	A massive yam.

Big people	Adults
Big thyme	A herb that is used as a remedy for colds and fever.
Black sage	A herb that is used for purifying the blood.
Black sea egg	Sea urchin that inflicts pain when the spikes penetrates the body. A marine invertebrate (Phylum echinodernata group)
Blade yuh tail	"A batsman making many runs off a bowler is ""blading his tail"""
Blew the pesh	Spend all the money
Blows began to pelt	A fight broke out.
Blue	Indigo blue block used to whiten clothes.
Bluggoe	Fruit of the banana or plantain family. It is shorter and thicker.
"Boise bande, Bob bon day"	Roupala Mantana.The bark of a tree. It is used as an aphrodisiac
Bol' face	A very demanding or pushy person.
Bom tourist	Beg the tourist for money
Bongaway	Out of control like a vehicle in motion without brakes.
Bonjay	Good God (Bon Dieu)
Bottom dollar	Last dollar
Boucan	"A place where cocoa, nutmeg or mace are dried and prepared for export."
Bounce up someone	To meet a person unexpectedly
Bow bow	A game patterned after the Western gunfight but played with toy guns.
Bowlie	The fruit of the calabash (Crescentia cujete) tree
Bowlie lantern	Lantern fashioned from the gourd of the calabash tree.
Bowzer	A gas station
Brango	Gossip
Brapps	Suddenly
Breadfruit	"Artocarpus altilis A large fruit , native of Polynesia. A must for the Grenadian dish known as oildown."

Break people tail	Beat up people
Breed	To impregnate a female
Breeze	A detergent
Breeze cyan pass	"This refers to people who stand so close to each other, not even the wind can pass between them."
Breeze out	"To relax, usually in a cool spot as under a tree."
Bridle	Whitish substance that forms from saliva at the corner of the mouth.
Brogues	Hard shoe football players wore in the 1960's.
Bruddah	Brother
Bubol	"Corruption, dishonesty"
Bucket ah drop	Heavy rainfall
Bud in cage	"To have a sweetheart, usually a woman in your house"
Bud pepper	A small slender pepper which burns the tongue when bitten. Bird pepper
Bugger	"Scamp, trickster"
Bull cow	Loose expression for cattle.
Bull pen party	A party where the number of men is far greater than the women present.
Bull pistle	The preserved penis of the bull
Bun bun	The food that sticks to the bottom of the pot.
Bunload	A large quantity of anything.
Bush tea	"Beverage made from herbs or plant leaves, natural remedy for sickness."
Bush yam	Wild yam.
Busload	A bus filled with passengers
Buss	Various meanings: denotes an action that is sudden.
Buss ah fall	To fall suddenly
Buss ah lime	To join friends for a hangout
Buss ah shit	To defecate in haste
Buss ah short cut	To take the shortened path to somewhere
Buss his pants	Tear his pants by an action like stretching or bending down

Bussing shots	Pulling the trigger of the toy gun which connects to the roll of caps to make a sound.
Butt	To bow like the spinning sequence of a kite in heavy wind.
Buttercup	Trumpet-shaped yellow flower. Allamanda cathartica Also called yellow bell.
Bwoy	Boy
Bwoy whey the hell yuh going with that?	"An expression of surprise, rejection or ridicule."
Bye Bye Blakey	"Good bye, I am leaving"
Cacabari	A colorful parrot fish with large scales
Calabash	Bowl made from the fruit of the calabash tree.
Calabash tree	Crescentia Cujete. The tree produces a large gourd-like fruit. A container is made from the shell after the pulp is removed.
Call dat George	"Be satisfied with something. The end of the matter, be contented with the situation."
Callaloo	The leaves of the dasheen plant.
Callaloo soup	"A soup made from the leaves of the dasheen plant blended with ochros, coconut milk and herbs."
Calypso	A musical and lyrical comment(social commentary) on any subject. It is usually composed for the carnival season.
Canboulay	The historical roots of the carnival. Also a term for the feast on the night before the carnival.
Candle spum	The liquid substance that forms when a candle is lighted.
Caning horse	Hitting the racehorse with a whip to make it run faster.
Can't go off	Can't defecate
Carrier	A metallic dish used as a food container. Popular with Grenadian school children

	during the 1960's.
Cassian	A type of waltz dance at the school graduation ball or other functions.
Catch ah glad	To be in a sudden happy mood usually marked by continual laughter.
Caway	Loose body action as the shaking of the hips.
Chang chang	An uneven haircut usually done in haste and without much care.
Cheap Grenadian chap	A Grenadian miser
Check out ah ting	Engage in courtship
Chicken snack	Chicken and fried potatoes
Chinaman	A method of bowling in the cricket game.
Chinatown	A popular entertainment spot that was located near the St. George's pier during the 1960's. The small restaurants were designed in the Chinese style.
Chinese plum	Small yellow plum roughly the size of a grape.
Chipping	Sliding step to the beat of the carnival music.
Christmas bush	A herb used for colds and fever.
Christmas cake	A cake made with fruits soaked in rum and wine. A must for the Christmas season in Grenada.
Cinnamon	Cinnamomum zeylanicum. Also called spice. Cinnamon sticks are made from the long pieces of bark that are rolled and dried.
Circle hole	Mythical hole in the sea that was said to engulf fishermen and their boats.
Clean that up	Ate it all
Clove	Cloves come from an evergreen tree in the Myrtle family. It is widely grown in Grenada.
Coal pot	A metallic device used for cooking. Coal is used as the fuel. Looks like a Japanese hibachi.
Cochoneel	"A plant of the cactus family, cochineal.

	It is used as a shampoo."
Cocoa sweating	The fermenting of the cocoa seeds in a box.
Cocoa tea	Beverage made from the dried cocoa (Thembroma cocoa) pod.
Coconut bat	Cricket bat make from the branch of the coconut (cocos mucifera) tree.
Cocorico	Kite made from the dried cocoa leaf.
Come up	"Pay up, pay for the service rendered."
Coming to come	"slow improvement, coming very slowly."
Commess	"Confusion, controversy"
Common	Vulgar
Commonness	"Vulgarity, loose behavior"
Compere	"Godfather of my child, friend"
Congoree	Millipede
Conkee	Food made with corn meal. It is usually wrapped in bluggoe leaf.
Coo coo	Food made with corn meal and cooked to become firm so it could be sliced..
Cool it	Relax
Cool out	To relax in the shade
Coolie kite	A kite make from two pieces of thin sticks from the coconut branch.
Coolie paw paw	Also known as Caraili. A bitter herb used for cooling the body. People also rub their skin with it when they bathe.
Coonumoonu	A foolish person.
Cork	To inhibit or restrict bowel movement. Trouble
Corn Hux	Corn cob
Corned fish	"Fish that is cleaned, salted and placed in the sun to be dried and preserved."
Cornrow	Hair braided into rows. It was very popular in Grenada during the 1970's.
Could pull ah good iron.	"Able to do hard work, could perform well"
Cow horn is never too heavy for its head	A load is never a burden if you are accustomed to it. The Lord will not give us more than we can bear.

Crab back	Delicacy made with crab meat and usually served in the shell of the crab.
Crappo	"Frog (From the French, crapaud)"
Crappo belly	Poor penmanship
Crappo smoke yuh pipe	You are in grave trouble
Crazy house	Abode of the mentally unstable.
Crease	The area where a batsman in the cricket game stands to face a bowler.
Crebo	Large black serpent which lives in damp areas.
Crimpeleen	A type of synthetic material used to make pants.
Cripple she backside	Brutalize her
Crocus bag	Sack that holds sugar. Jute sack
Crookery	Dishonesty
Crown cork	The cap of a bottle
Cry cry baby	Someone who cries often or easily.
Cuatro	Small guitar-like instrument with four strings.
Cuddah	Could have
Cuff	"The clenched fist, to punch someone"
Cuss	"Curse, profanity"
Cuss buds	People who constantly use obscene language
Custard apple	Relative of the sugar apple . It has a thick creamy custard-like pulp inside.
Cut backside	A proper flogging
Cut your nature	Reduce your sex drive
Cutlass	A tool that is similar in appearance to the machete. It is used to cut grass.
Cutlass pelting	Using the cutlass to cut grass etc
Cut-tail	A spanking.
Cutting style	Not wanting to be involved with something or someone that one feels is below his or her level or taste.
Cyan	Can't
Dam	Damn
Dasheen	"Edible starchy tuber, the leaves of this plant (callaloo) are used to make soup."
Dat	That

303

Dat good for me	"I deserve that, serves me right"
Dat ole man dey	That old man there
Dem	Them
Dem kind ah ting	A particular type of behavior
Dey	They
Dey go eat dem	They will eat them
Dey say	Rumors
Djhaley	A fisherman's practice of rewarding helpers who reel in the nets. They are usually given a portion of the catch.
Dog bed pants	Gray flannel pants the Grenada Boys' Secondary school students wore in the 1960's..
Dog muzzle shoe	A type of rubber sandal
Dog swim	To paddle like a dog in the water
Doh	Don't
Doh ask me	Don't ask me
Doh blam meh door	Don't slam my door
Doh gee me dat	Don't give me that
Doh gee me no	Don't give me any
Doh lie	Don't lie
Doh noe	Don't know
Doh worry	Don't be concerned about it.
Donkey heaven	A state of bliss (A make belief state of happiness)
Donkey years	A very long time
Doo	"To put a spell on, or curse someone with evil"
Doo Doo	"Sweetheart, term of endearment, doux, doux"
Dougla	Mixture of East Indian and African parentage.
Drink him out	Deliberately make his spend his money to supply drinks
Droging	Hauling load like a bag of cocoa on one's shoulder or head.
Drogue	To carry heavy load
Duck someone in the water	To push someone into the water head first.
Duff out	To leave suddenly

Dum dum	A foolish person
Dun	Done
Dun dat	Finished with that
"Easy, man easy"	"Relax, don't be so anxious, be calm."
Eh eh	No way
Eh?	What did you say?
Eights ah rum	A measurement of strong rum in a little glass
Every blessed cent	All the money
Fass	"Nosey, sticking one's nose in other people's business."
Fat pants	Baggy or roomy pants
Fat pork	A small pinkish fruit with a white pulp.
Father Christmas	Santa Claus
Fatigue	Giving someone a hard time.
Fellas	Men or boys
Fete	"A party that includes food, drink. and often dancing."
Fig	Banana
Fire in the Congo	"Lots of action, great entertainment."
Fire one	Have a drink
Firefly	A luminous night flying insect. Also called Candlefly.
Fish brawf	"Soup made with fish, root vegetables etc."
Flamboyant tree	"Delonix Regia, also known as Royal Poinciana. Its flaming red blossoms brighten the hillsides."
Flamma	A big ant that stings
Flex kite	A kite made from sticks of the coconut branch.
Fliers pants	A roomy pants made with very thin material
Flooding	A pants that is too short and leaves one's ankles or socks exposed.
Foot it up	Walk briskly.
Force ripe	Appearing more physically mature than one's age usually as a result of hard times.

Force ripe man	A boy who has the physical appearance of a man.
Force ripe woman	A girl who has the physical appearance of a woman.
Foreday Morning	The period before the break of day
Fowl cock	Rooster
Fowl Coob	Chicken coop.
Fraid	Afraid
French cashew	A red oblong to pear shaped fruit with white flesh
Gal	Girl
Galavante	To run all over the place. gallivant.
Galvanize	Corrugated zinc covering of houses
Gawd	God
Gee	Give
Gee me ah	Give me a
Geeze am bread	An expression of surprise
George Otway	"A very quick bath. The name originated from the very short baths George Otway, the undertaker used to give the dead."
Gimme	Give me
Give him his clothes	Curse him soundly
"Golden Apple, Pomsetay."	Pommecythere. A fruit with a sharp spiny seed. Called June plum in Jamaica.
Gospo	Fruit of the orange family.
Governor plum	Small edible berry of dark to purple color.
Grand charge	"To bluff, an action that is not backed up by deeds."
Grand move	Going through a motion but it is only a bluff.
Green Fig	Green Banana. It is usually boiled and eaten.
Green fig man	A man who loves to eat cooked green bananas.
Grin yuh teeth	Fake laughter
Grind	To gyrate against someone while dancing.

Grog	Rum
Groundnut	Peanut.
Groundnut sweetie	A dark flat candy with peanuts embedded.
Gru Gru	A small hard fruit with a nut inside. The plant (Acrocomia aculeata) belongs to the palm family.
Guayavearians	"Residents of Gouyave, a town in the parish of St. John's, Grenada."
Gun mouth pants	Narrow bottom pants
Gundy	The claw of a crab
Ha	Have.
Hardheaded	Slow to learn
Haul cutlass	Use of cutlass to cut grass etc
Haul yuh	Take yourself away from me.
Haul yuh scrutch	"Get away from me, leave me alone."
Haul yuh tail	"Get away from me, leave me alone"
Header	Diving into the water head and outstretched hands first.
Hear say	Information gathered through gossip
Hengibbit	A big evil person
Hengman	A man who hangs criminals condemned to die.
High science	Knowledge of the supernatural
High seat	The seat above the rear wheels of the wooden bus.
His bread and butter	"His livelihood, he depends on that occupation to make his living."
Hog plum	Spondias Mobin. A small yellow fruit.
Hopscotch	A child's game played by drawing boxes in a specific pattern and using an object to identify the position of a player who has to hop on one foot.
Horn	Cheating on one's partner.
Horning	Being unfaithful to your partner
Horse fly	A big fly found on the beach. It stings.
Hot	Sexually aroused
Hula hoop slipper	A rubber slipper
Huss	Hearse
In dem days	In those days

In truth	"Truly, It is a fact."
In yuh backside	In your behind
Irish potato	"The potato that was imported, not necessarily from Ireland."
Is come yuh coming	The reference is to the small pig who asked the mother pig why her mouth was so long. The young pig was told to wait he would get the answer.
It went well	It blended well.
Jab jab	"A traditional carnival portrayal. Otherwise called Devil mas. The masqueraders blacken their skin, and sometimes place horns on their heads."
Jack Spaniard	A large wasp that stings
Jail bud	Someone who is always serving time in prison. A recidivist.
Jam Session	A crowded party or meeting
Jamaican plum	Reddish plum that is eaten or used to make plum stew
Jammed me	Confined me to a small area
Janet Houses	Houses provided to the needy after Hurricane Janet struck Grenada in 1955.
Janet Truck	"Big public works truck that transported sand, cement, workers, etc."
Jim boots	A type of sneakers
Johnny Bake	A bake made without yeast and baked in a pot with fire on top and below to ensure that all sides are evenly baked.
Joke yuh making	You are not serious
Jook	"To prick, to pluck, to poke"
Jook down shirt	Shirt plucked down from the ceiling with a broom or stick.
Jooking board	A board with a step-like appearance used for washing clothes.
Jourvert	Means daybreak. Marks the start of the carnival in the streets on Carnival Monday morning. People dress in old clothes.
Jumbie	"Spirit, ghost"

Jumbie umbrella	Mushroom
Jump up	Dance in the carnival band.
Jun jun	"A smelly mixture made with old fish gills, rotten eggs and substances with obnoxious odors."
Junk	To cut off big slices from ham etc
Kajam	Muscular part of the foot behind the shin.
Kakajay	Mucus that forms at the corner of the eye.
Kee-kee-kee	Laughter meant to tease someone
Keeping duty	Traffic police officiating
Keg butter	A reddish salted butter.
Ketch	Catch
Ketch dey nen nen	To experience a difficult time.
Ketch she royal tail	She experienced a trying or difficult time.
Ketch yuh falling self	"Check yourself, show some respect"
Ketching yuh rass	Having a hard time
Kick the bucket	To die
Knock about	To wonder from place to place
Knock-about-mango	A mango also called Thin mango that was widely found in Grenada.
Knocking down rum	Consuming a great amount of alcohol
Knocking glass	Drinking together
Ko -kee -o- ko	The flower of the flamboyant tree.
Ko-kee-eyed	Crossed-eyed
Kuk kus	"One's private parts, penis"
La Diablesse	Devil woman said to have one human foot and one cattle foot.
Lambie	Conch
Lambie shells	The shell of the conch.
Lard pan	A tall tin can that contained lard or butter.
Last lap	The final hours of the carnival festivities
Later for you	"You are left behind, left out"
Laugh for so	"Excessive laughter, loud hearty laugh"
Lawd	Lord
Leapers Hill	Le Morne De Sauteurs. The place where

	the Caribs of Grenada jumped to their deaths rather than surrender to the French.
Leaven bread	A small tasty bread that was once popular in Grenada. It was wrapped in banana leaves and baked.
Leggo	Let go. Release. Also called breakaway.
Leggo beast	A woman who gets sexually involved with many men.
Leggo two planass on the man	Hit him twice with the broadside of the cutlass
Leh	Let
Leh me back me shirt	Let me prepare for action
Leh me buss yuh tail	Let me beat you up.
Lemon grass	A herb that is used as a remedy for fever and colds.
Lickrish	Greedy
Licks	"Blows, flogging, physical punishment"
Lift	A ride
Ligaroo or Loupgaroux	Vampire
Lighters	Wooden boats that were used to transport cocoa and nutmegs to the big ships during the 1960' and 70's
Lime	"To gather for casual chat, to hang our or loaf around."
Lite	A curse or spell put on people so that their behavior is considered abnormal.
Mace	The bright scarlet colored coat that surrounds the nutmeg.
Macintosh	Brown protective material that babies and young children slept on to prevent urine from soaking the mattress.
Macmere	Godmother of my child
Maco	"To spy, peep, someone who minds other people's business."
Madbull	Part of the kite that produces a sound when the wind hits it.
Make fares	Prostitute oneself for money
Make his panquaye droging goods	Earn a little money hauling goods for people.

Make up	"Resolve differences, disputes or conflicts and be friends again."
Ma-koo-koo	Swelling of the gonads
Male box party	A party where there are many men but very few women.
Mamaguy	"To make a fool of someone, to ridicule"
Mammy apple	Mammea Americana. Mammey apple. Has a brown leathery texture on the outside with deep orange flesh inside..
Man ah war	A battleship
Man better man	"A medicinal plant used for colds, fever and the flu"
Man on the run	A man who is always busy usually doing odd jobs.
Manicou	Opossum
Manish	A boy who acts or talks like a man. (Usually in a rude manner)
Maribone	Wasp-like insect that stings
Market Day	The day when the big food shopping takes place. Saturday.
Maroon	"A feast for people who help on a job. It is a community effort to help individuals build a house, clear land etc."
Mas	Carnival celebration
Mas costumes	Clothes the revelers wear on carnival day
Masanto	Bottle torch with wick used to provide light. Kerosene was used as the fuel.
Mauby	A drink made from the bark of the Carob (Colubrina reclinata) tree
Maypole	A dance. Each dancer holds a ribbon tied to the top of a pole. They dance around the pole and at the same time braid their brightly colored ribbons.
Me brudda	My brother
Mealybug	Destructive bug that wrecks havoc on plants.
Meh	My
Mess	"Defecate, feces"
Mind men	To clothe feed and generally look after men

Mint	The leaf of a perennial herb. Used for colds and fever.
Mong Mong	"Residents of Mount Moritz, Grenada."
Mongoose gang	Violent gang that existed when Eric Gairy was Prime Minister of Grenada during the 1970's.
"Monkey say cool breeze, baboon say wait a while."	"Life is good now but wait, things can change"
"Mooma, muddah"	Mother
Moosh	"To put flour, toothpaste or mixtures on one's face when that person is sleeping. A prank."
Mop	To beg
Mop ah ride	To beg for a ride
Morocoy	A land turtle
Morris chair	A wooden mahogany chair that was popular in Grenada during the 1950's and 60's. Some still exist.
Mountain dew	Illegally distilled white rum. Also called bush rum.
Muff	Patch of hair above the forehead
Music in yuh wire	Captivating music to make you dance
Nah	No
Nansi stories	Tales. Originated from Africa and featured a cunning Ashanti spider called Brer Anansi.
Nen Nen	Mother or Grandmother
Netballers	Those who play the netball game
Nice for so	Very charming
Niceness	Hospitality
Nigger boy sweetie	A hard locally made lollipop on a flex stick that became popular in St. George's during the 1960's.
Noe	Know
Number one	Urine
Number two	Feces
Nutmeg	"It is known botanically as Myristica fragrans. Both nutmeg and mace comes from the same tree. The scarlet outer coat is called mace, The brown seed is nutmeg."

O geed	An expression used when a foul odor greets one's nose.
Oaring boat	Rowing boat
Obeah	"Witchcraft, a form of sorcery"
Odesia	Reference to Rhodesia
Oh gorm	"An expression that denotes shock, surprise or indignation."
Oildown	"Famous Grenadian dish made with breadfruit, coconut milk, dasheen leaves and various meats."
Old Maid	Herb that is used as a treatment for diabetes.
Old year's night	New Year's eve
Ole	Old
Ole mas	Early carnival Monday morning portrayals that feature people bearing placards with satirical statements.
Ole rumbo	Seasoned rum drinker
Ole talking	Casual chatting
Once in a blue moon	Very rare occurrence
"One day for watchman, one day for thief"	"Everyone has an equal chance in life. You win some, you lose some."
One day one day congote'	You might get away with doing wrong today but one day it will catch up with you.
One More Buses	Small transportation buses that were popular in Grenada during the 1970's
Ooman	Woman
Orman	Almond
Oui	We
Out-ah-man	Cricket game in which one bowls or catches someone to get his chance to bat.
Outside ooman	"A man's mistress, also called his keeper."
Pace like fire	Very quick delivery of the cricket ball.
Pancup	"Drinking cup with a handle, made from a tin can. It was popular in the 1950's and 60's. Milo and Ovaltine cans were used to make the pancup."

Panmen	Musicians in the steel orchestra
Panquaye	A little money earned by doing odd jobs.
Papa Gawd	God
Papayo	Expression of surprise
Pappyshowing	"Fooling around, not being serious"
Pappyut	A foolish person
Parang	"Serenade at Christmas. Originally, people went from house to house singing Christmas carols. "
Park up.	To be stationary
Patois	French dialect
Peg ah bam bam	One side of one's butt
Pelau	"Special dish made with rice, chicken etc."
Pelting ah iron	Male engaging in sexual activity.
People for so	A large gathering
Pesh	"Cash, money"
Pickin'	The food the pigs eat
Pickin' pan	The pan that holds the food the pigs eat
Picture buss	An untimely break in the film during a show in the cinema
Piece ah wood	A piece of wood
Pink ah form	Performing very well
Piole twang	Spanish dialect.
Pit latrine	"Out house toilet, a pit dug in the ground with a seat and small wooden structure above for privacy."
Pitch oil	Kerosene
Pitching marbles	Playing the marble game
Planass	To hit someone with the flat part of a cutlass
"Play with dogie, dogie go lick your mouth"	"If you associate with people beneath you, they may take advantage of you."
Po- po	A baby or very small child
Poe	"A chamber pot, bed pan, Posey, potty"
Poke	Staying put at the cricket wicket. The objective is not to score runs but to remain at the crease.
Police	Penis

Poor fella	A remark denoting pity for someone
Pope ah ride	To beg for a ride
Posing off	Relaxing in style
Praise	"Prayer said for the dead usually accompanied by singing, eating and drinking. The wake"
Pre-cut Janet Houses	Prefabricated houses that were popular in Grenada after Hurricane Janet in September 1955.
Provisions	Root vegetables as yams and potatoes
Pudden	Pudding
Puff	To eat so much food that it leads to stomach problems.
Pugatay	A pod that itches the skin. Also called cowitch.
Pull brakes	To stop suddenly
"Pum, poom"	Pass wind
Puppa	Papa
Put ah licking	Devoured
Put out of the runnings	Could no longer compete
Rainfly	Insect like an ant with wings that come out after heavy rainfall.
Ram crammed	Filled to capacity
Rap	To hit someone behind the head with the palm of one's hand. It was an initiation for new students.
Rapped the vibes	Sang the songs
Rass	Ass
Rastas	Followers of the Rastafarian religion who are usually distinguished by their dreadlocks.
Red ants	Tiny red ants that sting painfully.
Red skin	Light complexion
Red spot	A soft drink
Rounders	A game similar to baseball but played without the bat.
Ruction	A noisy outbreak
Rum punch	"A popular drink made with lime, nutmeg, rum etc."
Rum shop	A small shop where rum is sold. A hang-

	out for drinkers.
Saga boy	"A flashy dresser, a man who dresses in fine clothing to attract women."
Saga ting	Fancy or stylish actions
Sah	Sir
Sailor words	Obscene language
Saltfish	Pollachius pollachius. Cod fish
Saltfish souse	"Delicacy made with codfish, hot pepper, onions, tomatoes, vegetable oil etc."
Sandbox	"A natural laxative, the shell of the fruit is used to make necklace pendants."
Santa Maria bush	A herb used as a remedy for colds and fever.
Sapodilla	"A brownish fruit, round in shape with a fleshy edible pulp"
Scope the scene	Look around carefully
Scrutch	Crutch
Scrutch up	To arrest a person by holding the waist band of his pants from behind and pulling upwards.
Sea bath	A swim in the sea
Sea cat	Octopus
Sea grape	Grows near the beaches in clusters and has a purple color when ripe.
Sea moss	A sea algae used to make a popular drink
Sea pum pum	An aquatic mollusk
Searchlight	Flashlight.
Senna pod	A purgative
Set up	To stay up at night
Shack shack	The fruit of the Flamboyant tree
Shado Beni	A plant used as a remedy for fever
Shake ah leg	Get up and dance
Shango	"A religion/dance with connections to the Orisha/Shango of the Yorubans of Africa. The ritual includes drumming, sacrifice and chanting."
Shittings	Loose bowels
Shortknee	A carnival portrayal. The revelers wear

	a thin masks and mirrors attached to their clothes. They throw power into the air.
Shuddah	Should have
Simi dimi	"Making strange signs with one's hands or body, strange antics, mumbo jumbo"
Ska	Jamaican dance/music that was popular in the 1960's.
Skanking	A reggae dance involving raising the feet high to the beat of the music.
Skin up their faces	An expression denoting aloofness or scorn.
Skin yuh teeth	Fake laughter
Skinup	Chinep or guinep . Small green fruit with soft jelly-like flesh. Grows in bunches.
Skull school	"To skip classes, truancy."
Sky Red	The name originates from the period in the 1950's when there were riots in Grenada led by Eric Gairy. Many of the estates were set on fire.
Skylark	To fool around when something important must be done. To idle
Slack our kites	Fly our kites
Sling ah kite	To bring down someone's kite by attaching a stone to a string and flinging it over the thread of the kite.
Slingingshot	A small catapult
Smartman	"One who manipulates others, a conman"
So and so.	Loose term to define a person. Also a profanity (Haul your so-and-so)
Soapfroth	Soap suds
Soca music	A blend of soul and calypso music
Social women	Women whose actions depict them as aristocrats when they are not.
Soft Shoes competition	"Football competition played at Tanteen, Grenada in the 1960's. The players used soft shoes or played without shoes."
Solo	A soft drink

Something else	Any action or person that is strange or unusual.
Sorrel	A drink. The coat that surrounds the seed of the sorrel plant is dried and boiled to make a popular Christmas drink. The plant is a member of the hibiscus family.
Sou Sou	System of cooperative borrowing in which a group of people pool their money and distribute among them-selves periodically.
Soucouyant	A she-devil
Soursop	Annona Muricata. Oval shaped fruit with a delicious white pulp. It is covered with small spines that easily break off. Also known as Guanabana..
Souse	"Food made with codfish, pig or cow's foot with onions, pepper and cucumber in a sauce."
Spin	The spinning motion of a ball delivered in the cricket game.
Spin cufform	Summersault
Split the scene	Leave the area
Spooge	Music made popular in Barbados
Squinge up	Squeeze oneself in a corner
Squinge up his face	"""To make faces"" "
Star apple	" Round purple fruit with a pulp that is soft and sweet. When cut crossways, a star shaped pattern is revealed."
Sticky cherry	A fruit used as a glue or gel. It is edible but not recommended for food.
Stinging nettle	Plant with stinging hairs on the leaves and stem that can itch the skin.
Stone bruise	Painful lump on the heel or sole of the foot that develops when the foot knocks against a stone.
Stone mangoes	Pelt stones with the aim of hitting mangoes to make them fall.
Strupps	Sound that is indicative of the sucking of the teeth

Stump me toe	To knock my toe against an object
Stupidee	A foolish person
Sugar	Diabetes
Sugar apple	Annona squamosa. Knobby fruit with a green skin. It has many small black seeds and the flesh is soft and white.
Sunday food.	Special dinner prepared for Sunday.
Sunday shoes	The best pair of shoes reserved for church and very special occasions.
Swallowed a dictionary	Had a strong vocabulary
Sweet Drink	"Carbonated drink, soda"
Sweet oil	Olive oil
Sweetie	Any confectionery
Swizzle stick	"Manual blender made from the limb of a tree used to stir calalloo, porridge etc."
Tail	Rear end of a person
Tam	Woolen hat
Tambran	Tamarindus indica. The fruit of the tamarind tree. The fruit grows in clusters and the shell is brittle.
Tambran ball	Candy made with the tamarind fruit. It is rolled into a ball
Tampee	Marijuana
Tania	Edible root that is cooked and eaten like potatoes and yams.
Tania log	"Porridge made from tania, spices and condense milk"
Tanty	Aunt
Tatou	Armadillo
Taybae	Confusion that stems from gossip or arguments
Tear lash in the ham	Devour the ham
Tearing tail	Wrecking havoc
Tess	A hostile or very aggressive individual.
The first hand	The first payment in the sou sou or partner association.
The longest rope has an end	Your troubles will not last forever. Everything has an end.
Throw down a drink	Take a drink of rum or other alcohol
Tief	Thief

Tinex	A brand of condom
Ting	Thing
Ting bang ba lay lay.	Bacchanal
Tings	Things
Tink	Think
To be straightened out	To be disciplined
Tongue lashing	A proper cursing
Torching crabs	Using a flashlight or other light to catch crabs at night.
Travo people	Road workers
Trim	Haircut
Trini	Trinidadian
Turned over	Capsized
Two two	Feces
Umpteen years	Many years
Under his oil	Drunk
Vekou	A carnival portrayal. The masqueraders wear long gowns and heavy wooden boots.
Vex	Angry
Vienna Bread	A popular Grenadian bread that was popular during the 1960's. It was fluffy in the middle and pointed at both ends.
Voop	Wild stroke with the cricket bat some-times made with the eyes closed.
Voose	Also known as grand charge. To bluff
Wares	"Dishes, cups, plates etc"
Wash yuh foot and come	"Anyone can come, no big preparation is necessary."
Washicong	Sneakers that was popular in the 1960's and 70's.
Water boots	Tall rubber boots gardeners wear
Water Cresses.	Herb that is used as a cooling for the body.
Water more than flour	Conditions real bad
Watergrass	".A vine that is used to feed rabbits, pigs and other animals."
Waternuts	Coconuts with the soft jelly inside.
Waters for the back	Nourishing soup to make one strong to enhance sexual performance.

Western	A very quick bath.
Wha	What
Wha ah talking 'bout	What I am saying
Wha go on dey?	What is going on?
Wha happen Bwoy?	What is happening boy?
Wha happening dey?	How is everything?
Wha yuh expect	It is to be expected based on past actions or decisions.
What is joke for school children is death for crappo	"What you think is funny may be dangerous, offensive or lethal to others."
What sweet in goat mouth does be sour in its bam bam	Sometimes your words or actions will come back to haunt you.
What the heck its Christmas	Because it is Christmas we will put more effort into our work.
What the hell	An expression of anger or frustration
Where horse reach donkey does reach	"I may not be as smart as you are or as fast as you are but I will get there, nevertheless."
Whey	Where?
Whey him?	Where is he?
Who have cocoa in sun must look for rain	Things may not always be rosy and one has to prepare for the unexpected and expected.
Whose tail to buss	Who to punish or inflict pain upon.
Wicked with the cricket bat	A prolific batsmen in the game of cricket.
Wid	With
Willowpeak	Narrow pointed hair above the forehead.
Windball	Tennis ball
Wine-ing	Rotation of the hips and waist
Woe pa	An expression denoting sadness. A lament
Womanish	A girl who behaves like a woman. (Usually in a rude manner)
Wood slave	"A lizard that usually resides in the house, gecko"
Words in place sah	The appropriate words are used
Work ah ting	"Perform an act, to try something"
Worthliss	"Worthless, good for nothing"

Woye	An expression of fatigue or pain
Wrong side	The inside of the garment worn on the outside.
Yam	An edible tuber
Yeah bwoy	Yes boy
Yes sah	Yes sir
You playing the rass	You are making a fool of yourself.
Youngsters	Children
Yuh	You
Yuh bounced up	You met someone by chance
Yuh father is a glassmaker?	You are blocking my view.
Yuh mad or wha?	Are you crazy?
Yuh tink	You think
Yuh tink we easy	"We are not simple, we use our heads, we could be unreasonably demanding."
Zaboca	Avocado. Also called pear in Grenada
Zandolie	Lizard
Zeba Pique.	A plant that is used for fevers and colds.
Zooty	Plant that itches the skin
Zupp	To hit someone's marble from a distance during the game